MW01258229

unlearning
anxiety & depression

JOSEPH J. LUCIANI, PH.D.

author of the internationally bestselling Self-Coaching series

unlearning
anxiety & depression

the 4-step
Self-Coaching
program
*to reclaim
your life*

GOODMAN BECK PUBLISHING

Copyright © 2020 by Joseph J. Luciani
All rights reserved.

No part of this book may be reproduced in any form or by any means,
electronic or mechanical, including photography, recording, or by any
information storage and retrieval system or technologies now known
or later developed, without permission in writing from the publisher.

Goodman Beck Publishing
PO Box 253
Norwood, NJ 07648
goodmanbeck.com

ISBN 978-1-936636-15-0

Library of Congress Control Number: 2019955917

Printed in the United States of America

10 9 8 7 6 5 4 3 2 1

First Edition

To my darling granddaughter Elia Rose,

I held you in my arms only hours after you were born.
That moment frozen in time. Your little body calm and serene,
the only sound…that of the angels whispering, she is love, she is love.

CONTENTS

PART I

1

Anxiety and Depression: Living with Chaos

What comes to mind when you think of the word *anxiety*? How about when you think about the word *depression*? These very words seem to stir up feelings of uneasiness, dread...confusion. After all, when you're hijacked with symptoms like sadness, crying, fatigue, appetite disturbance, sexual dysfunction, fear, worry, and difficulty concentrating, it's hard not to feel desperate and hopeless. And make no mistake, anxiety and depression are not *just* in your mind—they're whole body problems with biochemical, neurological, and emotional underpinnings.

There's no question that anxiety and depression can become very serious, if not life threatening, problems, especially if ignored or left untreated. They can run through your life affecting not just you, but your family, your friends, your career. Although anxiety and depression can disrupt your entire life, they have a weakness, an Achilles heel—a weakness that can be exploited! And that's what this book is about: a Self-Coaching approach that can help you exploit this weakness and liberate yourself from a life of unrelenting emotional struggle.

Before getting into specifics, there's a story (adapted from Dulce Rodrigues's children's story *The Frogs' Race*) about a frog and a wall of a problem that will prepare you for everything else that follows in this book.

Thumper

There was once a swamp that was completely encircled by a large, formidable stone wall. The frogs in this swamp had never seen beyond the wall. For generations there was speculation as to what was on the "other side." One day the chief frog decided to organize a race that would culminate in a leap up the wall that would, once and for all, settle the argument as to what lay beyond the wall.

The day of the race came and five of the bravest, strongest frogs lined up at the starting line. A sixth, a latecomer known as Thumper, quietly joined the others. Thumper, in contrast to the five other contestants, wasn't much to look at. He was thin, frail, and altogether rather sickly looking. The six frogs crouched at the starting line waiting for the race to begin. The chief's gun sounded and the race was on!

[Before continuing with this story, you should know that frogs are terrible pessimists prone to doubt, incessant fears, and unbounded negativity. It's a fact.]

As the competitors raced toward the wall (with Thumper trailing far behind), the pessimistic, hysterical spectator frogs began to scream and howl, "Stop, don't do it, you'll get hurt! You'll kill yourselves! Stop now!" As the race progressed and the crowd's warnings continued, one by one, the now leery frogs began to drop out of the race until only one frog was left, Thumper. Thumper, undeterred, approached the wall and with a mighty leap, almost made it to the top. As he hung on for dear life, the crowd was becoming frantic, yelling, "What if you can't hold on?" "Drop down, we'll catch you." "Don't be a fool, you can't make it!"

But Thumper was determined. Inch by inch he kept climb-ing...higher...higher, until he reached the top of the wall. And it was at this point that Thumper became the first frog in the history of the swamp to ever see beyond the wall!

The reason Thumper was able to succeed where no other frog had was because Thumper was deaf!

A Swamp Called Emotional Struggle

What are your hysterical frogs? They're the thoughts that pummel you with doubt, fear, and negative thinking; thoughts that discourage and prevent you from getting over your wall of anxiety or depression. These thoughts rise up from a murky psychological swamp we commonly refer to as insecurity. In the next chapter you'll learn how insecurity provides the fuel for *all* emotional struggle that follows. For now, simply be aware that once you learn to turn a deaf ear to insecurity's toxic (frog) thoughts, you will begin what I call an *unlearning* process capable of retraining not just the way you think and feel, but the actual structure of your brain itself.

As you begin to restore a healthy emotional balance, you will simul-taneously be restoring the balance of valuable brain chemicals that have been depleted by the chronic stress you've been living with. If you take medication for anxiety or depression, in time you may find that you can reduce or even eliminate the need for ongoing medical support. My lips to god's ears, right?

By learning how to extricate yourself from the endless distortions of insecurity-driven thinking (typified by doubts, fears, and negatives) you will be retraining your brain to stop the emotional stress and chemical depletion that fuels your life of suffering. When I talk about retraining your brain, please know that this isn't hyperbole; I quite literally mean reshaping the anatomy of what scientists have come to call our "plastic brain." And once you begin to "rewire" your brain through a self-coached process of systematically eliminating reflexive, toxic thinking, your natural balance and resilience will return. It's what biologists call homeostasis, from the Greek words for *same* and *steady*, referring to the fact that all living things have self-regulating mechanisms that, given the opportunity (in our case, by eliminating insecurity's frog-thoughts), will actively seek to maintain the stable conditions necessary for survival.

Self-Coaching,[1] in plain everyday language, offers a framework to help you understand how insecurity inadvertently becomes the underlying motor that drives a life of control, desperately trying to overcome feelings of vulnerability. But rather than overcoming vulnerability and making us feel more secure, insecurity-driven thinking only leads to anxiety and depression's further loss of control. The answer isn't trying to side-step insecurity, it's learning to become more secure and self-trusting. This is the end-game of Self-Coaching—building your self-trust muscle. Learning to coach self-trust will restore your natural, homeostatic capacity for genuine happiness. But first, let's take a closer look at what it means to retrain your brain.

Static Brain, Plastic Brain

Can the brain really be retrained? The answer is a resounding yes, but for most of the twentieth century, it was assumed that the brain was a static, unchanging organ whose capacity was determined by your genetic makeup. Let me illustrate this twentieth century, *static-brain* mindset by telling you about the origin of a personal, destructive static-mindset that began with my "inability" to spell.

Early on in elementary school, in spite of my efforts, I wasn't a very good speller (actually, I was a terrible speller). We had to memorize twenty

---

1. Cognitive Behavioral Coaching (CBC) would be a more descriptive way of describing my technique, however, I feel that the term Self-Coaching is simpler and more user friendly, which is why I've chosen to use it throughout this book.

words a week, which doesn't sound like much now, but I vividly recall seeing the pained frustration on my mother's face as she tried night after night to quiz me on my words, telling me, "Joey, concentrate! Concentrate!" Even then, I felt exposed and embarrassed. Perhaps I was too antsy and couldn't sit still long enough to concentrate, but don't get me wrong, whatever the reason, it wasn't that I wanted to flub my words, I just did.

By the time I reached high school, my spelling insecurities had morphed into an almost phobic fear of writing (no spell check back then), which itself then morphed into a laissez-faire complacency about schoolwork in general. Since I had concluded that my inability was, in fact, a mental shortcoming, I began to accept my dismal academic fate along with my lackluster grades. I wish I had known what I know now, that current research suggests that there's a neurological glitch in about 20 percent of people that makes them chronically poor spellers. I think I could have lived with a "glitch" rather than the pronouncement that I just wasn't that smart.

Fast forward. Going through college (which if it weren't for pole vaulting, never would have happened) and graduate school, I wasn't quite sure what to make of my consistently improving grades. I attributed this mainly to my tenacity rather than to any actual ability, which, as it turns out was partially true, but I'll get to that in a minute. One thing, though, was unmistakable—startling in fact—I began to notice improvement, especially in my writing skills. I even had an English professor who, impressed with an essay I had written, asked me if I had ever considered majoring in English. Talk about startling! For the first time in my life, rather than feeling defensive and exposed about my writing, I was actually beginning to feel a fledgling sense of confidence. So how is it that my agony became my ecstasy?

There's no question that through my repetitious labor (a.k.a., tenacity) and struggle during my college years, I was forcing my mind—my brain—to adapt and change. Simply put, my brain grew—it grew because I was *exercising* it. The ability for the brain to grow in response to learning is called neuroplasticity. And if, in fact, the brain is pliable, "plastic-like," what's to say that anxiety and depression, like my entrenched negative mindset, can't be undone with proper Self-Coaching exercise? Unlearned?

Okay, okay, I realize that anxiety and depression aren't simply "mindsets." But I am going to ask you to suspend any preconceived notions you may have about anxiety and depression and, at least for the moment, consider the possibility that if, indeed, the brain itself can structurally be changed through learning to expand its actual capabilities, then why *wouldn't* it be capable of "unlearning" anxiety and depression? And herein lies the crux of my thesis: in order to unlearn something, it has to first be learned, thereby becoming a habit—a neurological wired pattern in your brain. You may think, *surely anxiety and depression aren't learned!* Keep reading.

Pathways in the Brain

I live in northern New Jersey, which to my knowledge was settled some ten thousand years ago by the Lenni-Lenape Native American tribe. There were three main branches of the tribe, and a web of paths was worn into the hardwood forests of New Jersey allowing the tribes to move from tribal village to village. As the European colonial intrusion began around 1650, slowly these paths were seized by the colonials who began a more robust traffic with horses and carts. Eventually, during the early 1700s, strawberry farming became a major industry in North Jersey, as wagons filled with produce heading for New York City began to further widen and formalize these once foot paths. Today, these same paths have been transformed into multi-lane county roads.

It helps to think of your physical brain as possessing, not paths and roads, but neural pathways that transmit information traffic. If, like the expansion of the Lenni-Lenape footpath, one of your neural pathways were to become more frequently traveled, that pathway would eventually be transformed from a pathway to a super neural highway—a habit-loop.[2] Just as a neural pathway for a particular strategy to control life can be formed by repetitious usage, so too can the same pathway become abandoned by disuse as we form new, more healthy habit-loops in our brain.

When you learn about controlling strategies in Chapter Seven, you will not only be assessing your particular go-to strategies that offer you a *sense* of control when struggling with anxiety or depression, but you will also be identifying structural neural pathways (habit-loops) that currently exist in your brain. The good news is that your brain is always changing—it is neuroplastic—and with a Self-Coaching approach to unlearning anxiety and depression, you can not only neutralize these old neurotic neural pathways, but you can begin to forge new super neural highways devoid of the confounding effects of insecurity.

Neuroplasticity

In 2000, neuropsychiatrist Eric Kanel won the Nobel Prize for discovering that learning quite literally changes the brain's structure. It helps to think of the brain as you would any other muscle—exercise it and it will grow. Although the implications of this discovery referred to intellectual functioning, such as my writing and academic skills, they can also be applied to changing the neurological structure of your brain responsible for sustaining any habit—habits such as anxiety and depression. (And yes, I did say, "habits!" More on this in a moment.)

Mind-Brain Unlearning Note

Self-Coaching can teach you how to exercise, stimulate, and retrain your brain—allowing you to reclaim your life free from chronic suffering.

2. In his book *The Power of Habit*, Charles Duhigg popularized a term called "habit-loops" referring to a neurological "loop" that governs any habit behavior.

You may think my talking about reshaping your anatomical brain is rather farfetched. If so, let me tell you about a fascinating study done by Eleanor Maguire, Katherine Woollett and Hugo J. Spiers from the neuro-imaging center at the University College, London, and you decide.

London cab drivers are required to memorize a map of the city including some twenty-five thousand streets and landmarks. It's a gargantuan learning process that can take years to accomplish. Upon successfully completing a test called the Knowledge of London Examination System, the driver is granted a license. The study followed a group of trainees, taking periodic snapshots of the cabbies' brains using MRI imaging. Over time the researchers found an increase in the grey matter—nerve cells in the brain where processing takes place—in the hippocampus, which is the part of the brain responsible for navigation. As impressive as these results are, the researchers went a step further, demonstrating that London bus drivers, who drive the same route every day and are not required to "navigate"—therefore not required to "exercise" the hippocampus—did not show an increase in size of that organ.

Another compelling study conducted by lead author Corinna M. Bauer of the Massachusetts Eye and Ear Infirmary using multimodal magnetic resonance (MR)-based imaging demonstrated that the brains of people who are born blind make new connections in the absence of visual information. These connections result in enhanced compensatory abilities such as heightened sense of hearing, smell, and touch as well as other cognitive functions. This research demonstrates that the structural, functional, and anatomical changes in the brain found in those with blindness are not present in normally sighted people.

I realize that the term itself, neuroplasticity, may seem quite intimidating, but fear not, you won't have to become a neurobiologist to begin to dismantle anxiety or depression. All you need to know is that the exercises in this book are designed to rewire your brain. Like the Fiddle Leaf Fig plant in my office, I don't need to understand plant photosynthesis to keep my plant healthy and growing; I just need to be sure to continue my regime of watering, fertilizing, and pruning. The psychology and Self-

Coaching components of the program in this book, like my watering and fertilizing, are all you need to follow in order to rewire a healthier brain.

In fact, let's keep it really simple. All you need to know going forward is that learning changes your brain. You may have already concluded from the above discussion that negative learning (thinking) changes your brain negatively, and positive learning (thinking) the reverse. What's critical is for you to understand that what goes on in your mind—the thoughts that you allow (or resist)—aren't just mental; they produce electrical chemical events in your brain that either contribute to your suffering or diminish it. And, as you'll see throughout this book, by understanding and appreciating the fact that *thoughts change chemistry*, you'll be more likely to take your Self-Coaching program more seriously. How? One thought at a time.

Mind-Brain Unlearning Note

There's no question that the brain, like any other muscle in your body, will grow in response to consistent, targeted stimulation, i.e., learning.

Psychology + Coaching + Neuroplasticity

Psychology is considered a social science, neuroplasticity is considered a biological science, so, what would we call coaching? Certainly not a science in the strict sense of the word, but for our purposes of Self-Coaching, how about we simply call it a motivational science? Okay, with this in mind, let's link our three *sciences* together. In order to rewire your brain (the biological science) and begin to unlearn anxiety or depression, you need to extricate yourself from insecurity-driven, distorted thinking (the psychological science), and, this is important, in order to liberate yourself from toxic thinking you are going to need to sustain your Self-Coaching training over time (the motivational science).

Perhaps you're still insisting, *I need therapy, not coaching!* If this sounds like you, then it's important to dispel, at least for now, any notion you may have that what you're about to read is just another "coaching" book, lacking any "real" science, offering simplistic, worn-out, you-can-do-it prescriptions. So, in this chapter I will give you as much of an overview as I possibly can to help you understand what years of working with anxiety and depression in my private practice, as well as my own early emotional struggles, have taught me about eliminating anxiety and depression.

To be clear, it wasn't my years of formal training and education that ultimately shaped my thinking about anxiety and depression—it was the common-sense insights that I gleaned over the past four decades of private practice. I say "common sense" because I've come to see that therapy doesn't have to be a mysterious journey through the abstract weeds of unconsciousness. What separates us from a liberated, healthy, happy life isn't dependent on an endless dissection and interpretation of past trauma. It *is*, however, dependent on actively dealing with here-and-now reflexive, destructive patterns and habits of thinking that, unless challenged actively and directly, will follow you through life.[3]

Take, for example, a self-declared chocoholic. Do you think it matters why they ate that first Hershey's bar twenty years ago? Of course not, for the chocoholic, it *only* matters that he or she dig their heels in and abstain now. It doesn't matter if the habit is smoking, biting your nails, or crippling, endless loops of insecurity-driven thinking. When it comes to breaking any habit, unless you actively challenge, neutralize, and replace it, it "ain't going anywhere."

Anxiety and depression may not be addictions, but addiction-like, they are capable of becoming entrenched habits that mold and shape your emotions, your chemistry, and your actual brain's anatomy. Fortunately,

---

3. As you'll see in upcoming chapters, I'm not suggesting that one's history is unimportant. Clearly, having an understanding of the historical forces that shaped your emotional life can shed light on the "why" you struggle, while giving you added perspective. Self-Coaching, though, isn't dependent on these historical insights and is primarily concerned with the "how" you extricate yourself from the habits of the past that are contaminating your present life.

our "plastic" brain is quite capable of forming new neuronal pathways and replacing old destructive habits with more adaptive, healthy ones. It's this plasticity that enables me to tell you that, with proper self-coached training, you don't have to go on living with anxiety and depression.

Yes, but, why Coaching?

I want to come back to why, as a psychologist-coach, I felt it necessary to link coaching with psychology and neuroplasticity. When I was writing my first Self-Coaching book back in the nineties, to my knowledge there was no such thing as a life coach, career coach, health and wellness coach, relationship coach, or the hundreds of other "coaches" that have sprouted up since then. When I first formulated my Self-Coaching program, the only "coaching" I had in mind was athletic coaching. For those old enough to remember, the Knute Rockne kind of coaching. This is why you shouldn't confuse Self-Coaching with the coaching movement of the past fifteen years.

Readers familiar with my previous book *Self-Coaching: The Powerful Program to Beat Anxiety & Depression* (Wiley, 2007) will recall how it all began when a cousin of mine wanted advice for the anxiety and panic he had been struggling with for years. He had been to therapists and tried numerous medications, all with no discernible results. I wasn't about to engage in any kind of formal therapy with him, but he was family, so I couldn't abandon him either. We began to have regular talks, which, as it turns out now, were seminal to my thinking about anxiety and depression.

What was crucial for me was that he was my cousin and *not* my patient. (Note: I truly dislike using the term "patient." But "client" seems too business-like, and simply using "person" could cause confusion in the discussions that follow. So for now, forgive the medical implications as I stick with "patient.") With my cousin, I was able to take the gloves off and be much more direct, which was quite a departure from typical office demeanor of passivity and reflective responses to my patients. I was, for example, able to be quite assertive, refusing to listen to his persistent whining about how he was never going to get better, that he was suffering from a mental illness like his grandmother's, and like her, was going to wind up in an institution.

We grappled a lot at first because of his stubborn adherence to his pessimistic conclusions. Until one day, getting impatient with one of his hysterical rants, I said, "Stop thinking of me as a psychologist who has all the answers. Think of me as a coach." My cousin, a former college football player, inspired me to add, "What do you think would have happened if you told your football coach you were too scared to get in the game?" Smiling, my cousin replied, "He would have kicked my butt!" I added, "I want you to imagine that you're *that* coach and you're going to get in the face of your hesitations and kick butt! Nothing's going to change unless you coach yourself to get off the bench and stop cowering in self-doubt and fear."

Although my in-your-face approach didn't have any immediate effect on my cousin's entrenched insecurities, it did set the tone for our ongoing talks. Most importantly, it got my cousin to stop relying on me to "save" him with an abracadabra psychological insight because now I was "coaching" him to start taking a more active role in his own recovery—to get off the bench.

From those early, serendipitous exchanges with my cousin I came to see that traditional therapy alone, at least for me, was too...abstract, too passive, and too removed from the action necessary to "get in the game" (i.e., stop yielding to insecurity). I realized that a better approach would be to meld a solid, sensible psychological format with motivational coaching—an approach that empowers rather than infantilizes. All too often in therapy, the therapist becomes the parent-like "authority," leaving the patient to assume a child-like role of waiting to be told how to feel better. My cousin presented himself to me as a victim, and by definition, victims are powerless. He was not powerless. Nor are you powerless!

With anxiety and depression, it's easy to feel victimized by the "voice"[4] of self-doubt and pessimism, insisting that you "can't," that "it's too hard." In order not to be bullied into passivity, there needs to be another "voice," and that's the empowered voice that inspires, ignites, and fuels your optimism. That voice can and will come from your inner coach. You'll see.

Mind-Brain Unlearning Note

Bottom line: Self-Coaching is all about insight and action.

Becoming your own therapist-coach may seem like a tall order, especially if you're feeling sapped by depression or depleted by chronic anxiety. But keep in mind a very important Self-Coaching principle: *feelings aren't necessarily facts!* Just because you *feel* you can't doesn't make it so. You have unlimited potential for liberating yourself from a life of struggle. We see this all the time with human feats of unbelievable determination. Just ask Fauja Singh, the "Turbaned Torpedo," who in 2011 (at the age of one hundred) completed the 26.2-mile Toronto Marathon! How about Herbert Nitsch, an Australian free diver who, on one breath, was able to dive 702 feet below the surface. Or Dean Karnazes, an American ultra-marathoner who completed fifty marathons in fifty states in fifty days. And then there's Wim "Iceman" Hof, a Dutch adventurer who climbed Mount Everest and Mount Kilimanjaro wearing only shorts! Don't *ever* underestimate the power of determination or the human potential to turn the impossible into the possible.

---

4. When referring to our inner dialogue, it's helpful to think of these thoughts as inner "voices." It's as if "someone" in your mind is talking and you're either listening or ignoring the chatter.

Doctor, Am I Normal?

Forty years ago, when I started my first graduate internship, I was assigned patients mostly with mild to moderate anxiety and depressive complaints. Although I didn't fully realize it at first, whenever I was assigned someone who was taking anti-depressant medication, I felt somewhat... intimidated. I found myself approaching them differently than those who weren't taking medication. I wrongly felt that someone who *had to* take medication was different from someone who didn't have to take it. My perception was that those who were medicated had more *serious* problems. They, unlike my more "normal" patients, were...mentally ill. After all, they needed medication!

I look back on those early days with pained hindsight. Back then, I assumed that when it came to anxiety or depression, there were two varieties: a kind of "normal" emotional struggle related to stressful life circumstances and a darker, more pervasive struggle not necessarily connected to life circumstances. I was drawing a line dividing normal psychological adjustment from mental illness. I recognize now that, although my thinking had some merit, what was flawed was my seeing two distinct manifestations of these struggles rather than one continuous progression.

Think of a cigarette smoker addicted to nicotine. With a smoker we can make a distinction between mild (less than a pack a day) to moderate smoking (a pack a day) to heavy smoking (two packs or more a day). Whether mild, moderate, or heavy, all represent degrees of nicotine addiction. In the case of a cigarette smoker, it's easy to understand how, in time, a nicotine habit can progress from an occasional few cigarettes to multiple packs a day. It's critical to understand that with anxiety and depression there is also a similar progression.

It seems that most patients I work with for their anxiety or depression hold similar misperceptions to my early, black-and-white thinking. If, for example, I'm working with someone who's struggling too much with debilitating symptoms, and I mention that medication could help, there's a moment where the air seems to leave the room. Finally, the heavy silence is broken by, "You mean, I *need* medication?" You see, they too have come to feel they have crossed a line where they are no longer normal. After all, *normal* problems don't require medication. Right? Wrong! As you might guess, I see things quite differently now.

If we're to avoid a normal versus abnormal (or worse, mentally ill) way of thinking, then we must adopt what might best be called a relativistic view—not just of anxiety and depression, but of emotional struggle in general. What may begin with mild symptoms of worry or moodiness can progress over time into debilitating symptoms of hopelessness, despair, and so on. Just as a cigarette habit is reinforced by smoking many cigarettes over time, a *habit* of anxiety and depression must also be reinforced by insecurity-driven thinking. Hold on a minute! Anxiety and depression are habits? I realize this sounds rather heretical, especially if you've always thought of your struggles as, well, an *illness*.

With a physical illness, a virus or bacteria invades your body and you become ill. With an infection, you are quite literally a victim of this nefarious agent. I hope to convince you that with anxiety and depression you're also being victimized, not by some outside agent or illness, but by a toxic, habituated kind of thinking (and perceiving) that has eroded and shaped you mentally, chemically, and when it comes to your actual brain, anatomically. And once you understand the cumulative effects of this destructive type of thinking, you can begin to retrain your brain to slow down and eventually unlearn how to stop the erosion, thereby allowing your normal resilience to be restored. Saying this differently, you can begin to experience life without the overlay of anxiety and depression.[5]

One reason you may have difficulty accepting the notion that anxiety and depression are habits is because of the traditional psychiatric view that has dominated the field of psychology (not to mention our media) for at

---

5. Although it may appear that I use the term brain and mind interchangeably (a concept that will be dealt with extensively in the chapters ahead), for now understand that when I refer to the brain, I'm referring to the neuroanatomical organ that houses your thinking mind.

least the last seventy-five years—a view that embraces a medical model of illness. Words like "patient" (my use of "patient" not excluded), "diagnosis," "illness," "mental hospital," etc. all continue to reinforce a medical model of psychology.

I see this all the time in my practice. Someone, for example, may enter therapy with a smorgasbord of distressing symptoms, but not until I put a label on it (required for insurance purposes), like Major Depression, Generalized Anxiety Disorder, Obsessive-Compulsive Disorder, etc., do I hear a gasp. Now that they have a "label," it's as if I just handed out a life sentence. For many, putting a diagnostic label on their struggle is further evidence that their life has been hijacked.

If this describes you, then consider the alternative: rather than feeling powerless and victimized by your struggle, what if the truth is that you are *not* powerless? What if you are inadvertently feeding your struggles with misguided, insecurity-driven thinking? And what if instead you could learn to retrain your brain to starve the thinking that fuels your struggles? If you're willing to consider this proposition, then let me give you one bit of encouragement that will be repeated in many ways throughout this book: *All habits are learned, and all habits can be broken. All habits! Even anxiety and depression!*

What's in Your Bucket?

Not only do you need to change how you think about your anxiety and depression, it's also important to make a distinction between your life before you became anxious or depressed and your current life of suffering. I realize that for some people this may not be possible, as anxiety and depression may reach far back into their childhood, but even with someone with a relatively recent onset of symptoms, there usually isn't a specific tipping point where you go from feeling your normal everyday self to feeling anything but normal as you grapple with depressed or anxious feelings. Rather than a specific tipping point, typically anxiety and depression are usually the result of a gradual transition caused by the corrosive effects of insecurity that invariably lead to emotional stress and chemical depletion.

The best way to think about the effects of chemical depletion is to think of your brain as a bucket containing the chemicals (serotonin, dopamine, etc.) responsible for your emotional balance. Imagine stress to be a metal punch capable of poking holes in the bottom of the bucket. A few holes created by life's inevitable challenges and frustrations don't pose a significant problem, as your brain is capable of replenishing this loss through a biological process called hemostasis. But if stress becomes chronic, creating more and more holes poked in the bucket, in time, your body won't be able to meet the demand, thereby creating chemical imbalances. This is why anxiety and depression are not "just in your mind." They can, through a process of depletion, become whole body problems. And this is why medication that slows down this depletion works.

How We Generate Stress

"I worry about everything—getting sick, losing my job...I drive myself crazy. Why bother? Nothing makes me happy anymore." When you become identified with destructive, insecurity-driven thinking, you are inadvertently creating a tainted version not only of yourself, but also the world you live in. It's important for you to know that your perceptions of yourself, your life, and your world, are all simply interpretations and judgments that you make—they are not facts. The truth is that you, your life, and your world are neither good nor bad, black nor white. It all depends on your perceptions and judgments.

Let's say, for example, that a company has to lay off ten of its workers. Four of the ten may become anxious and panicked, another four may wind up moderately depressed, while two of the ten may not be bothered at all, remaining optimistic that something else will come along. The point is, losing your job doesn't *make you* get anxious or depressed. As Epictetus, a second century slave turned philosopher, put it, "It's not what happens to you, but how you react to it that matters."

Fourteen Hundred Reasons
Why You Can't Afford to Ignore Stress

If you go back as far as I do, you may remember the 1969 song "War," with the lyrics, *War, what is good for? Absolutely nothing!* That's how I feel about stress. What is it good for? Absolutely nothing![6] Stress will ultimately pave the way toward a life of emotonal struggle. Need some convincing?

There's a structure in your brain called the amygdala, which becomes activated when we feel threatened (real or imagined). The amygdala informs another part of your brain, the hypothalamus to start what's called the hypothalamic-pituitary-adrenal (HPA) response. Here's where it gets interesting. Your hypothalamus begins to mobilize your pituitary gland, which in turn triggers your adrenals to activate your sympathetic nervous system to release, ready for this? One thousand, four-hundred stress related chemical reactions in your body. Phew!

Oh, and by the way, there can be NO stress or anxiety without amygdala/hypothalamus activation. In Part III you're going to be given the Mind-Talk steps that will teach you to tame your amygdala response.

Mind-Brain Unlearning Note

The more vulnerable and insecure you are, the more susceptible you are to being adversely affected by life's stressful and challenging circumstances.

---

6. When I refer to stress in this book, I'm mainly referring to neurotic, insecurity-driven stress. A hot water tank busting in your basement or getting a flat tire, will typically cause an understandable amount of stress, but stress that is proportionate to the circumstance and time-limited, isn't the kind of stress that leads to anxiety and depression.

Mental Mutiny

Typically, we see our thoughts as having a life of their own: "I just can't stop worrying," or "Do you think I want to feel this miserable? I try, but I just keep thinking things are hopeless." Certainly, when it comes to emotional suffering, we don't decide to suffer! Well, not consciously. How is it that our thoughts can turn against us, torture us, and worse, even make us not want to live? To begin to understand this mental mutiny, you need to understand that your thinking (especially self-sabotaging thoughts) doesn't occur in a vacuum; it is directly influenced by the unique combination of characteristics that form what we call your personality.

Whether you describe your personality as being hypersensitive, overly emotional, pessimistic, optimistic, worrisome, upbeat, introverted, or extroverted, you're talking about a here-and-now snapshot of who you've become. In this moment, you are the end result of all the developmental experiences, positive and negative, that have shaped you (and your brain). But when it comes to understanding the sabotaging thoughts associated with anxiety or depression, you need to know that these thoughts are the byproduct of insecurity that has shaped your personality.[7]

Think of a stack of coins, each coin representing a life experience. As the stack grows, if you add a bent coin or two, or three, what happens? The stack begins to tilt. Eventually as more coins continue to be added to the already tilting stack, the stack falls. The bent coins represent the insecurity that results from early trauma, separation, loss, illness, and so on. The stack falling represents the onset of anxiety or depression. Since Self-Coaching is about here-and-now problem solving, it isn't essential that we analyze every bent-coin experience in your history. It doesn't matter whether your potty training was too strict or too lenient; it only matters that you re-stack the coins, ensuring that you don't allow insecurity to add

---

7. Although there are genetic predispositions that may lower your threshold to becoming more anxious or depressed, these influences can best be thought of as tendencies rather than life sentences.

any bent coins going forward.

So, what are today's bent coins? They're current and chronic habits of insecurity-driven thinking (doubts, fears, and negatives) that sabotage, discourage, deplete, and distort your natural and full potential. Unless you learn to understand how you inadvertently feed these habits that tilt your life toward chronic anxiety or depression, and what you can do to starve them, you can't expect to liberate yourself from struggle. As with any habit, you need to learn how to take the right action to interrupt these patterns (habit-loops) and begin to retrain your brain.

Let me ask you a few serious questions. I won't sugar coat it. Are you serious about committing yourself to a progressive program that can challenge the entrenched habits that sustain your misery? Are you ready to put in the necessary effort to retrain your thinking and your brain? Are you ready to reclaim your life that has been snatched away from you by the faulty habits of anxiety and depression? And are you ready to understand that if you remain passive and victimized by insecurity-driven thinking, nothing will change? If so, then it's time to get started.

2

Two Words That
Will Change Your Life

What if I were to tell you that there are two simple, uncomplicated reasons why you suffer from anxiety and depression? No doubt you would find such an oversimplification rather preposterous. But before getting to these reasons in this and the next chapter, let's take a look at why you need a new, simplified perspective. After all, if you're like most people who have tried to understand why your life has become so twisted and tormented, you've probably spent most of your time scouring the weeds of your past looking for clues as to "Why?" And you've likely come out of those weeds still feeling anxious and depressed.

You've probably been convinced that the key to your liberation from suffering lies in finding the sine qua non, the cause—the truth that will set you free. Although there is some validity to approaching your struggle with a traditional perspective that assumes you need to find the "why," in my opinion, it's too myopic. If, for example, someone were to point to a brick wall and ask you what it is, you'd simply say, "It's a brick wall." You don't need to go up to the wall and inspect each brick to finally conclude that it's a brick wall. The same goes for anxiety and depression; you don't need to explore every historical "brick" of your past in order to see and understand the bigger picture—the here-and-now wall of a problem.

Traditional Psychology vs. Self-Coaching

I'll be the first to admit that Self-Coaching doesn't sound as sexy as psychoanalysis, which is why I wanted to include this rather illuminating but disturbing experience I had as a patient with a not-so-good Freudian psychoanalyst. I mention this, my first therapy experience, simply to highlight how easy it is for a "naive" patient to spend an inordinate amount of time and money not getting better. Perhaps even more importantly, to highlight the importance of redefining our expectations of what therapy, psychology, and healing "ought" to be. All this to prepare you to open yourself up to a more unorthodox approach—a Self-Coaching approach—to ending your struggle.

Shortly after graduating from college, I found myself struggling with anxiety. Having majored in psychology, I thought being a patient myself would be a great way to feel better and experience the process of therapy firsthand. And, of course, back in the early seventies I assumed that the gold standard of therapy had to be psychoanalysis. I mean, if you're going to buy a car, why not the Jaguar rather than the Ford? Right?

Although my analyst wanted me to come five days a week, I could only afford two sessions a week, and this was at a staggering twenty-five dollars a session (thank god for my wife's teacher's insurance). I was instructed to free associate. You know, talk about whatever comes to mind: school, finances, jobs, the color of his rug (it was a nauseating, faded orange)... all this while he silently took copious notes. Other than his asking the occasional, perfunctory, "How do you *feel* about that?" or offering a few dream interpretations, that was about it. Even when pushed, he was loath to give an opinion, and would typically deflect with, "It's more important what *you* think about it." After one particular session where I discussed a seemingly mundane dream about a bug on the back of my leg, he sat back in his leather recliner and offered a rare interpretation: "You obviously want to be intimate with your mother!" Obviously? Seriously? Oedipus be damned.

I may have been young (early twenties) and psychologically quite naive, but his dream interpretation left me scratching my head, stirring up questions not only about the value of therapy, but about Doctor So-and-So as well. Whenever I expressed my misgivings about therapy, he would point out that I was resisting, projecting, having transference issues, or was in denial. How do you argue with opinionated Freudian logic? Especially when you don't even understand the terminology! I finally decided that enough was enough and made a decision to terminate therapy and go off to graduate school in California. Can you guess his response? He *adamantly* advised against it, warning that I needed more work!

Finally, an opinion!

This, as you might imagine, created a wave of anxious thinking. Maybe I wasn't seeing things clearly. Was I, in fact, resisting? In denial? What if he was right? I began to feel like there was a ticking anxiety time bomb in me just waiting to explode. And yet, in spite of his ominous warning, plus my general state of anxiety and ensuing trepidation, my gut was telling me something quite different.

Something in me knew I had to roll the dice and get to California to pursue my dream. Unfortunately, I arrived in San Diego with my analyst's words still haunting me: *You need more work.* Regardless of my ambitions, I couldn't stop ruminating and "what-iffing." After all, who was I to challenge the *doctor*, the authority, the purveyor of sanity? Confused, worried, and angry, I somehow managed to focus on my school work as the months began to slip by. As you might guess, there was no anxiety meltdown! NO MELTDOWN! I probably wouldn't be writing this book had I listened to my "doctor."

There is a postscript to all of this. About four months after leaving for California, I did receive a letter from Doctor So-and-So apologizing for his "counter transference." Although I can't remember his words exactly, I believe he said that *his* analyst insisted he write to me apologizing for not being truthful (i.e., lying). The details are not important. But even to this day, I hope I never run into him face-to-face! (It's a Jersey thing.)

Let's Be Fair

Okay, so hold on, let me be fair. In every profession there are the good, the bad, and the ugly. Even though my experience with Doctor So-and-So was truly an "ugly," I was to find out that it was, in fact, an anomaly. Since that first disappointing therapeutic experience, I've had many training analysts (a requirement of my clinical education was to have a new individual therapist every year as well as a group therapist, not to mention my years of post-doctoral training analysis). Each and every one of these psychologists, psychiatrists, and psychotherapists taught me, helped me, and inspired me.

What Should be the Goals of Therapy?

In my estimation, if therapy isn't making sense and translating to everyday real-life experience, it isn't therapy at all; it's nothing more than a psychological analgesic. Growing up Catholic, I know the powerful analgesic effect that going to confession has on your psyche. You walk out of that confessional feeling cleansed, liberated, and one hundred psychological pounds lighter. For many people, therapy is just such a cathartic experience. In confession, you are absolved of your sins by a priest; in therapy you feel absolved because of your efforts to connect the dots of your past to your present suffering. With Doctor So-and-So, even though I would spend an hour prattling on about my historical "bricks"—without ever achieving any closure—I must admit, I always walked out of his office on an analgesic high. I didn't have to understand what was going on—after all, with all of Doctor So-and-So's copious notes, surely we were getting somewhere. As they say, hope springs eternal.

You might be wondering why my rather disturbing therapeutic experience mentioned above didn't turn me off to psychology forever; actually, it did just the opposite. More than ever, I realized I had unfinished business—I still wanted to know "why" I continued to struggle with anxiety, but more importantly, I simply wanted to feel better.

Breaking with Tradition

From the very start of my Ph.D. program I was introduced to many other psychological schools of thought. Since the Freudian method still left a sour taste in my mind, and was no longer my gold standard, I opened myself up to other possibilities. After a few brief infatuations with Gestalt therapy, Transactional Analysis, and so on, I had the good fortune of taking a course called Myth and Symbol, with John Sanford, a well-established author, Episcopal minister, and Jungian analyst, that left me totally enamored with C.G. Jung. My goal after getting my doctorate was to pursue the one hundred hours of required training analysis (which I eventually did) in order to enter the C.G. Jung institute in New York (which I didn't).

It was during my "Jungian" years that I had a discussion with another psychologist at the mental health clinic where I was working. He was a behaviorist who tried in vain to convert me to the notion that a technique called behavioral modification was the most expedient way to eliminate self-destructive behavior. In the arrogance of my youth, and with the ongoing infatuation I had with all things Jung, I remember feeling somewhat sorry for him. After all, how was it possible for anyone to approach psychology by completely ignoring the unconscious (as behaviorists do)? Poor guy had no idea of the collective unconscious, of archetypes, and the symbols of the unconscious. His views seemed so simplistic to me. That was over forty years ago. Looking back, I wish I had listened a bit more carefully to what he was saying. It might have saved me years of weekly trips to New York City for my training analysis.

Don't get me wrong, from a purely intellectual standpoint I'm glad I went through my "formal" training. But from a practical standpoint as a psychologist in private practice, well, it wasn't so helpful. My patients weren't getting much better by my helping them understand transference, archetypes, dream interpretations, or childhood memories. As I started to become desperate, I found myself beginning to stray from the traditional Jungian fold. I tried using hypnosis and bio-feedback, and began to drift toward more of an eclectic approach—a little of this method, a little of that concept—whatever seemed to work. Long story short, I still wasn't getting results, at least the kind of convincing results I was seeking.

When it came to offering tangible solutions to anxiety and depression, I invariably found myself in an endless rabbit warren of dead ends. I vividly recall Mary, a young lady in her early twenties who I had been working with, who was suffering from anxiety and panic attacks. After a thorough, historical exploration we found that her anxious, worrisome mother had set the stage for Mary's early perceptions that the world was a very dangerous place not to be trusted. What's important was that Mary's adult fears, worries, and "what-ifs" were indistinguishable from her mother's. There it was! Or so it seemed at the time. The problem for me arose when Mary came back the next week and asked, "Now I know *why* I worry, it all makes perfect sense, but I still can't stop doing it. What can I do?" I can't remember what I told her, but I know I didn't have an adequate answer for her. All my previous training left me stumped. After all, once someone connects all the ah-ha, historical dots, there shouldn't be any reason to go on suffering, right? Not quite.

Like Mary, I too had questions. I remember thinking, *What else can I do as a psychologist?* I simply wasn't feeling comfortable offering palliative (supportive) therapy, especially when every session seemed to be a rerun of the previous one. To be honest, I was beginning to feel like a charlatan, holding out hope for my patients when I was hopelessly floundering myself. In fact, during those initial days of private practice, I began to seriously think about finding another career. It just didn't feel right offering a rudderless form of Joe Luciani psychology to my patients. I did some serious soul-searching as well as consulting with various colleagues who all encouraged me to stay the course, indicating that they experienced similar frustrations in their own professional growth.

The only thing that kept me going was that I knew that my patients were, in fact, feeling supported, understood (regardless of my confusion), and hopeful, which appears to be the reason why they kept coming back (recall the "analgesic" effect mentioned above). One thing that was beginning to evolve, perhaps because of my frustrations, was that I was gradually beginning to change my traditionally stoic, reflective posture and instead, I was becoming more of an "active" participant in the sessions. I wasn't afraid to encourage and often "mirror" the attitude that I felt was missing in my patients. For example, with a depressed patient, I might inject a bit of energy, hope, or encouragement. For an anxious patient, I might encourage them to challenge (reframe) emotionally distorted hysterical thinking with more objective, less contaminated thinking. Things were seeming less dire as I began to shift my own intuitive gears. I began to feel more hopeful. Still, I needed more than hope.

It was at this point that my cousin, who you may remember from the last chapter, called asking me to help him with his anxiety. Finally, I was ready to break away from following any particular school of thought and start to trust my own psychological instincts. That's not to say that I threw the psychological baby out with the bathwater, which is why, if you happen to be a student of psychology, you will notice eclectic elements of other orientations expressed in Self-Coaching. In fact, I fondly recall working with a psychology graduate student who told me, "I see you employ a lot of Albert Ellis's Rational Emotive Therapy in our sessions." I had never read Albert Ellis! I went home that evening and ordered a book by him, and son of a gun, my patient was right; there were similarities. Same goes for Aaron Beck's Cognitive Behavioral Therapy (CBT), which I read after writing my first Self-Coaching book on anxiety and depression back in 2001.

I'm just glad I developed my Self-Coaching insights before being introduced to Ellis, Beck, and others, simply because it confirmed for me something that I've always felt about psychology: there are universal conclusions that anyone working with patients for a long enough period of time will come to realize. Well, maybe not anyone. Sometimes a therapist's personal evolution is stunted by an archaic, rigid adherence to a particular psychological dogma. You may recall my analyst's pronouncement, "You obviously want to be intimate with your mother!"

Think of a bicycle wheel where each of the spokes represents one of the many different psychological approaches to choose from: analytic, psychodynamic, dialectical behavioral therapy, cognitive/behavioral, etc. Using my spoke analogy, although there are many approaches (spokes) to choose from, they all point toward the "hub," which represents the ultimate objective—emotional healing. I happen to be partial to my Self-Coaching-spoke approach for a few reasons:

1. It's user friendly. Self-Coaching from its very inception was designed to minimize the dependency of a patient on his or her therapist.

2. The concepts make common sense. You don't need a Ph.D. to understand what's going on and what you need to do to progress.

3. By treating anxiety, depression, and emotional struggle as habits, you eliminate the need for endless interpretations. You learn what you're doing that feeds these habits and what you can do to starve them.

4. By learning specific exercises that require active practice, you actually restructure your brain. Old brain-habits are neutralized (unlearned), and new positive habits are established.

5. *And now, as promised at the beginning of this chapter, the two words that will change your life—insecurity and control.*

Here's the CliffsNote on insecurity and control: once you understand that insecurity is the source of your suffering and that trying to compensate by (over) controlling life is your neurotic remedy, you will begin to see that anxiety, depression, worry, compulsion, phobias, and even addictions are all feeble attempts to ward off vulnerability in a world where self-trust, confidence, and hope have been compromised.

Insecurity

Let's start out with a discussion on insecurity and pick up the concept of control in the next chapter. Insecurity is a term often confused. So, what exactly is insecurity? In my previous book *The Power of Self-Coaching* (Wiley, 2004) I offered the following (along with an updated insecurity quiz that follows):

- Insecurity is a feeling of vulnerability and/or helplessness.
- Insecurity results most often from childhood psychological wounds—real or imagined.
- Insecurity is the faulty perception that you can't handle life or some aspect of life.
- Insecurity is based on emotional distortions, not necessarily facts.
- Insecurity becomes a habit of thinking and perceiving.
- Insecurity minimizes the possibility for accurate self-perception.
- Insecurity becomes worse over time.
- Insecurity eventually feels like a natural part of your personality.
- Insecurity is a habit, and all habits can be broken.

Before we go any further, let's use this short quiz to get a general idea of how insecurity may be contributing to your emotional struggles. A life contaminated by depression or anxiety will *always* be fueled by insecure thinking. I've yet to see an exception to this rule. The converse is equally true: the more secure you are (or become), the less your life will be damaged by insecurity's corrosive effects of worry, doubt, fear, or negativity. Since insecurity can often be subtle, even unconscious, it's important to begin to shed as much light as possible on this all-important component of your anxiety or depression.

Please read the following questions carefully, but don't overthink your responses. The quiz is not meant to be a precise assessment of your personality; it's only intended as a helpful guide to predicting your general level of insecurity. You'll find that as you progress with your Self-Coaching training, coming back and retaking this quiz can offer valuable feedback about your emotional growth.

Circle your responses as being "Mostly True," "Sometimes," or "Mostly False," as they generally pertain to your life. Answer every question, even if you have to guess. Scoring is at the end of the quiz.

T S F	I'm overly shy or uneasy with strangers.
T S F	I lack self-confidence.
T S F	I'd rather be at home than going to a party.
T S F	I often feel I'm not smart enough.
T S F	I don't feel that I have enough money.
T S F	I'm pessimistic.
T S F	I often wish I were better looking.
T S F	I don't feel I'm as good as others.
T S F	I tend to feel like a sham; if people knew the real me, they wouldn't like me.
T S F	In relationships I tend to cling.
T S F	I'm afraid to get too close to others.
T S F	I would be much happier if I didn't worry so much.
T S F	I have too many fears.
T S F	I usually hide my real feelings.
T S F	I find it difficult to say no.
T S F	If someone's quiet, I might think they're angry or upset with me.
T S F	I often wonder what people *really* think of me.
T S F	I'm always comparing myself to others.
T S F	I tend to be a jealous person.

T S F   I'm not okay.

T S F   I often feel guilty.

T S F   In any relationship, it's only a matter of time before
               people find fault in me.

Score each "Mostly True" response two points, each "Sometimes" response one point, and each "Mostly False" response zero points. Tally up all your points.

Your Score: _____

A score of 1 – 11 indicates a mild degree of insecurity. A score of 12 – 18 indicates a moderate level of insecurity. If you scored 19 or more, this indicates a substantial interference from insecurity. Record your score and remember to periodically retake this quiz as you progress through your Self-Coaching/brain retraining program. You'll see your trust-building efforts reflected in your improved Insecurity-Quiz scores.

You Weren't Born Insecure

Regardless of your Insecurity-Quiz score, do NOT feel discouraged. For starters, recognize that having insecurity isn't an exception—it's the rule. To a greater or lesser extent, everyone has insecurity. Although it's the underlying reason why you suffer with anxiety or depression, it remains an acquired habit—not a life sentence! But how does insecurity become such a ubiquitous habit in the first place? For starters, no one grows up in a perfect world. No one has perfect parents. No one escapes loss, illness, frustrations, or separations—no one escapes life's inevitable feelings of vulnerability.

The dictionary defines insecurity simply as a lack of confidence or assurance. Most people will tell you that it's an unsafe, doubting kind of tension that you feel from time to time. From a Self-Coaching perspective, insecurity is an anticipation of danger, vulnerability, or helplessness, high-ly correlated with a lack of self-trust. The good news is that you weren't born insecure; you *learned* to be insecure. As mentioned above and worth repeating: insecurity is an acquired habit. And like any other habit, it can be broken.

When it comes to insecurity, there's usually a point, depending on the challenges you face, where you begin to experience emotional stress. It helps to think of a thermostat that has been set according to the strength of your insecurity. A very insecure person, whose thermostat has been set very low, will require only a minimal loss of control to trigger emotional struggle, whereas a relatively secure person with a minimal amount of in-security will have a thermostat that has been set much higher, which will require much more trying circumstances before triggering an emotionally stressful response. The goal of Self-Coaching is to reset and raise your thermostat's set-point, thus increasing your tolerance to any and all life challenges, at which point insecurity is unable to continue to generate and fuel anxiety and depression.

Don't Waste Your Money

I've been talking a lot about my past, but if you'll indulge me just one more Joe Luciani anecdote (I promise), I think it will help shed more light on the nature of insecurity and its ability to shape our personality and our mental health. You may recall that in the last chapter I talked about how insecure I was about my academic "inabilities." Well, I didn't quite tell you the whole story. I didn't tell you about a rather painful—and embarrass-ing—encounter I had with my high school guidance counselor that, as they say, *sealed the deal* when it came to my feeling insecure.

Before telling you my encounter with Mr. M, let me just reiterate (in my defense) that for me, high school was about sports, dating, and hang-ing out. On rare occasions—very rare occasions—I would manage to take home a book or two, but not often. In my senior year my mother insisted on setting up an appointment with my guidance counselor, Mr. M, to discuss college. The meeting, to the best of my recall, went like this:

My mother started out by thanking Mr. M for holding the meeting. Getting right to the point, she began, "I want to discuss what college Joe might attend next year." After a long, long silence, Mr. M, looking first at my mother, then at me, and finally back at my mother, said, "Don't waste your money." That was it! Trust me, even though this was more than fifty years ago, you don't forget something like this.

As I look back at how devastating (and inexcusable) Mr. M's response was, I realize that the real devastation was what happened in the years after high school where I tried to hide my embarrassing "secret" about my intellectual shortcomings. I told you about my college and eventual successes in the last chapter, but I didn't tell you that during those formative years I wasn't insecure just about my academic skills; I became almost paranoid that others, like Mr. M, would see that I was a sham, a person—*wasting his money*—who shouldn't be in college.

You may wonder why Mr. M's "advice" had more of an influence on me than my actual, successful academic performance over the years. As you'll see in the chapters that follow, one of the biggest contributors to anxiety and depression is the inability to differentiate facts from emotional fictions. I was ruled by the fiction that I was intellectually inferior. The fact that I was able to accumulate A's in my college classes was irrelevant; nothing seemed to be enough to topple my faulty perceptions. It never occurred to me that my dismal high school performance had everything to do with the fact that I never bothered to study! I see this behavior all the time with my patients. They're able to tell you that their feelings and insecurities are ridiculous, but nevertheless, they go on spinning and spinning the fictions of insecurity that keep them imprisoned.

Remember the stack of coins in the last chapter? Surely, "Don't waste your money" was a major, bent-insecurity-coin experience for me. With the exception of extreme trauma associated with post-traumatic stress disorder, it's important for you to understand that one "bent-coin" experience won't necessarily evolve into a neurotic *habit* of insecurity. For that to happen, there needs to be an accumulation of toxic-shaping experiences as you grow up. These cumulative experiences—illness, loss, frustrations, parenting issues, and yes, traumas—create a sense of vulnerability (in full disclosure, there were other "bent coins" in my stack, but who's counting). Suffice it to say that some coins are bent more than others. My careful effort to try and hide my "secret" was no doubt a major contributor to my stress and anxieties, but not the only factor. Once you begin to slide down that slippery slope of allowing insecurity to shape your thinking and perceptions, you're on your way to a life of suffering. Insecurity is pervasive, resistant to challenge, and as a habit, life defining.

Calling Out Insecurity

Some may recognize their own insecurity, saying, "I'm too insecure to trust anyone." While others may deftly camouflage it with rationalizations, excuses, or deflections, saying, "No, of course I'm not scared (i.e., insecure); I'm just not comfortable in social situations." The common thread that runs through all expressions of insecurity is a hesitation to trust self and life. Without trust, you find yourself feeling too vulnerable. You don't have the confidence necessary to simply let life unfold. In my situation after Mr. M's pronouncement, I was unable to trust who I was. I clung to the irrational belief that, in spite of my academic accomplishments, my performance was all a sham covering up my inescapable, inherent flaw.

Insecurity attempts to prepare you for anticipated chaos. This is what we commonly refer to as worrying. After all, you don't worry about things going right! As Mark Twain said, "I've had a lot of worries in my life, most of which never happened." A friend of mine told me about his mother's even more poignant, but opposite, spin on this notion: "Don't tell me worrying doesn't work. Most of the things I worry about never happen." A person with adequate self-trust lives in the here-and-now moment with the confidence to believe that they can handle life as it unfolds. An insecure, untrusting person is either mired in past regrets or in anticipation of future chaos.

Case Stories

Throughout this book I will refer to actual material from my work with patients in order to show how Self-Coaching applies to everyday situations with everyday people. I find that these stories, along with my added commentary, provide an effective tool in helping you to get a more practical application and understanding of various Self-Coaching concepts. For clarity, I've chosen to use rather discrete examples of either anxiety or depression, when, in fact, anxiety and depression are often comingled together. Each story was selected to best exemplify the concepts currently discussed in the text. Also, do keep in mind, whether you suffer specifically from anxiety or depression, these stories illuminate the underlying common denominator of both—insecurity and its influence on shaping your struggles. I therefore encourage you to read all the stories in this book in order to more fully understand the mechanisms involved in emotional struggle. Let's take a look at how insecurity can not only define a life, but also destroy one. [Note: The examples that follow are actual examples that have been significantly altered to protect any personal identifying information of my patients.]

Officer Mike

Mike, a twenty-eight-year-old police officer, former marine, and mixed-martial arts black belt, became visibly defiant at my mentioning the possibility of insecurity. He said, "There is no [expletive deleted] way I'm insecure! I can't afford to be insecure!" But even for this seemingly secure police officer, there was no other explanation for his recent panic attacks and his unfounded, hysterical jealousy toward his wife. So, when I tried to soften the blow by rephrasing my assertion, "Would you agree that you have insecurities regarding your wife's behavior?" he still was having nothing to do with a term that in his estimation connoted weakness. He said, "No! I don't have insecurities; she can't be trusted."

Interestingly, Mike wasn't able to explain a recent, rather intense panic attack that sent him to the emergency room thinking he was having a heart attack. He attempted to sidestep the issue by saying that it probably was due to his feeling physically depleted due to his shift work and the one-too-many coffees he drank that night. I would have given him some slack with this if it weren't for the fact that he had been having somewhat less intense, but similar attacks on and off for the last six months. At this early stage of therapy, Mike wasn't ready to confront his insecurity demons, which for him suggested not only weakness, but also less manliness. Considering the fact that the only reason he came to therapy was because his wife threatened to leave him if he didn't, I knew I had to tread lightly. At first!

There was no question that Mike was a formidable and competent law enforcer. There was also no question in my mind that Mike was suffering from anxiety. And where there's anxiety there's insecurity. In this case the jealousy was just the tip of the iceberg. The jealousy, along with his infrequent symptoms of panic, were the only outward manifestations of insecurity that showed. His insecurity had everything to do with the one thing he prided himself on: being in control.

From being a marine, black belt, and policeman, Mike, for the most part, felt powerful, capable, and secure. Until his marriage, his tough-guy persona (Mike was reprimanded twice by his chief for getting too physical) gave him the illusion that he controlled life and people. As it turned out, the one thing he couldn't control—his wife (his Achilles heel)—became the crack that allowed insecurity and anxiety to enter the picture.

Prior to marriage, Mike didn't recall having any problems. He had it all figured out: if you're strong and powerful enough, you don't ever have to feel insecure. After marriage, he inexplicably encountered a wave of insecurity that toppled his previously constructed façade of security. His marriage began to fracture only months after the wedding, his wife going to live with her mother after telling him she was tired of being bullied.

Without going too deep into Mike's past, suffice it to say that from an early age, being the class tough guy, intimidating others, and never showing weakness was his response to his emotionally abusive, alcoholic, bully of a father. He said, "There was no way I was going to cry when my old man belted me. I wouldn't give him the satisfaction," which is why when we first met, he informed me, "There is no [expletive deleted] way I'm insecure!"

Where There's Smoke, There's Fire

I mention Mike's story in order to introduce you to the concept that insecurity and control are the smoke and fire of anxiety and depression. Mike had always known how the traumas of his past had shaped his life; he just didn't understand how it was *still* shaping his life. There's no question that past trauma can, tsunami-like, travel with you through life, leaving you desperately—consciously or unconsciously—trying to escape from a world that was broken. Our present world may no longer be broken, but we continue to act as if it is. And this is why someone like Mike had to control and bully life—it was because of his habit of insecurity that he insisted he wasn't about to be vulnerable.

Looking Ahead

Unlike Mary's insecurity mentioned earlier in this chapter, or Mike's, not all habits of insecurity can be traced back to childhood, and clearly not all insecurity is a result of a specific trauma, but *all* insecurity, regardless of what instigated it, becomes a precursor to a life of control. In the next chapter you'll see more clearly how a life spent trying to circle the wagons of control sets in motion an inevitable crash and burn of emotional struggle.

3

Anxiety & Depression:
It's All About Control

In high school biology I learned that all organisms avoid pain and seek pleasure (e.g., the absensce of pain in more primitive organisms). I would like to offer a second Self-Coaching imperative: all organisms (including you and me) instinctually hate being out of control. Absolutely hate it! Here's an interesting fact: the Moro reflex is a startle reflex normally present in all newborns. If an infant feels a sudden loss of support, as if falling, the arms and legs will first spread out (startle response) followed by a coming together as if grasping something.[8] It's thought that the Moro reflex may be a vestige from our primate evolution where a newborn monkey, losing support (feeling out of control), will try to regain its hold on the mother's body as a way to prevent falling—which for primates typically high up in trees, could mean death. The primal fear of being out of control is no doubt intimately related to what we typically refer to

8. My granddaughter Elia, at four months old, transitioned from her swaddle to a more modified swaddle that allows more arm movement. The reason for the swaddle, other than offering a comforting facsimile of the womb, is that the Moro reflex is rather strong and will cause the baby to startle and wake up crying.

as our survival instinct. When it comes to life, we are, in fact, survival-controlling machines.

The instinct to want to be safe and in control is not confined to primates. Just this morning I noticed a small spider walking across my desk. I'm not fond of spiders, especially since my days in San Diego where under every kitchen sink was pasted a warning sticker with a picture of a black widow spider sporting a menacing red hourglass marking. Anyway, I was about to smack the little fellow with a book, when, no doubt sensing my threat, it began what can only be described as evasive maneuvers. In one of the most remarkable feats of desperation I've ever seen, it hopped, jumped, zig-zagged, and dodged my every attempt to squish it. Having evaded my whack-a-mole assault, the little fellow skittered off harassed but unharmed. Ya gotta be impressed with the power of the survival-control instinct.

Good Control, Bad Control: Setting Your Internal GPS

From a Self-Coaching perspective, there are two types of control—healthy and unhealthy. Healthy control is essentially a prudent attempt to do what it takes to maintain our safety, health, and well being. The operative word here is "prudent," suggesting a sensible and practical response to real-life vulnerabilities, which is why we buckle up before driving, take vitamins, or look both ways before crossing the street. Unhealthy control, on the other hand, is anything but prudent, sensible, or practical. Take, for example, a man suffering from obsessive-compulsive disorder (OCD) who feels in control only when he ritualistically checks and rechecks his stove ten times before leaving the house, a woman with social anxiety who feels in control by avoiding eating or drinking in public, or someone suffering from depression whose dark thoughts often begin to drift toward suicide as a grim way of ultimately controlling (stopping) their suffering.

Healthy versus unhealthy, the motive in either case is the same—wanting to be in control (or needing to feel less out of control), which is a basic homeostatic instinct. Like my hopping spider, you and everyone else are just trying to avoid suffering and struggle by maintaining control over our lives. That being said, the question remains, *how is it that our basic, healthy, survival instincts to be in control of our lives can leave us feeling even more out of control? Aren't instincts supposed to protect us?* The answer is *yes, but*—there is a but. Sometimes the control we seek isn't the result of an actual life challenge; it's a response to distorted, reflexive, insecurity-driven thinking. A recent experience driving home from a friend's house in Long Island will illustrate this point.

My wife and I were not familiar with how to get back to New Jersey, so we set up our GPS, clicking "Go home" on our device. Little did we know that my daughter had previously used our car and had reprogrammed the GPS's "home" directions. We were driving along in quiet conversation, when my wife asked, "Why does that sign say Midtown Tunnel?" We had never been in the Midtown Tunnel, but we assumed we were in good GPS hands. After a few more miles, we realized we were, in fact, headed due south rather than north and home. We were lost! It wasn't the GPS's fault that we were lost; it was only following my daughter's programming. And this is my point: unhealthy control is the product of misguided directions given by insecurity's *programming*. And like our GPS excursion, unless you reprogram your mind and your brain, you too will be heading in the opposite direction from where you want to wind up.

Mind-Brain Unlearning Note

Anxiety and depression are the result of faulty brain programming.

Insecurity + Control

In the last chapter we learned how the doubts, fears, and negative thinking of insecurity generate feelings of vulnerability that leave us feeling out of control. In order to understand the retraining necessary to unlearn and liberate your life from struggle, you need to see how the chronic stress of trying to overcontrol life leads to both emotional and chemical depletion. It's this depletion (which is why medication works) that becomes the precursor to anxiety and depression. Take a look at Ray, a patient I was working with whose phobic fear of dogs will illustrate the profound, corrosive influence of trying too hard to control life.

Ray's Story

Although Ray had never actually been traumatized by a dog, for some inexplicable reason he had become immobilized by an anticipation and gripping fear of being bitten. Ray was a jogger who, because of his fears, opted for running on the more trafficked county roads rather than the quiet streets of his suburban neighborhood. His logic was that home owners along these busy routes were less likely to leave their dogs outside without being leashed. From time to time, if he did encounter someone walking a dog, he would hastily cross over to the other side of the street, keeping one eye on the dog, all the while wondering, *Is that guy holding the leash tightly enough?* Eventually Ray, rather than addressing his fears, gave up jogging outside altogether and bought a treadmill.

Initially Ray came into therapy because of anxiety and related issues. His dog phobia didn't come up at first, since Ray had already "solved" that problem with his treadmill. One day, coming to my office and getting out of his car, Ray saw my neighbor's loose dog meandering about in front of my home/office. Ray sat in his car for fifteen minutes waiting for the dog to move on before daring to walk the twenty-five feet to my office entrance. When he entered, Ray was red-faced and visually agitated. When I asked him what happened, all he said was, "That damn dog!" I had a sense there was much more to this and asked that he tell me more about his dog encounter. (I should tell you that Lucy, my neighbor's adorable West Highland Terrier who terrorized Ray, isn't that much larger than your average cat.)

Ray told me that he had recently developed an irrational fear of dogs and had no idea why. Pressing him, I asked him to tell me what it was about dogs that made him anxious. What came out was quite illuminating. According to Ray, "Dogs know no fear. They only know aggression. When I'm around a dog, if that dog decides to bite me, nothing I do matters. It will attack. With people, I can reason, talk to, get them to understand, but how do you reason with an out-of-control dog?"

It wasn't the dog that was out of control; it was Ray's imagination that made him feel out of control, which is why he did everything in his power to control his encounters with dogs. He tried carrying pepper spray but decided it might cause more problems by getting a dog more agitated. He purchased what he described as a dog "zapper," which was supposed to emit a high-pitched sound that, allegedly, would deter an aggressive dog. But one day while passing a barking dog locked up in a car, Ray decided to experiment and give him a "zap." No effect! So, Ray's ultimate Plan B solution, as mentioned above, was to buy a treadmill.

Before discussing this further I'd like to reintroduce you to a term briefly mentioned in Chapter One: "habit-loop." For now think of a habit-loop as a dog chasing its tail (no offense, Ray). Ray's habit-loop (which was repeated over and over again during the course of a jog) would look like this:

anticipation/hypervigilance >>
sight (or thoughts) of a dog encounter >>
anxiety about being bitten >>
avoidant behavior >>
reduction of anxiety >>
anticipation/hypervigilance

So how in the world could such an intense, phobic, habit-loop come about if, in fact, there had never been a traumatic canine encounter? As it turned out, Ray's dog phobia was just the tip of a control-iceberg. It quickly became apparent to me that Ray was a dyed-in-the-wool control freak. His life was a compulsive nightmare of everything from never being late (which was why Ray was so agitated coming in late to our session); obsessions about health, physical appearance, money; numerous superstitions; and indecisiveness. When it came to his marriage, he was a tyrant, needing to control every decision from where to go on vacation to what TV shows to watch, even insisting that his wife load the dishwasher according to his exacting specifications. His wife, adding to his stress, had recently told him she felt like a prisoner and wasn't going to take it any longer.

Controlling life made Ray feel less vulnerable. It seemed perfectly reasonable to him to insist that life—and wife—comply with his blueprint on how things ought to be. I should point out that Ray wasn't complaining about the ongoing effort required to keep all his worldly ducks in a row. But he was becoming increasingly troubled by a free-floating, chronic anxiety along with the stress and effort involved in trying to anticipate and prevent an emotional "duck" mutiny. As incredible as it seems, Ray never connected his anxiety to his compulsive need to control every aspect of his life.

In Ray's world, there was an implicit set of rules and expectations, but unfortunately some things in life just don't play by the rules—you guessed it, dogs! Ray finally conceded that no matter how hard he tried when jogging in the suburban "wilds," there was ultimately nothing he could do to totally eliminate the possibility of getting bitten. In Ray's black and white world, if you aren't 100% in control, then you're out of control. And for him, being out of control just wasn't an option. It came down to one conclusion: he had to stop running outdoors. Although he hated running indoors on his treadmill, he gladly accepted boredom instead of the chronic stress and fear he faced when running outdoors. What price control?

In order to keep the above discussion focused primarily on the nature of Ray's need to control, I purposefully omitted a prolonged discussion of his history—the "why"—he became such a compulsive over-controller. Suffice it to say that Ray was the apple that didn't fall far from the tree of his excessively rigid parents who only dealt in life's blacks and whites. Ray's rather uneventful history, which he happened to describe as "perfectly normal," serves as a good example of how less than traumatic, subtle environmental factors (e.g., overcontrolling, anxious parenting) can conspire to create problems. And as a postscript, if you haven't already anticipated where this is going, after a month on the treadmill, Ray couldn't stand the boredom; he longed for the open roads. But that was too scary, so he decided to give up running and put his treadmill on Craigslist.

Why Do I Feel out of Control?

So, maybe you're thinking that you're nothing like Ray. Okay, but what's important is to understand that regardless of your unique array of symptoms, anxiety, depression, and the need to overcontrol life are typically associated with one or more of the following:
- Adverse shaping influences (especially during your developmental years) that have molded your personality
- Excessive stress generated by trying to chronically overcontrol life
- Life challenges that overwhelm your controlling strategies
- Your general state of psychological and physiological resiliency
- Genetic factors that may predispose you to both anxiety and/or depression

The "Why" and "What" of Anxiety and Depression

According to medieval philosophers, the goal of alchemy was to obtain the philosopher's stone, a substance capable of turning base metals into gold. The starting point required for the creation of the philosopher's stone was called the prima materia, or "first matter." When it comes to anxiety or depression, the prima materia—the starting point—is insecurity. Insecurity is the fertile soil from which all feelings of vulnerability (i.e., loss of control) and suffering originate. Let's expand the discussion from the last chapter on how insecurity is an inescapable part of growing up in an imperfect world. By understanding the circumstances that set the stage for insecurity to develop, you begin to have a better idea of "why" you struggle.

As we've discussed in previous chapters, there's no question that understanding the historical reasons for your insecurity can offer some valuable perspective. But from a Self-Coaching perspective, understanding the "why" you suffer, as enlightening and helpful as it may be, isn't as important as the "what" you're going to do about it. If you're trying to quit smoking cigarettes, do you think it matters *why* you took that first cigarette? Of course not. For someone trying to quit smoking, the historical "why" they started smoking is completely irrelevant to breaking the here-and-now nicotine habit. And when it comes to cigarette smoking, clearly, understanding alone won't do a thing to help you break your habit.

With anxiety and depression, though, there definitely is *some* relevance (the gasp you just heard came from traditional analysts). The reason I say "some relevance" is because you need to understand that the past will *not* set you free. There's a saying that if you're duck hunting, you can never *aim* a duck to death. Translation: you must pull the trigger. With anxiety and depression, your history is important, but pulling the "trigger" is more important. What's the trigger? Actively applying the Self-Coaching steps outlined in Part III of this book.

There's no question that understanding the influences that have shaped your insecurity puts you in a better position to recognize how the past is mirrored in the habit-loops of the present—habits conspiring to trip you up. This expanded historical view of your struggles can often be motivating. It makes the irrationality of suffering more understandable. We humans do better with knowing what's in the dark. But once again I must offer a disclaimer: although Self-Coaching is definitely enhanced by having historical insights into your struggle, it is by no means dependent on these insights in order to unlearn anxiety and depression. Let's expand this discussion.

Mind-Brain Unlearning Note

Definition of Neurosis:
A confusion of the past with the present.

The question remains: just how important is it to spend years (as is often the case with traditional analysis) dissecting and analyzing the past, trying to get to insecurity's prima materia? As helpful as understanding the shaping influences of your insecurity can be, breaking the habits of anxiety and depression *can* be done in the absence of these insights. I've had many patients over the years who just didn't have clear memories of their childhood. Without the assistance of a therapist, it's difficult to accomplish this historical "dissection" on your own; it's a forest-for-the trees problem. By developing a here-and-now, facts-versus-fiction, Self-Coaching approach, the habit-loops that reinforce anxiety and depression can be unlearned as you actually begin to rewire your brain and reset your mind without any retrospective detective work.[9] The bottom line: habits are learned, and habits—all habits—can be broken. Your job will be to find out how you have been inadvertently feeding and reinforcing your habits of anxiety and then begin a Self-Coached process of starving them.

---

9. One reason why retrospective data isn't crucial to Self-Coaching is because the here-and-now *you* is an aggregate of everything that has preceded you. Your past is reflected in the present, which is why the habits of today are the habits that must be broken.

4

Non-Nurturing Shaping Influences

As previously mentioned in Chapter Two, insecurity is an inescapable part of growing up in a world where there are no perfect parents, where loss, illness, frustrations, or separations all contribute to feelings of vulnerability for the growing child. When it comes to insecurity, there's no question that a child growing up in a nurturing environment where there is love, encouragement, and stability will fare much better than a child growing up in a non-nurturing environment. Before moving on to the application of Self-Coaching in the chapters ahead, it's important to take a closer look at what constitutes a non-nurturing environment—these are the catalytic forces that determine the extent of one's legacy of insecurity.

Non-nurturing forces can be the result of direct influences, like growing up with an abusive, alcoholic parent, being bullied or teased at school, or being traumatized by the death or separation of a loved one. Other less direct shaping stimuli could be a struggle with an undiagnosed learning disability or not being popular in school. As impactful as these circumstantial influences can be on the developing ego, perhaps the most substantial contributor to later insecurity is whether or not the parental environment was nurturing or non-nurturing.

Molding and Shaping

Have you ever tried to "throw a pot" on a potter's wheel? You start off with a lump of damp clay slapped onto the center of a wheel that begins to spin. As you apply gentle pressure with your hands, the lump begins to be transformed, first into a tubular column, then as you insert your thumbs at the top of the column, it widens, you press down more, the column becomes squatter, and finally, voila, a pot is born. Or not—sometimes the slightest wrong movement causes the entire thing to wobble, then collapse. The beauty of working with clay is that if you're not satisfied with the outcome, you simply pound down your clay and start again.

Think of your brain as that pliable lump of clay. Life experiences rather than your hands are the forces that continually mold, shape, and determine your end form (the you that's reading this book right now). Unfortunately, when corrosive, shaping life forces have had a hand in your development, the end result—the adult *you*—may wind up riddled with anxiety or depression. The sad truth is that once you become anxious or depressed you will most likely stay that way unless you realize that, through the neuroplastic capacity of your brain, you can neutralize old habit-loops while reshaping new ones. In a sense, you can throw a new "pot." Regardless of how hopeless or discouraged you feel, you absolutely can be released from your distorted perceptions of self and life. And the proof, as they say, is in the pudding. You'll see.

I Had a "Normal" Childhood, so Why Am I Anxious and Depressed?

Many patients I've worked with report coming from relatively happy, loving, nurturing environments, yet their suffering appears to be no less than the person from the broken, abusive, defective home. How can this be?

How can relatively "normal" parents inadvertently promote the insecurity that invariably leads to a life programmed for anxiety and depression? To answer this, you should understand that not all anxiety and depression are a result of a completely dysfunctional, non-nurturing environment. Far from it. The confusion often occurs when, for example, I ask a patient to tell me about their childhood and they assume I'm looking for dysfunctional, alcoholic, abusive, or criminally neglectful parenting—the really bad stuff. They say, "There wasn't anything terrible about my childhood. It was unremarkable. Nothing terrible. You know—normal."

So how can an "unremarkable, normal" childhood environment lead to anxiety and depression? It turns out that the word *dysfunctional* must be understood in a relative sense, just as with the word *normal*. Both terms refer to behavior that occurs on a relative continuum and are not meant as yes-or-no labels. As I learned in graduate school, these are statistical concepts, not people concepts. Let's take, for example, a "relatively" normal, but mildly indifferent, egocentric parent. Such a parent might have enough self-awareness (or sense of guilt) to recognize their profound selfishness and make a conscious effort to "do the right thing" by getting more involved in the child's life. In which case, although the child may feel "relatively" secure and happy, they never quite feel secure and loved enough. As the saying goes, there is one true love and a thousand different copies.

Another example might be a somewhat overcontrolling, anxious, worrywart of a parent. In this scenario it would be hard for a child not to become sensitized to life's dangers—the what-ifs—thus setting the stage for a worrisome, anticipatory anxiety to emerge. Interestingly, most children of worrywart parents will often misinterpret mom or dad's excessive worrying as an expression of love rather than what it really is: an expression of the parent's insecurity. I only mention this because oftentimes when reflecting on our past, we have a tendency to misinterpret, minimize, romanticize, or otherwise excuse our parents. We may feel a sense of guilt or even shame for implicating them in our current struggles. After all, as I hear often from my patients, "They did the best they could," which may be true, but this doesn't excuse parents from having shortcomings. Nor does it mean you're being disrespectful or unloving to your parents if you recognize the objective truth.

By recognizing the similarities between your present-day insecurities and the nurturing/non-nurturing environment provided by your parents (as well as other significant shaping influences) during your early developmental years, you give yourself an important edge. You gain the ability to step apart from your own personal mental congestion and recognize how your present struggles have been shaped by your early learning and conditioning—the programming of your brain. As mentioned in the last chapter, understanding the past gives additional perspective to the question, "*Why* am I struggling?" And, as many patients have told me, it makes them feel less crazy to know that anxiety and depression don't just happen (like a mental illness). There's always a backstory.

The Non-Nurturing Environment

For the sake of simplicity, rather than going too far afield discussing the countless other, nonparental circumstances and influences that may affect a child's development, such as illness, loss, separations, poverty, a broken home, etc., I've chosen to focus on four non-nurturing parental styles that I feel are most closely associated with later susceptibility to anxiety and depression. As mentioned above, keep in mind that a "nurturing versus non-nurturing environment" is a relative thing. Think of it as a continuum that ranges from a wonderful, loving, nurturing milieu to a dysfunctional, corrosive, non-nurturing one. Most will find their experiences somewhere in between these two extremes.

The four categories listed below are general descriptive, non-nurturing parental characteristics that are best seen as ranging from mild, to moderate, to severe. Although I list these as discrete categories, it's not uncommon for there to be some overlap between the categories. They are:

- The overcontrolling, anxious parent
- The codependent, clinging-vine parent
- The indifferent, unloving parent
- The defective, abusive parent

Mind-Brain Unlearning Note

When reading through the four non-nurturing parental categories below, try to keep an open mind. Recognize that, even though the descriptions that follow illustrate rather extreme or blatant examples, it's up to you to make a relative judgment as to the severity or subtlety of these influences on your life.

The Overcontrolling Anxious Parent

Back around 1969, overly anxious, controlling parents began to be called "helicopter parents." Helicopter parents have a tendency to hover over their children—helicopter-like—micromanaging every aspect of a child's life, saying, "Watch out!" "Don't pet that dog!" "Don't eat that." The child becomes merely an extension of the parent's anxieties, fears, and insecurities. In an attempt to stay one step ahead of anticipated mayhem, helicopter parents just can't help jumping in and getting involved. Too involved!

It's not just about being cautious with present dangers either. Overcontrolling, anxious parents always have one eye on what's ahead. My cousin, a kindergarten teacher, had a recent encounter with a determined helicopter parent that says it all. On the first day of class she received a note from a mother asking that she offer a curriculum that would accommodate her five-year-old son's ambition to become an astrophysicist. Thinking this was meant as a joke, my neighbor was flabbergasted when the irate mother approached her after school one day angrily asking why no curriculum had been offered. When my cousin balked at the request, the parent threatened to go to the principal, superintendent, and the local papers! True story. Hell hath no fury like a helicopter parent scorned.

Why have so many people lost so much perspective? Part of it is cultural, where parents seek every advantage for their child in order to remain competitive in what is perceived to be a dog-eat-dog world—a world where other anxious parents are relentlessly seeking the same advantages. But it mostly has to do with the parents' own anxieties and insecurities, where, short of wrapping their child in bubble wrap, they obsessively try to insulate the child from any and all of life's slings and arrows.

Another less obvious factor has to do with affluence. As Baby Boomers (along with the affluence passed on to the Generation Xers) began to experience the prosperity of a post-World War II recovery, they set in motion a new brand of overcontrolling, anxious parent who can overcontrol because now they can afford to. No to be denied, the generations following the Gen Xers (Xennials, millennials, etc.) have the time, the money, and the wherewithal to schlep kids from Karate school to SAT tutors, to soccer practice, and home for takeout. Life has steadily evolved, not just around the child, but *through* the child. I guarantee, if you watch any of the old fifties sitcoms like *Leave it to Beaver* or *Father Knows Best*, you can't help but notice how the archetypical parents of that era were involved more as observers rather than active participants in the lives of their children. Seems weird, huh?

More and more I invariably find that my adult patients who were parented by overanxious, controlling parents are more likely to become insecure, anxious (worrywarts), controlling, fearful, and emotionally ill-equipped to handle life. And why wouldn't they be? For the most part, they weren't required to figure things out, to deal with adversity, to think and problem-solve, or to develop self-confidence and a sense of security. This was all done for them. Most times, not being overprotected isn't a bad thing. And sometimes even experiencing failure once in a while can be transformative. Participation trophies, anyone?

The Codependent, Clinging-Vine Parent

There's an important difference between the overcontrolling parent and the codependent parent. Where the overcontrolling parent is invested in controlling and protecting every aspect of a child's life, the codependent parent lives vicariously through the child in order to compensate for their own shortcomings. Because of their own emotional neediness, this is a parent who, rather than being the source of emotional stability for the child, uses the child to feed their own fragile ego.

Just this past weekend I ran a 5K race and was about to pass a father with a young boy, perhaps seven or eight years old. The boy was crying hysterically, trying to tell his father, "I can't do it. I want to throw up...I have to throw up! Dad, please stop! Please!" The father had him by the hand not only refusing to let him stop, but literally dragging him along, screaming, "Shut your mouth. You're not going to throw up. You're going to finish this [expletive] race. Do you hear me?!" Of course, I gave this father a piece of my mind, only to get a "mind your own damn business" response.

A codependent parent lives in a black-and-white world where they are never wrong and must always control at any cost. This episode solidified for me the fact that for many parents, children are seen as nothing more than extensions—if not protectors—of the parent's ego. My guess is that the kid did finish the race, and I suspect the father was fuming all the way home, upset and offended by his son's lack of grit. After all, I suspect that for this codependent parent, his son insulted his (the father's) masculinity. And how do you think this kid must have felt, being such a miserable disappointment to his father? There's a good chance that one day down the road as an adult, he'll be sitting in an office like mine asking, "Why do

I feel so inadequate?"[10]

Do keep in mind that it's never the child who is responsible for a code-pendent relationship to develop. For this to happen, there must be a par-ent who is neurotically unable to separate their emotional needs from that of the child's, whereas the child's dependency on his or her parent is a realistic, survival need of the developing child. Like a vine clinging to a post, a codependent parent sends mixed messages—sometimes they're the post to which the child is encouraged to cling, and sometimes they're the vine looking for the child to, consciously or unconsciously, support them. Take for example a mother I worked with whose husband ran off with a neighbor's wife. Wounded and depressed, the mother spent most of her days in bed crying. She constantly told her son, "Mommy needs you now more than ever. Daddy's gone and I need you to be strong for Mommy." This poor ten-year-old boy, like it or not, had to assume the burden of becoming Mommy's "post."

For many parents the codependency may be subtler, often masked in more socially acceptable forms, but none more prevalent (and obvious) than youth sports. When I played Little League back in the fifties, our field was strewn with pebbles, potholes, and weeds, not to mention the makeshift chicken-wire backstop. And if an occasional parent did show up for a game, they would have to stand, as there were no bleachers to sit on. And yet no one complained. We had a great time.

Today I live a block away from the Joe Henry Little League field. (In my day, fields didn't have names. Mine was simply called the "ball field.") The Joe Henry field has a weed-free, manicured lawn, an in-ground sprin-kler system, a tarp that gets rolled out to protect the infield from rain, lights towering forty feet in the air for night games, an electronic score

---

10. Note: I imagine that the boy mentioned in the 5K race was experienc-ing an existential crisis. Physically, he felt he just couldn't continue the race, but emotionally, he didn't want to disappoint his father. Since he had to be dragged along, crying and complaining, he wound up becoming the inad-equate, disappointing son. And it's likely this wasn't a one-time crisis for this kid.

board, announcer, snack bar, sunken dugouts, practice batting cages, and so on.

On game day, the bleachers fill up fast, the folding chairs encircle the outfield fence with its bright yellow protective plastic cap, and, lest I forget, along the entire outfield fence are local advertising signs that can be purchased for a mere five hundred dollars a season. I ask you, what do you think is the mentality behind wanting to have their sons and daughters compete in such professional settings? My answer: whether it's Little League, soccer, football, or basketball, for many parents this is very serious business and, oh yes, very personal. This sign hanging on the Joe Henry fence says it all:

Reminder from Your Child
—I'm a kid
—It's just a game
—My coach is a volunteer
—The umpires are human
—No college scholarships will be handed out today

Mind-Brain Unlearning Note

The overcontrolling anxious parent may also be overly involved, as is exemplified in youth sports, but the difference is that the anxious parent is trying to protect the child from defeat, humiliation, and so on, whereas the codependent parent is using the child to gratify or compensate for their own ego deficits.

Many codependent parents feel victimized by life. And youth sports are just the ticket to give them a vicarious shot at what they lack—a sense of empowerment. Unfortunately, it's the child who, each time he or she walks out onto the field, must bear the weight of each parent's neurotic desire to win, win, win. Directly or indirectly, just like the boy in the 5K race mentioned above, there's no escaping the pressure and guilt connected to the child's feeling that they *must* perform in order not to incur the disappointment (if not the wrath) of a crestfallen parent.

Feeling like an appendage of the codependent parent's ego, this child has a hard time trying to figure out whether they are the post or the vine, leaving them feeling profoundly ambivalent and distrusting of the chaotic world they live in. When a child is treated as a hostage to a parent's neediness, how could it be any different? As you'll see in Part III of this book, the process of unlearning anxiety or depression is all about developing the self-trust *muscle*. Unfortunately, codependent children typically grow up with an atrophied self-trust muscle.

When Overcontrolling and Codependent Parents Go Amuck

Recently a federal investigation termed Operation Varsity Blues has uncovered the largest college-admissions scheme ever by the Department of Justice. Fifty parents, including Hollywood stars and top CEOs, were charged with fraud in a scam to secure admissions to such prestigious schools as Yale, Stanford, USC, and other big-name schools. They all participated in an elaborate plot that involved changing exam scores, falsifying student biographies, as well as Photoshopping images of students participating in sports they had actually never played. These parents would make charitable donations (upwards of over six million dollars in one case) that would funnel money to college athletic coaches in exchange for fast-tracking these "student-athletes" through the admissions process.

From what you've read about overcontrolling (helicopter) and codependent (clinging-vine) parents, this scam shouldn't surprise you. There's no question that most parents would do just about anything to get their child into the school of their choice. But there's a fine line that separates doing "just about anything" and fraud. For an affluent, overcontrolling or codependent parent, the temptation to bypass the rulebook and secure the status of a prestigious university may be, well, at least for the fifty parents charged in this particular scandal, irresistible.

Perhaps the helicopter parent simply wants to protect little Sally or Johnny from a life-crushing rejection, or the codependent parent can't wait to start wearing that Ivy League sweatshirt around town, but make no mistake, whether it's a helicopter or codependent parent, when it comes to their child, if there's a way, rules be damned.

The Indifferent Unloving Parent

An indifferent parent is a parent whose own life and personal needs supersede their child's. This type of parent may be openly neglectful, distracted, or simply too selfish to establish an adequate and loving relationship with the child. One patient I worked with recalled, "My mother never seemed to care about me. It was my grandmother who dressed me, read to me, who loved me. My mother was so involved at the country club, her golf, her committee work...she was the star with everyone else. She wasn't mean to me; she just never had the time. I remember once when I came home with a bleeding knee, she was on the phone with one of her girlfriends. I stood there hysterically crying and pointing to my knee. She cupped her hand over the mouthpiece of the phone and told me to go upstairs and show grandma. I did, and grandma took me to the hospital where I got four stitches."

As you can imagine, growing up with distracted, indifferent parents invariably leaves a child assuming, "Guess I'm just not good (lovable, pretty, smart, important) enough." Although I refer to the indifferent parent as distracted and egocentric, sometimes you have a selective indifference, which is the case where one of the children stands out as a star child and the other the forgotten child. The star child brings accolades from teachers, coaches, friends, and family. The proud but selectively indifferent parent may forget to attend to the less-fortunate child. Although times have definitely evolved, there still remains a selective bias in many cultures for boys. I admit, growing up in an Italian family, there was a difference. In fact, my cousin Celeste (with whom I grew up in the same house as a "sister") will tell you today that I was "El Rey," the king. Well, maybe not quite a king, but she does have a point.

If you've never seen the 1980 movie *Ordinary People*, I highly recommend it if you're interested in a depiction of an archetypal, indifferent mother. You'll never forget Mary Tyler Moore's Best Actress role as Beth, a mother whose love for her son Buck, who died in a boating accident, leaves her unable to love or relate to her other son Conrad. In one poignant exchange, Conrad, pleading with his mother about why she never visited him when he was in the psychiatric hospital, exclaims, "You would have visited Buck if he was in the hospital." Beth replies, "Buck would have never been in the (psychiatric) hospital!"

The Defective, Abusive Parent

There are many psychologically wounded parents who suffer from alcoholism, debilitating anxiety and depression, personality disorders, drug addiction, and so on. As you can imagine, a defective parent's ability to provide an adequate nurturing environment is limited by the extent of their dysfunction. It may produce neglect, emotional or physical abuse, erratic and inconsistent attempts to show love, or simply a depravity of character. But regardless, children who grow up in these homes are the children of chaos.

In such an environment, the emergent ego doesn't stand a chance of developing a sense of trust or confidence in life or self. Instead, what evolves is a world strewn with emotional land mines. Nothing is stable or reliable, and any misstep by the child can trigger pandemonium. In this environment, there is no relief other than the intermissions between periods of tumult. Because of the tenuous nature and unpredictability of day-to-day life, these children live in constant fear of abandonment, rejection, guilt, and shame. Insecurity, for all intents and purposes, becomes an inescapable legacy of these children, which invariably manifests itself in their adult lives.

Many adult-children of such dysfunctional homes live provisional lives, always waiting for the other shoe to drop, which happens to be a relevant idiom. During the late nineteenth century, tenement apartments in New York City were built with the bedroom of one apartment situated above or below the others. Someone sitting on a bed in the bedroom above you would drop a shoe, "thud," and you, in bed below, waiting, knew that it was only a matter of time before the second shoe would follow—it was inevitable. A child growing up with a defective parent, where periods of stability are merely preludes to the inevitable next storm, has no choice but to live with the chronic apprehension of the chaos to come. "Thud."

Children of defective parents will often bring this expectation of relationship chaos into a marriage, where it can become a self-fulfilling prophecy. Jealousy and distrust act as a relationship cancer that will eventually create the "expected" toxic environment: "See, I knew this wasn't going to work. You never really loved me." In more casual relationships, in an attempt to compensate for their apprehension and fear of emotional retaliation, they often become obsequious people-pleasers, always trying to avoid the anticipated wrath and rejection inherent in any relationship. Emotionally, there is always a profound distrust that there can ever be stability and love in a relationship. How can there be when the fear of abandonment, rejection, or reprisal has been structurally imprinted on the child's brain?

Because of the unpredictability of growing up in a threatening, erratic environment, these adults, devoid of any sense of security and self-trust, often become overly dependent, fearful, and terrified of abandonment. And ironically, they tend to gravitate toward defective, often abusive partners—partners who mimic their distorted expectations of love. To an outsider, it seems inexplicable, for example, that someone being physically abused will, time and time again, return to the abusive partner. Only when you begin to see the twisted perceptions of trying to be loved by a parent unable to love can you understand the reflexive insecurity that accepts abuse as a prelude to being loved. And sometimes we never over-come it, as is the case with Denise, a retired postal worker who came into therapy because of her anxiety and growing depression. Her story is of a tragic, lonely life devoid of intimacy.

Denise's Story

Denise's retired life was a simple one. A few casual acquaintances, two cats, and an unwavering routine of housework, shopping, and watching YouTube videos. It was only because of her darkening depression and anx-iety that her life of solitude and distraction had become problematic. She attended ACoA (Adult Children of Alcoholics) regularly, and although she kept to herself, she considered her meetings a vital part of her life. In therapy she told me about growing up in a broken home, never knowing her father, where she did her best to please her alcoholic, mercurial moth-er. Denise's mother was young and attractive and would bring home a constant stream of men to drink and sleep with. Denise vividly recalls the arguments, the shouting, things crashing, and at times, seeing her mother emerge from the bedroom bloody and disoriented, only to sit down at the kitchen table and pour herself another drink.

Denise was frightened, alone, and left to her own resources to feed herself, mend, wash her clothes, do her homework, and help with the housework. Denise's mother didn't work but always had enough money for the rent and food. Denise was quite certain that she was a prostitute. Somehow Denise managed to get to school each day, where she isolated herself and avoided making friends, lest anyone find out about her em-barrassing home life. At home, responding to her mother's often used admonition, "Children are to be seen, not heard," she built a kind of nest made up of old clothes in the back of her closet. It was here that she would retreat each night when her mother would tell her, "Mommy's going to be busy tonight. You'd better not be a problem." It was in her "nest" where she hid a stash of cookies, magazines, and books, mostly fairy tales. Her favorite was the Ugly Duckling.

That particular night after my session with Denise, being only casually familiar with the story of the Ugly Duckling, I went online to read it. It tells the tale of an abused and lonely duck who wanders off aimlessly, enduring a life of solitude and hardship. One day, seeing a flock of swans, he decides, "I will fly to those royal birds...and they will kill me because I am so ugly." The Ugly Duckling is shocked when the swans accept him, only to realize by seeing his reflection in the water that he has grown into one of them—a magnificent swan! The Ugly Duckling spreads his beautiful wings and flies off with his new family. It was that story, more than anything else, that gave nine-year-old Denise the only comfort she recalls feeling during those early years. Unfortunately for Denise, she never found her "swan family" to fly off with.

5

Depression

When Supreme Court Justice Potter Steward was asked to define pornography, he replied, "I know it when I see it." The same can be applied when trying to define anxiety or depression—*you know it when you feel it.* As self-evident as this statement may seem on the surface, it falls far short of explaining not only the specific symptoms of anxiety and depression, but also the causative factors that contribute to these struggles. To this end, let's begin our discussion by taking a more in-depth look at depression.

Mind-Brain Unlearning Note

In Chapter One I discussed how terms like normal versus abnormal can distort our perceptions and wind up creating needless obstacles in therapy. The same goes for labels such as generalized anxiety disorder, major depressive disorder, obsessive-compulsive personality disorder (OCD), and so on. As detrimental as labels can be, causing many to feel victimized, these labels do serve a useful function for communicating and codifying clusters of symptoms.

Depression

If you tell someone that you're feeling depressed, they'll no doubt understand what you're talking about. Feeling empty, sad, down in the dumps, worthless, or just plain blah are often commonly experienced with depression. The dictionary generically defines depression as a "pressing down," which is precisely what the emotions associated with depression feel like—a weight on your shoulders, an overwhelming feeling of dread and hopelessness that presses down on you, making life difficult if not impossible. The reason everyone understands what depression feels like is because we've all, from one time or another, felt depressed. Feeling depressed is often a normal, albeit difficult, part of being human in a world of struggles, setbacks, and loss. But the depression we feel when *pressed down* in response to challenging life circumstances is quite different from what is commonly referred to as a clinical or major depression.

Clinical Depression

When it comes to depression, it's important to understand where you fall on the relativity continuum. On one end of a continuum are mild, transient feelings of sadness, while on the other end are symptoms characterized by persistent, life-altering distress.

Mind-Brain Unlearning Note

Hopefully at this point in the book you're beginning to embrace the Self-Coaching perspective that when it comes to all things psychological, relativity matters. Big time!

From a mental health perspective, the various forms of depression are delineated by specific, clinical criteria as described in the Diagnostic and Statistical Manual of Mental Disorders (DSM-5), published by the American Psychiatric Association. As different as some of the classifications are—substance/medication-induced depression, disruptive mood dysregulation disorder, persistent depression, etc.—they do share a list of common traits, such as the presence of a sad, empty, or irritable mood, accompanied by physical and cognitive mental changes that significantly affect your ability to function normally.

A clinical/major depression refers to a severe, life-altering depression. Although its symptoms might be identical to the grief experienced after the death of a loved one or a depression in response to dire circumstantial events (financial disaster, divorce, etc.), clinical depression is mostly differentiated by the persistent, self-generated nature of such suffering.

Circumstantial Depression

From a Self-Coaching perspective, it's important to differentiate between clinical depression and what I call "circumstantial" depression. Although a devastating circumstantial trauma can generate the same array of feelings, such as intense sadness, insomnia, appetite disturbance, cognitive impairment, guilt, and so on, the critical difference is that a clinical depression is generated and sustained by the inner erosion caused by insecurity, while a nonclinical, circumstantial depression is driven by stressful external events. The severity of the symptoms may be the same, but one is driven from the inside-out (insecurity), the other from the outside-in (circumstance). Although there can be some confusion when trying to differentiate one from the other, especially when there is overlap between these depressions, typically a person suffering from a circumstantial, nonclinical depression (not insecurity-driven), will eventually regain normal functioning as stressful life circumstances abate, while the person with a clinical depression will sustain a depression because the cause—insecurity—continues to fuel it.

Quite often, there's a fine line as to where a circumstance-driven depression ends and a clinical depression begins. This is important because many clinical depressions are triggered by circumstantial events. Let's, for example, imagine that Bert has been wrongly accused of embezzling money from his company. Bert comes home from work feeling terribly upset and out of control. He feels that everyone at work must be thinking he's a crook. As the investigation goes on at work, Bert starts to get more and more depressed as he finds himself withdrawing, crying spontaneously, unable to eat, not leaving his apartment, and just wanting to sleep all day.

Clearly we would call this a circumstance-driven depression. But what if I told you that Bert has had significant insecurity issues most of his life? If this is the case, we might suspect that his circumstance-triggered depression would, at some point, become contaminated by his reflexive, pessimistic, worrisome insecurity. Then there would be a commingling of both external (being falsely accused) and internal (insecurity) influences. A line from the play *Man of LaMancha* captures this situation quite nicely: "Whether the pitcher hits the stone or the stone hits the pitcher, it's going to be bad for the pitcher." In Bert's case, there's a possibility that even if he's exonerated at work, his now pessimistic distrust of life itself (after being falsely accused) could combine with his insecurity to evolve into a clinical depression characterized by incessant doubt, fear, and negativity.

Mind-Brain Unlearning Note

A notable exception to what I call circumstance-driven depression/anxiety would be one of the trauma-related disorders, of which post-traumatic stress disorder (PTSD) is most familiar. PTSD, for example, is a psychiatric disorder that can occur in people who have experienced or witnessed a traumatic event such as a natural disaster, a serious accident, a terrorist act, war/combat, rape, or other violent personal assault. Symptoms of PTSD can last for months, and at times years, after the trauma.

It's best to consider depression/anxiety associated with severe trauma as an exception to my dichotomy, i.e., circumstance-driven versus insecurity-driven depression. But do keep in mind that with the exception of PTSD, you'll find it helpful to distinguish between circumstantial and insecurity-driven depression and anxiety.

The circumstantial grief I felt after my father's death will help to illustrate this point. (I know, I keep promising I won't continue to offer any more Joe Luciani stories. I lied.) When I was in my late teens my fifty-two-year-old father died unexpectedly of a heart attack. I flew home from college and entered my home filled with teary-eyed family and friends who solemnly escorted me into the living room to see my mother. Seeing her sitting there crying, yet managing to smile when she saw me, was heart-wrenching. Getting through the wake wasn't easy, as everything around me seemed cast in dark shadows; nothing seemed right. I felt that nothing would or could ever be right again. How could it be?

I was depressed. I had no appetite, couldn't sleep, and wanted to be left alone to process my feelings. But since I was surrounded by loved ones, I wasn't given the option of retreating. In fact, after the funeral I was quite literally dragged into the kitchen and offered a shot of scotch from my cousin Justin. The kitchen conversation started slowly, awkwardly, but shortly progressed (or regressed, depending on your viewpoint) to what I would call downright…well, hilarious, as we lovingly reminisced about my father's legendary, rather harmless displays of temper throughout the years, like the time he was trying to unsnag a fishing line and wound up throwing his fishing pole, mine, and my cousins' poles overboard, all while calling on all the saints to witness. Even now, I recall how grateful I was standing there in the kitchen, to have had such a pleasant—albeit temporary—respite from my emotional pain on that day of the funeral.

In the days and weeks following the funeral I would go sometimes for many hours without feeling sad at all, and then, *wham!* I would be walloped by a wave of profound, gripping sadness that would hit me like a freight train, which typically dissipated just as suddenly. Grief is a processing—a recalculating—as our psyche tries to somehow grasp and assimilate this new incomprehensible reality that has been cast upon us. A clinical depression may also feel incomprehensible, but there are no lasting waves of joviality or humor, no respites, no *time healing all wounds*. There is instead only a persistent, unrelenting darkness of mood embraced and fueled by feelings of self-loathing and worthlessness.

Homeostasis Revisited

Our bodies and minds have been engineered by eons of natural selection to maintain emotional and physical equilibrium; this is called homeostasis. A biological illustration of this is what happens in the advanced stages of starvation when fat reserves in the body have become depleted and we switch to proteins as a major source of energy. Muscles, which are the largest source of protein in our body, become quickly depleted. As our bodies continue to deteriorate and break down, psychologically there is a corresponding shutdown seeking to mitigate further depletion by gradually shutting down the psychic motors with symptoms of withdrawal, apathy, and listlessness—symptoms, coincidentally, not dissimilar to depression. In the advanced stages of starvation, your homeostatic mechanisms, both psychologically and physically, are desperately trying to do one thing: enhance your possibility of survival. As stated in previous chapters, human beings physically as well as psychologically abhor losing control. Our bodies and our minds are designed to reflexively do whatever we can to regain control, i.e., survive.

If we accept the premise that natural selection would never favor traits that seek to harm us, how do we explain depression? How in the world can we look at depression as not being harmful? What purpose does it serve other than to ruin our lives? To try to explain this seeming paradox, let's go back to our starvation analogy. Only when you weigh the damaging effects of starvation (depleting fat reserves, muscle loss, etc.) against the potential survival value of slowing everything down and not dying (for example, a starving person on an island eventually getting rescued), can you see the inherent "wisdom" of homeostasis. No doubt it's easier to see the survival value of why our body does what it does in the absence of food, but it's not so easy to understand how depression has any value whatsoever. Let's consider this possibility more carefully.

In a nutshell, depression (and anxiety) are attempts, albeit last-ditch attempts, to minimize further psychological loss of control. Bear with me on this. Here's another useful analogy: My home is equipped with various circuit breakers designed to protect my electrical circuitry from an overload, which could lead to a fire. Depression acts like a psychological circuit breaker. As the cumulative effects of insecurity lead to our feeling more and more out of control and vulnerable, stress invariably begins to accumulate, taxing our psychological circuits, resulting in both a chemical and mental depletion (recall our bucket analogy from Chapter One). The brain's "circuits" become emotionally overloaded, eventually reaching a critical point of depletion. At this point the circuits begin to shut down to prevent further meltdown. By giving up, retreating, not caring, and withdrawing into yourself and from life, you are essentially shutting down (depressing) the psyche from further harm.

Clearly depression doesn't solve any of your worldly problems, but it does serve a homeostatic purpose of preventing further overload. Think of it this way: In my home, if a circuit breaker trips in order to prevent fire, I will no longer have electricity. It's a good-news-bad-news scenario—I would be sitting in a dark house, no TV, no lights, no doing the wash or other normal house functions, but I won't have a fire! When feeling overwhelmed and out of control, withdrawal of energy and closing down normal functioning can be seen as a defensive maneuver designed to insulate us from that which we feel we can't handle—life. And just as my darkened home loses its functionality without electricity, with depression you also lose "normal" functioning. Listen to John, a thirty-six-year-old divorced pharmaceutical salesman whose deepening depression provides a good example of a circumstantially driven depression morphing into a clinical depression and tripping his "circuit breaker":

> I've been feeling down for a long time, ever since I lost my job a year ago. At first, I tried to hide it from my friends and even my family, telling them I was working from home. I tried really hard to find another job, but unfortunately, after gaining close to fifty pounds, I looked terrible. I'm sure that had something to do with always being told, "We'll get back to you."
>
> I began to flounder. Without working I didn't know who I was; I had no identity. The first thing anyone would ask me was, "How's the job search going?" And every time they'd ask, it felt like they were mocking me…judging me, hell, I don't know. I would make up some cockamamie story that I had a few irons in the fire, trying desperately to change the subject.
>
> I ran up over twenty thousand dollars of credit card debt, which just about depleted my entire savings. I looked terrible, felt terrible, and began to feel sorry for myself. I'm thirty-six, divorced, unemployed, fat…I feel like such a loser.
>
> Lately, for no reason, especially after too many beers, I find myself crying, always with the feeling, *Why me?* I don't want to give up, but I guess I already have. I stopped looking for work two months ago. I rarely leave my condo, which I know I'm going to have to sell before my savings run out, but I just can't imagine cleaning up this dump for a sale.
>
> I've become a hermit. I used to see the guys regularly for our weekly golf. Guess they got the hint; they don't even call anymore to ask if I'm going to join them. But even if they did call, I don't think I could handle any kind of joking around, not to mention the "advice" they'd be giving me. It's just not worth it.

I haven't had a date...I can't remember how long it's been. I have no interest in sex, which really depresses me. That's when I pull into myself and start to drink or binge. The one thing that scares me most is that I keep thinking, *Why bother? What's the point?* I know I'm not suicidal, but sometimes thinking of ending this struggle is appealing.

John's "circuit breaker" had been flipped to the off position. Feeling out of control, desperate, and overwhelmed by his circumstances, he retreated from a life that he could no longer control, into a hopeless life of withdrawal and despair. It's this retreat that is so often associated with depression. And here's what's critically important for you: depression is not a self-sustaining problem. Like any habit, it has to be fueled to persist. John's insecurity, as you can see from his intake report above (which is something I ask new patients to provide), was constantly badgering him with chronic negativity, doubt, and fear. In order for John or for you to flip the circuit breaker back to the on position, you first have to—just as with a real circuit breaker—reduce the load that is overpowering the circuits. John had to learn how to stop fueling his depression/insecurity.

Evaluating Your Depression

Self-Coaching is designed to give you a systematic program for cutting off insecurity's fuel supply, enabling you to break the habit-loop of depression. With more severe depression a Self-Coaching approach can still be a valuable asset. However, because of the seriousness and depth of such a depression, Self-Coaching is best used as an adjunct to working with a mental health professional who will also help you determine if medication might be appropriate. I know for many people, as soon as the word *medication* comes up, they begin to cringe. When it comes to a serious, clinical depression, it helps to see medication as a therapy facilitator, giving you a level playing field from which therapy as well as your own Self-Coaching efforts can be maximized.

If you're currently in therapy, I strongly suggest sharing this book with your therapist. I've received a great deal of feedback from psychologists and therapists of every persuasion telling me how helpful my books have been for their patients. A few years ago, I gave a lecture at New York's Ninety-Second Street Y. After the lecture a woman approached to tell me how much she benefited from the talk. "However," she said, "I'm a psychoanalyst and your approach seems to go against my whole philosophy. But what you said makes common sense. Where can I buy your book?" About a year after the lecture this same woman contacted me through my website and wrote, "Just wanted to thank you again and let you know that I give a copy of your book to every new client."

Causes

Multiple risk factors can lead to the development of a clinical depression. There are three risk/prognostic factors listed in the Diagnostic and Statistical Manual (DSM-5): temperamental, environmental, and genetic/physiological.

Temperamental

According to the DSM: "Neuroticism (negative affectivity) is a well-established risk factor for the onset of major depressive disorder, and high levels appear to render individuals more likely to develop depressive episodes in response to stressful life events."

Self-Coaching Perspective: Neuroticism refers to the perceptual and cognitive distortions created by the erosion of thinking that is fueled by insecurity. As we begin to feel more and more out of control, we begin to compensate with strategies of control designed to protect us from harm. Unfortunately, living a life of control isn't natural; it requires ongoing energy and effort, which generate stress. It's the cumulative effects of stress and concomitant loss of control over time that can instigate a clinical depression.

Environmental

According to the DSM: "Adverse childhood experiences, particularly when there are multiple experiences of diverse types, constitute a set of potent risk factors for major depressive disorder. Stressful life events are well recognized as precipitants of major depressive episodes...."

Self-Coaching Perspective: Adverse childhood experiences create a state of vulnerability/insecurity where, depending on the frequency and chronicity of these toxic experiences, the child begins to feel more and more out of control. Instinctually, the child begins, through a trial-and-error process, to develop protective strategies (avoidance, worrying, anticipating, etc.) to feel less vulnerable. Keep in mind, it's not the stressful life events that lead to depression; it's how we react to and interpret these events that does! The more your life has become compromised by control, the more likely you are not to have the resilience to endure more stress.

Genetic/Physiological

According to the DSM: "First-degree family members of individuals with major depressive disorder have a risk for major depressive disorder two-to-fourfold higher than that of the general population.... Heritability is approximately 40%...."

Self-Coaching Perspective: There seems to be little debate that depression can have a genetic component. But it's imperative to view this not as a life sentence, but a *tendency* towards depression. It's true that your "plastic" brain may come pre-wired—to a certain degree—however, this "wiring" is constantly being modified and changed by your experiences throughout your life. You may be more susceptible, or "pre-wired," to have a lower threshold to depression, but just like with a genetic disposition toward alcoholism or obesity, this doesn't mean you will become an alcoholic or obese. If insecurity is left unchecked and if your life becomes caught up in a compulsive, ongoing, controlling struggle, you will be at risk. The bottom line is that genetics or not, insecurity is the variable.

Depressive Disorders

Major Depressive Disorder

If you feel you're holding your own and managing your life in spite of a mild to moderate depression, then a self-managed program may give you all the tools you need to begin to turn the tide and reclaim the liberated life you seek. Because depression can be a serious, life-threatening condition, let's take the following self-assessment to determine whether or not you may be suffering from a major depressive disorder. Take a look at the following checklist and put a check next to any symptom you've been experiencing for more than two weeks:

- ☐ Depressed mood nearly every day for most of the day
- ☐ Significantly reduced interest or pleasure in all, or almost all, activities
- ☐ Significant weight loss or weight gain, or increased or decreased appetite nearly every day
- ☐ Sleep disturbances: inability to fall asleep or excessive trouble staying awake during the day
- ☐ Agitation with increased, purposeless physical activity (e.g., restlessness, hand wringing, pacing, tapping fingers or feet, etc.) or a significant slowing down and decrease in physical activity
- ☐ Fatigue, tiredness, lack of energy nearly every day
- ☐ Feeling worthless or excessive, inappropriate guilt nearly every day
- ☐ Reduced ability to concentrate or think, or indecisiveness nearly every day
- ☐ Frequent thoughts of death or dying, frequent suicidal thoughts

without a significant plan, or a specific plan to commit suicide

Although the checklist doesn't rate the severity of the symptoms listed, if you checked five or more of these symptoms and the quality of your life has significantly diminished, you may be suffering from a major depressive disorder and should consider contacting a mental-health professional to further evaluate the extent of your depression.

Major depressive disorder is a serious form of depression affecting millions of adults, with symptoms typified by a profound state of despair, hopelessness, worthlessness, dejection, loss of interest in usual activities, and so on. Although medication and psychotherapy are essential in treating major depression, Self-Coaching can be an ongoing adjunct to your treatment, as well as providing a long-term strategy for preventing or minimizing future occurrences.

With a major depression the need for antidepressant medication (see discussion that follows) should be explored, especially if you've been struggling with suicidal thoughts or fantasies. If, in fact, you're feeling out of control and flirting with suicidal thoughts, you should waste no time and contact a health care professional immediately! If you don't know who to contact, call 911 or go to your nearest hospital emergency room. Depression can and will distort your perceptions and judgments. As hopeless as you may feel, the truth—the real truth—is that there *is* hope—even if you can't see it.

Persistent Depressive Disorder (Dysthymia)

The essential feature of a persistent depressive disorder (dysthymia) is the length of time the symptoms have persisted. Check any of the following symptoms that you've experienced for at least two years:

☐ Poor appetite or overeating
☐ Insomnia or trouble staying awake during the day
☐ Fatigue or low energy

☐ Poor concentration or difficulty making decisions
☐ Feelings of hopelessness

If you've experienced a chronic depressed mood for at least two years and have checked two or more of the above symptoms, then you may be suffering from dysthymia. Typically, someone suffering from dysthymia will be suffering from a chronic, depressed mood, which they will describe as always being sad, listless, or down in the dumps. Dysthymia doesn't necessarily disable a person's functioning, but can greatly inhibit it. Although individual counseling and medication are helpful with dysthymia, Self-Coaching is an extremely valuable and effective strategy for unlearning the "blahs."

Substance/Medication-Induced Depressive Disorder

The diagnostic features of substance/medication-induced depressive disorder can include the symptoms of a major depression. The essential difference is that the depressive symptoms are connected to the ingestion, injection, or inhalation of a substance (such as illicit drugs, alcohol, or certain prescribed medications), and these depressive symptoms exceed the length of intoxication, physical effects, or withdrawal of the drug.

Depressive Disorder Due to Another Medical Condition

The most important diagnostic feature of depressive disorder due to another medical condition is that there is a chronic period of a depressed mood or significantly reduced interest or pleasure in almost every aspect of life and is related to the physiological effects of the medical condition.

Evaluating Your Depression

In order to evaluate your depression, it's important not only to look at your mood, but also to scrutinize any changes in your behavior or functioning. A mild depression may be experienced as a kind of emotional "flatness," leaving you saying, "I'm bored most of the time. Nothing seems to excite me anymore." Using this same example, a moderate depression may find you staying home more often, avoiding friends, feeling lethargic, and admitting that you're feeling "down" most of the time, every day. With a major depression, what was a "down" intensifies, leaving you in a much darker, dispirited mood, as you find yourself withdrawing more completely from friends and family, sleeping excessively, not wanting to get out of bed. Your grooming, which was always important to you, just doesn't matter as you find yourself with recurrent thoughts of, *Why bother?* Or worse.

Depression Severity Scale

If you come down with a cold or flu and you want to know how sick you are, what do you do? You take your temperature, right? If it reads 99 degrees, chances are you're not going to fret; perhaps you'll head to the drugstore for some over-the-counter aids. But if your temperature reads 103 degrees, you treat the matter differently. You know you're sick—really sick—and you'll probably give your internist a call. Unfortunately, there is no depression thermometer. But we can approximate the degree intensity of your depression in a similar fashion—not according to degrees Fahrenheit, but in degrees of severity ranging from mild to severe.

I've reproduced a Depression Severity Scale from my previous book *Self-Coaching: The Powerful Program to Beat Anxiety and Depression* (Wiley, 2007) to help you plot the intensity of your depression. As you progress from left to right along the continuum, notice that the symptoms are cumulative—that is, moderate depression can include any or all of the mild symptoms, whereas severe depression can include any or all of the mild and moderate symptoms. Do keep in mind that, although it's possible, this chart does not suggest that either mild or moderate depression will necessarily progress into a major depression. Take a look at the continuum and estimate at what point you place your depression.

Depression: A Severity Scale

1   2   3   4   5   6   7   8   9   10

Mild
Depressed mood, apathy, lethargy, decreased performance, decline in interest or hobbies, reduced spontaneity, "blah" feeling, occasional depression, functioning may be strained but remains mostly unimpaired

Moderate
Intensification of all mild symptoms, occasional bouts of crying or tearfulness, worry, mildly impaired general functioning, fatigue, anxiety, social difficulties, possible appetite disturbances, disturbed or excessive sleep, difficulty with concentration and memory, diminished interest in sex, depressed most of the time with occasional periods of distraction, susceptibility to illness, low frustration tolerance, feelings of hopelessness

Severe
Intensification of all mild and moderate symptoms, normal life functioning is minimal or completely shut down, recurrent thoughts of death and/or suicide, depressed all the time

Why Medication

You may recall my faulty perception as a graduate intern that patients who took medication were different from more "normal" patients, whose emotional struggles didn't require medication. As you've read, my perceptions have thankfully evolved since my myopic days as a young intern. Unfortunately, for many people who suffer from depression or anxiety, the thought of taking medication brings up many similar misperceptions and fears, which is why it's important to have a more informed understanding of the benefits of antidepressant medication, especially with any depression that significantly erodes the quality of your life, where normal functioning has been severely compromised.

With moderate to severe intransigent depression, medication is often an essential adjunct to therapy, which is why I call medication a therapy facilitator. Studies have shown that with moderate to severe depression, therapy or medication alone is not as effective as combining the two. Recalling from Chapter One the image of a bucket with holes punched in the bottom, the psychological depletion ("leakage") caused by insecurity poking holes in the bucket begins to challenge the homeostatic balance of chemical neurotransmitters (serotonin, dopamine, norepinephrine) associated with depression and anxiety.

From a Self-Coaching perspective, if you stop the "leak" (insecurity and our neurotic attempts to control life) then the depletion slows or stops to a point where emotional balance can be restored—naturally. If the erosion is so great that adequate habit re-formation cannot progress, then medication, by slowing down the rate that the brain breaks down these mood-balancing neurotransmitters, creates more balance and emotional resiliency for therapy (habit re-formation) to proceed. This is why combining medication (restoring chemical balance) along with therapy (stopping the source of depletion) can not only be an effective course of action, but a life-saving one as well.

If you're considering taking medication it's important to understand that certain antidepressants work better for some people and not others. It's also not uncommon to try different medications during treatment. Some people may also require more than one medication to achieve optimal results. Working with your doctor, you can discuss the risks as well as benefits of antidepressant medication in order to optimize your treatment. It's important to keep in mind that taking medication isn't an exact science where one size fits all. Although the prescribing of these medications is far from being haphazard, it is essentially a trial-and-error process to assess your unique requirements.

Although there are a number of different classes of antidepressant medication, the most common medications for depression are the selective serotonin reuptake inhibitors (SSRIs: Celexa, Lexapro, Luvox, Paxil, Prozac, and Zoloft) and the serotonin and norepinephrine reuptake inhibitors (SNRIs: Cymbalta, Effexor, Khedezla, Fetzima, and Pristiq). Both SSRIs and SNRIs have a relatively more benign side-effect profile than older medications such as the Tricyclics, Tetracyclics, or MAOIs, which are often prescribed when other SSRIs or SNRIs don't work. This, combined with the ease with which patients can be withdrawn safely from them, makes the SSRIs and the SNRIs a typical first choice of many physicians when treating depression.

When considering these medications, realize that it typically takes several weeks before the drug reaches a therapeutic level, which means you won't feel any different when you first start taking these. If your struggle is intense, do keep in mind that the sooner you start this "buildup," the better.

What If I don't Think I Need Medication?

What if you're feeling depressed, but you just don't feel *that* depressed? Do you still need to consider taking medication? If your day-to-day functioning seems adequate, and emotionally you're holding your own and getting by, then you may be suffering from a mild-moderate depression, in which case medication more than likely isn't necessary—but *change* is necessary. Your Self-Coaching, unlearning efforts are geared to liberate you from insecurity, thereby eliminating the source of psychological and chemical drain that lead to depression. Once you stop the drain, you'll be able to restore your chemical balance naturally.

Beating depression using a Self-Coaching approach requires that you have:

- A working understanding of what you're doing that fuels the habit of your depression as well as an awareness of what's necessary to starve this habit.
- A progressive, *unlearning* program of exercises capable of training you to restructure your brain and your thinking.
- A natural capacity—or one *facilitated* by medication—to sustain the training required to reach and liberate your life from emotional struggle.

If you're capable of managing these three goals, then you can genuinely expect to conquer depression.

Mind-Brain Training Strategy

While reviewing the descriptions of depression found in this chapter, make a list of the symptoms you encounter on a day-to-day basis. Using the Depression Severity Scale, estimate the degree of severity of your depression. This estimate will serve as your baseline as you progress through your Self-Coaching training. Periodically you may want to repeat this exercise, not only to note your progress, but also to ensure that you are not getting more depressed. You'll find that an awareness of your progress can act as a source of motivation and encouragement.

6

Anxiety

Let's begin this discussion with my dog Lulu and her anxiety reaction when going to the veterinarian. I don't know what kind of sensory apparatus dogs have, but Lulu would begin shaking uncontrollably just driving down the block as we approached the vet's office (I wonder if dogs suffer from a kind of canine PTSD). I don't think it would be too anthropomorphic to suggest that Lulu was, indeed, feeling anxious that something unpleasant was about to happen. Although we might be tempted to say that Lulu was worrying, or perhaps even having a canine panic attack, I feel this would be a bit of a stretch.

But not all animals are like Lulu. Take for example a deer who regularly visits my rose bushes for lunch. My boisterous protestations invariably produce an ear twitching, seemingly anxious, frozen assessment of the situation. As my rose-chomping nemesis sees that I pose no real threat, he casually resumes his munching. Whether deer or dogs, once the threatening stimulus is removed, there is no anxiety—at least none that I can detect. Lulu never seemed to have to recover from her visit to the vet, and the deer continued to nonchalantly feast on my roses. One moment anxious, the next totally calm.

My point is that animals, when confronted with a threatening stimulus, respond with what has commonly been called the fight-flight-or-freeze reaction,[11] which is an immediate physical and mental readiness for…whatever. An instinct perhaps best described as: "don't get killed." If no threat is assessed, the animal quickly returns to a natural, unruffled state. Animals are simply "present." No threat, no anxiety. We humans aren't so lucky when it comes to anxiety. For us, we need to add one more reaction: fight-flight-freeze or *fester*.

Unlearning Healing Note

Fight-Flight-Freeze-Fester

A wound that "festers" becomes progressively inflamed and irritated—anxiety does exactly the same thing!

A patient I was working with who had just returned from Europe told me about a traumatic event that happened to him in a busy train station.

While my patient was walking through a crowded train station, a man in front of him stumbled. Reaching down to try to help the stumbling man, my patient never felt the hand behind him, slitting his pocket with a razor and removing his wallet from his back pocket. With less than a week left to his vacation, my patient spent the rest of his sightseeing in a hypervigilant, anxious mode. Wherever he went, he imagined a hand reaching into his backpack or pocket, snatching his camera, or clawing for his cell phone. He wound up having a miserable week worrying about being mugged again. It wasn't until he boarded the return flight for New York that he began to relax. The reason my patient, unlike Lulu or the deer in my garden, had such a miserable week was because of something exclusively human: the ability to worry and anticipate that more bad things were going to happen.

---

11. Stress experts have added "freeze" to what has traditionally been referred to as the fight-flight reaction. In the wild, many predators react to movement by freezing. A "frozen" deer, for example, may go unnoticed.

This uniquely human capacity to worry and anticipate future confrontations has been both a reason for our evolutionary success and, unfortunately, the cornerstone of all anxiety disorders. Many eons ago when our genes were going through the laborious trial-and-error process called natural selection, our ancestors had to compete in a hostile world. Without claws, protective shells, or wings to flee, there was only one place to look for a selective "advantage": our brain. With a larger brain, humans were more than capable of learning to survive the rigors of the primeval world teeming with predators, climate challenge, and hostile competing tribes. Of all the mental functions that ensured our survival, our ability to anticipate and prepare for future events—the ability to ponder, worry, and be concerned about life's "what-ifs"—was, no doubt, one of our most valuable assets.

The dictionary defines worry as feeling uneasy or concerned. These feelings are what we might call the psyche's early warning system. Let's face it, a too-complacent cave person might very well have wound up as breakfast for a saber-toothed tiger.

Mind-Brain Unlearning Note

Worry versus Anxiety

It may be a bit misleading to refer to worry (which I attribute only to humans) and anxiety as distinct, separate expressions. Worrying happens to be an integral component of all anxiety disorders, and perhaps it would be more accurate to think of worrying and anxiety as a conjoint expression, i.e., worry-anxiety.

Normal or Neurotic?

Everyone worries, right? If so, are we, in fact, genetically programed to worry about threatening future events? Then by extension, are we doomed, to a greater or lesser degree, to be anxious? The answer is *yes*. We seem to be programmed to worry and yes, we seem to be programmed to get anxious. But there is a caveat. Both worrying and anxiety can be either perfectly normal or terribly neurotic.

Mind-Brain Unlearning Note

Neurotic versus Normal

Neurotic, a favorite word of psychologists, is a term that can lead to some confusion. From a Self-Coaching perspective neurotic worry-anxiety is based on insecurity-driven, emotional "fictions" rather than on objective facts.

• Neurotic worry-anxiety is exaggerated, ruminative, and disproportionate to a real or imagined threat (the "what-ifs," etc.).

• "Normal," non-insecurity-driven worry-anxiety is a proportionate reaction to a factual threat (impending surgery, loss of a job, upcoming blizzard, etc.).

Sometimes, because of circumstances, it can be confusing to know whether you're dealing with a "normal" or "neurotic" type of anxiety (for emphasis, in this chapter I'll refer to anxiety as worry-anxiety). Take a look at an email I recently received and see if you think this is a reasonable, proportionate reaction to my patient's mother's colonoscopy:

> My mom has her colonoscopy tomorrow. I can't stop shaking. Can you help me think more rationally about this? It's very unsettling to me. I haven't slept all week worrying about this. What happens if something shows up? I just lost my grandfather. I'm not ready for this! I'm so afraid to lose my mother too or to have something be wrong. It's all the medical stuff that's scary to me.

A young neighbor we know has colorectal cancer and is not doing well. It all makes me nauseous. How do I not let these things scare me so? I'm not really sure if I'm scared for those I love or for myself. I can't stop these thoughts. How do I let them go? I wish I could think more positively and stop feeling so…frightened. Can you drop me a note back?

After reading this email you might be tempted to feel that it's not so unusual to be somewhat worried about the results of a loved one's colonoscopy. True. But the excessive, disproportionate worrying, the difficulty sleeping, the physical reactions, and the ruminative quality make it quite clear that this person, although reacting to a legitimate stimulus, is also reacting to a more diffuse type of anxiety that crosses the line between normal and neurotic.

Normal anxiety is proportionate to an immediate danger or circumstance. This would be illustrated by Lulu or the deer in my garden: once the threatening stimulus is removed, both the worrying and the anxiety of the moment quickly dissipate. Neurotic anxiety, though, is not time-limited, nor is it tethered exclusively to the aggravating stimulus. If, for example, Lulu *was* neurotically worrying, then we would expect that she would be shaking in her bed late at night worrying when the next veterinarian visit was going to be scheduled.

Anticipation versus Worrying

Before going on, it's important to clarify that *anticipating* future events isn't the same as *worrying* about future events. Although we'll be discussing this conundrum more thoroughly in the next chapter, for now it's important to understand that the essential difference—anticipating versus worrying—has to do with the infusion of insecurity.

Clearly we dispassionately anticipate upcoming life demands all the time. We have appointment books, pay bills on time, get our flu shots, and leave early for work when the forecast is for nasty weather. Worrying on the other hand drifts from the objective facts into a subjective realm of insecurity-driven fictions. *Anticipating* a challenging weather forecast may cause us to feel a bit insecure, uneasy, or tense as we mentally prepare ourselves for what might be a real challenge. What's critical is the amount of insecurity or feeling of vulnerability that's generated. I realize this can get a bit confusing, since sometimes insecurity itself can be a reasonable and proportionate reaction to a perceived threat, while other times insecurity can be anything but reasonable and proportionate. The following hurricane example will help to clarify this important point.

Let's say you hear there's going to be a Category 5 hurricane. If you then begin to anticipate your possible needs, collecting flashlights, batteries, water, and so on, this would be both a prudent and proportional anticipation of the storm to come. You might even look up at the tree limb hanging over your house and have a passing worry-thought (or two) about it landing on your roof.[12] This reaction would be totally within what we might call the "normal" range of being somewhat anxious and concerned. This would also be an example of what we might call a reasonable degree of insecurity—feeling vulnerable and relatively helpless to the approaching storm. When describing a normal range of reacting, it's important to keep in mind the qualifiers: *prudent and proportional.*

But when insecurity dominates the picture, then what was proportionate becomes exaggerated, uncontrollable, and ruminative. Visions of the trees crashing, roofs collapsing, and you being crushed swirl unchecked in your mind as you begin to feel your neck muscles tightening, your heart beating faster, and your headache pounding. Let's be clear: even the prudent person preparing for a storm might be feeling a good deal of stress and a reasonable amount of fear. This a good thing. Remember our instinct: *don't get killed.* When worry, stress, or fear are connected to a specific threatening stimulus, and our reaction is proportionate to that stimulus, then we can say that our anxiety is a normal, instinctive, protec-

---

12. Worry is essentially an anticipation of things going wrong. We don't worry about things going right.

tive reaction. But when insecurity takes the helm and begins to steer our thinking in a more hysterical fashion— "I'm going to die! We're all going to be killed!"—flooding our bodies with the stress chemicals adrenaline, norepinephrine, and cortisol, then what might have been a proportionate reaction becomes neurotic.

Control, as you read in earlier chapters, is the survival reaction to feeling vulnerable. It also happens to be the cornerstone of anxiety. When because of fear, real or imagined, we begin to feel threatened and out of control, we worry. The healthy person's worries are, as we've been discussing, proportionate and directly related to the stimulus. The healthy-thinking person has sufficient self-trust that allows them to believe—trust—that they will handle what life throws at them. It's this self-trust that keeps worrying in check. For someone lacking self-trust, the opposite is true.

Without the ability to believe or trust that you can handle life, then the only thing left is to try to do something—anything—in order to feel less vulnerable and out of control regarding a perceived future threat. But when there is nothing that can actually be done about, for example, an upcoming colonoscopy, we begin to ruminate, "What if I have cancer? What if…?" We do this because, as you'll read in the next chapter, worrying can become a neurotic attempt to avoid, sidestep, manipulate, or superstitiously influence what frightens you. But like a hamster on a wheel, we just keep spinning with what-if, what-if, what-if. This is called rumination. Since the future is merely a concept and doesn't exist, then we are dealing with a cascade of ominous fictions perpetrated by insecurity—not here-and-now facts.

Just this past week I was driving to the hospital for a minor medical procedure. I began to imagine how painful it was going to be. I caught myself in this reverie and admittedly, with some difficulty, willfully decided not to speculate as I turned up the music in my car. To my surprise, with a shot of lidocaine, I never felt any pain. Zero! Whether it's a medical procedure, an IRS audit, or a divorce, the only thing worry will do for you is to reinforce the fact that you're afraid to, as they say in AA, *Let go and let God*—to let go of worry-anxiety and risk trusting that you'll handle what's ahead.

Panic Attacks

When it comes to neurotic worry-anxiety, even the smallest challenges, real or imagined, can initiate our "don't get killed" mental and physical reaction as we go from normal defense mode to Defcon 1 mode. So if we accept the premise that we are, indeed, genetically engineered survival machines, how do we explain the devastation that neurotic worry-anxiety can have on our lives, especially when a panic attack can leave us feeling totally out of control and defenseless? Surely, feeling panicky and out of control would have no survival advantage—at least no rational advantage.

To answer this, I go back to my circuit-breaker analogy from the last chapter about depression. If you recall, when the circuits were overloaded, depression was an attempt to flip the breaker to the off position to prevent further meltdown. Anxiety is the opposite. When, because of mounting insecurity, we get caught in a destructive habit-loop of worrisome, doom-and-gloom fictional prognostications (the what-ifs), our instincts do whatever it takes to regain control over what we now perceive to be our threatened lives. And unlike depression's flipping the breaker to the off position, with worry-anxiety thinking we continue to replace the smaller breaker with larger and larger ones in order to handle the increased load, not of electricity, but of stress.

The overload on your brain circuitry is caused by the stress of relentless worry-anxiety thinking that flows unchecked. Over time, as your suffering escalates, you increase your anxiety "amperage" (stress), putting more strain on the circuit breaker. Let's imagine that your brain's circuit breaker has become compromised over time by the persistent demands put on it, and instead of functioning properly and tripping off to protect the circuitry, it malfunctions and remains on in spite of the overload. If this were to happen in your home there would be no more electrical regulation; there would be a fire. Psychologically, the loss of any emotional regulation is what we call a panic attack.

With a panic attack you begin to hysterically feel yourself losing more and more control, and as your rational judgment and perceptions become hijacked, you say, "Oh, my god, I've got to get out of this elevator! My heart is pounding...I'm having a heart attack!" Often these faulty perceptions (having a heart attack, going crazy, etc.) are associated with intense and gripping emotional and physical symptoms. Emergency rooms are no strangers to these attacks, and when the would-be victim of that imagined heart attack is told, "There's nothing wrong with you. You *just* had a panic attack," they are only partially relieved, unable to believe that their racing heart, lightheadedness, and disorientation were "all in their mind."

Feeling a panic attack under extraordinary or life-threatening circumstances is understandable. In a situation of true and extreme danger—a situation where, for example, you're being physically assaulted—at some point your rational thinking brain is taken over by a more primitive part of your brain called the amygdala, which is the primary structure in your brain that triggers the fight-or-flight response designed to accomplish one thing: survival. And typically, survival requires action, not problem solving or rational thinking. While in this hyper-survival mode, your brain is now on autopilot, where you will do anything and everything to survive—anything!

Ironically, a panic attack driven by insecurity is no different emotionally or physically—adrenaline rush, increased heart rate, shortness of breath, sweating, etc.—from one produced by the prospect of actual mortal danger. If you've become more of a chronic worrier, constantly stoking your insecurities, then it doesn't have to be an actual trauma that precipitates an attack; it could be your general state of apprehension and emotional exhaustion, where a crowded elevator, going over a high bridge, flying, being caught in traffic, public speaking, or taking a test could trigger an attack.

I should point out that because of the cumulative, draining effect that worrying and stress can have on your overall self-confidence, sometimes a panic attack will just seem to *come out of nowhere.* Don't be misled; panic attacks do come from somewhere—from the depletion of your self-trust and confidence—leaving you precariously perched on a fence of self-doubt and fear, waiting to lose your balance. *[Note: a more complete clinical delineation of panic attacks follows in the description section of this chapter.]*

The Child-Reflex

From a Self-Coaching perspective, worry-anxiety is composed of two components:

- A feeling that you're out of control or beginning to lose control.
- A tendency to "catastrophize"—to make emotional mountains out of life's molehills.

As a prerequisite to the Mind-Talk unlearning steps that you will be introduced to in Part III of this book, it's important for you to begin to sharpen your awareness of the true reality, not only of situations that provoke worry-anxiety, but of all emotional struggle. To this end, one concept that has served me well with my patients is what I call the *Child-Habit-Loop* or simply the *Child-Reflex*. Although we'll be discussing this reflex more thoroughly in upcoming chapters and especially in the unlearning exercises ahead, I introduce it here in order to help you in your assessment of your worry-anxiety symptoms.

Since all emotional struggle has insecurity as its motor, it's important to understand that insecurity's roots were invariably established during your child-adolescent developmental years. This is important because insecurity expresses itself in the reflexive, primitive thinking and perceptions of the child. Compared to your mature, rational adult perceptions, the child perceptions are hysterical exaggerations that leave you feeling even more vulnerable and helpless.

To understand the Child-Reflex, imagine that someone followed you around filming you from your childhood into your early adolescence. If you were to watch these videos now, you might observe times when you became panicked about your father arguing with your mother, or a time when you were in your bed crying because you thought no one loved you. In another video you might notice that time in middle school where you were being unmercifully teased because of your weight. These images, captured on video, would show seminal moments of vulnerability that eventually shaped and molded the adult who you've become.

No matter how many times you watch the video, the child captured in those clips doesn't change—same fears, doubts, and misinterpretations. Just as these images are permanently recorded on the video, they are also permanently recorded—imprinted—in your brain. And it's these imprints that comprise the fabric of your insecurity today. The next time you find yourself worrying hysterically about an upcoming challenge, pause a moment and listen to what's going on in your mind. You will undoubtedly hear the voice, not of the mature, here-and-now you, but of a frightened, vulnerable child. This is the Child-Reflex.

Brain Training: Imprints

In order to fully grasp the concept of the Child-Reflex, it's important to understand how the past is permanently encoded in your brain, which is why in Chapter Three I defined neurosis as a confusion of the past with the present. Wilder Penfield (1891 – 1976), a groundbreaking researcher and surgeon, serendipitously found that while operating on patients with intractable epilepsy, if he stimulated certain portions of the temporal lobes of patients who were conscious (under local anesthesia), they were able to recall vivid memories (visual and auditory), dreams and smells, of past experiences. These memories were much more distinct than normal memory, and were often about things that had been forgotten. When Penfield stimulated the same area again, the exact same memory would pop up—an old song, a view of a childhood bedroom.

As with all habit-loops, the Child-Reflex expresses itself in a knee-jerk, reflexive fashion. It's what we call a stimulus-response. Take someone with social anxiety, who may be sitting quietly on a park bench when someone approaches and is about to sit on the same bench. The approaching person is the stimulus (perceived threat), and the reflexive, insecure response is worry-anxiety. All this happens involuntarily without any formal thinking, and it will go on happening unless we begin to insist on making conscious that which was less than conscious, and begin to actively neutralize the Child-Reflex.

The good news is that you are NOT your Child-Reflex. Raising your consciousness and being able to catch yourself when in the throes of Child-Reflex is the first step in understanding that you have a choice—a choice to interrupt, resist, and then, learning to use my technique of Mind-Talk, begin to neutralize (unlearn) this reflexive, insecure habit-loop.[13] This is the unlearning process required to liberate yourself from the distortions of the past and to then release your natural, uncontaminated potential for genuine happiness.

Neurotic Worry-Anxiety Descriptions

Let's take a look at the various clinical descriptions for neurotic worry-anxiety:

General Anxiety Disorder (GAD)

General anxiety disorder is characterized by the following symptoms:

- Excessive worry and anxiety
- Fatigue
- Feeling irritable, testy, or grouchy much of the time
- Feeling restless, keyed up, or edgy
- Difficulty concentrating or forgetting

---

13. Although habit-loops are, in fact, imprinted in your brain, by unlearning and neutralizing these neurotic habits, we render them impotent.

- Muscle tension
- Sleep difficulties (difficulty falling or staying asleep, restlessness, nonrestorative sleep)

There are several differences between GAD and what we might call "normal" worry-anxiety. First, those with GAD suffer from excessive worrying that typically interferes with everyday life functioning, while those dealing with normal worry-anxiety would not classify their anxieties as "excessive," and might even perceive their worries as manageable since they are able to step apart from these worries when required to function with day-to-day demands. Second, the worrying of those with GAD can occur without precipitant (e.g., a stressful, challenging circumstance), the quality of the worrying is more ruminative and distressing and will persist for a longer duration than normal worry-anxiety, and the range of worry-thoughts is less connected to a given circumstance and more diffuse in nature (finances, health, terrorism, etc.) Third, those with GAD are more likely to report physical symptoms resulting from their constant worrying and related difficulties with their jobs, relationships, and other significant life demands.

People with GAD spend their days feeling anxious and worrying indiscriminately. There can be a specific hook for worrying, like the person above whose mother was about to have a colonoscopy, or there can be a more diffuse kind of worrying about mundane things like making a doctor's appointment or not finding enough time to work out. I once worked with a man who worried about "later." He would sit for hours every morning worrying about whether he was going to be anxious *later* in the afternoon or evening. Whether there's a specific hook or not, those suffering from GAD will invariably find something to worry about.

We worry because we're trying to figure out how to feel less vulnerable. And when, because of insecurity, we have insufficient self-trust to believe in ourselves and our ability to handle life's challenges, then worrying becomes our go-to strategy to try to feel fortified and less threatened. Unfortunately, as we've discussed, worry begets worry, and a vicious cycle ensues:

vulnerability/insecurity >>

loss of control >>

worry to regain control >>

increase in anxiety >>

increased insecurity/vulnerability >>

more persistent worrying >>

more persistent anxiety >>

etc.

Panic Disorder

Typical symptoms associated with a panic attack:

- Palpitations, accelerated heart rate
- Sweating
- Shaking
- Shortness of breath
- Feeling of choking
- Chest discomfort
- Nausea
- Feeling faint
- Fear of losing control
- Fear of dying

People who suffer from panic attacks experience an abrupt, unexpected, disorienting surge of intense fear and discomfort accompanied by thoughts of impending doom. Although panic attacks are often unpredictable, they don't occur in a vacuum. Panic attacks are typically associated with a history of anxious, worrisome thinking, which, as you know by now, is highly correlated with insecurity.

It's not uncommon for someone to develop a fear of having a panic attack, especially when there has been a history of a previous attack. I recall a patient who had to go miles out of his way to get home from work each night because he had previously experienced two separate panic attacks on one particular stretch of the New Jersey Turnpike. Although there can be a trigger or cue that sets off a panic attack, sometimes an attack can seemingly come out of the blue. This can be a serious problem, especially when driving a car or operating machinery.

So much of psychology, as we'll be discussing in upcoming chapters, is a form of self-hypnosis/suggestibility. It's not at all uncommon for an anxious person to generate knee-jerk, associative triggers—like my turnpike patient—that will precipitate a panic attack. Such triggers can be related to phobias (extreme, irrational fears of a specific object or situation) such as fear of being on a bridge, in an elevator, or sitting in a crowded theater.

The trigger for most panic attacks begins with a self-suggestion: "I can't handle this!" (Although for someone already sensitized to worry-anxiety, a physical sensation like a skipped heartbeat, for example, can trigger an alarm: "I'm having a heart attack!") If this thought is embraced and amplified, stress chemicals will be released, causing a devastating smorgasbord of symptoms, such as your heart beginning to race, feelings of being smothered or choked, nausea, dizziness, profuse sweating, along with feeling like you're about to throw up, pass out, or die.

When in the throes of a panic attack there is absolutely nothing that helps. It's this place of total vulnerability and helplessness that is so devastating. The intense, disorienting fear and panic can make you feel like you're going crazy as you feel totally and completely out of control.

Social Anxiety Disorder

Typical symptoms associated with social anxiety disorder are:
- Anxiety about being exposed to possible scrutiny or judgment by others
- Anxiety that you will act in a way that will be humiliating or embarrassing
- Anxiety in most social situations
- Attempting to avoid social situations, but if endured, creating intense stress and anxiety
- Persistence of social fears, avoidance, and anxiety

It's not uncommon for most people to experience social fears and anxieties from time to time. And for most people these fears are mild and short-lived. But for someone suffering from a social anxiety disorder, the fears and anxiety are anything but mild or transient. Simple things like eating or drinking in public, making eye contact while talking, or using a public bathroom can all become insurmountable challenges.

From a Self-Coaching perspective, a habit-loop of insecurity has created a profound state of self-distrust and loss of confidence. This distrust is so pervasive that one is forced to constantly monitor every action, always trying to access the social dangers of the moment. Everyday life can become a living hell as someone with social anxieties tries to navigate in a world where they feel constantly in the spotlight, where every act is scrutinized and judged by others. I recently asked a socially anxious patient, "What makes you think that you are so important that everyone is judging you?" She responded, "I know they aren't, but *what if* they are?" This is the distorted logic of insecurity; it's the old "what-if" trap. And for someone with social anxiety and zero self-trust, it's imperative to figure out how to keep the lowest possible profile in order to avoid the possibility—any possibility—of doing something embarrassing.

Mark, a thirty-six-year-old fossil preparator, loved his job at the museum where he worked in isolation in the paleontology lab restoring fossils. He came into therapy because, as he put it, "I'm driving myself crazy." Specifically, it was his daily commute on the subway that was wearing him down:

> "When I first get on the car, if there are empty seats, I stand there frozen, sometimes for minutes, calculating which seat gives me the best chance to avoid eye contact. Then if I do decide I should take the seat, I feel everyone will think it's weird that I didn't take the seat when I first got on the train. The worst is when there's only one seat and it's between two people. I know what anyone else would do, which makes me more anxious. I'm sure everyone is wondering why I'm hanging onto the pole instead of taking the seat. I feel my face flushing as my anxiety goes through the roof. The only thought that gives me comfort is knowing I'll never have to see those people again."

Because of a profound lack of self-confidence, someone like Mark puts himself in a mental pressure cooker where, in order to avoid doing something that might be embarrassing, he has to figure out, in real time, every possible defensive action he might take to be safe. It's a grueling chess game of, *If I do that, then they might think….* All this rapid-fire contemplation taking place as the stress of inaction begins to send anxiety through the roof. But it's a no-win chess game, since no action comes with a guarantee of success. Seemingly, the only possible solution is avoidance. Avoidance is the neurotic solution; unlearning the habit-loop of insecurity is the ultimate *checkmate* solution.

Agoraphobia

Typical symptoms associated with agoraphobia are fear or anxiety about two or more of the following:

• Using public transportation

- Being in open spaces
- Being in closed spaces
- Being in a crowd
- Being outside and away from home

For the agoraphobic, the above situations, when they cannot be avoided, create fear and anxiety that is out of proportion to the actual situation. With agoraphobia it's all about control—control with a capital C. (Note: any phobia that is isolated and not associated with any of the other avoidant situations listed above would technically be considered a *specific phobia* rather than agoraphobia.) Take fear of flying. If you're a "white-knuckler," no one has to remind you of the reasons why you'd rather drive or walk to your vacation destination than fly—and many people do just that. For some, when there's no alternative other than to anesthetize themselves with alcohol or Xanax, flying is a nightmare.

Anxiety can build sometimes days or weeks prior to the flight while anticipating a panic attack that's sure to happen. It doesn't matter that the National Safety Council says the odds of dying in an automobile are 1 in 98 for a lifetime, while the odds of dying in a plane accident are 1 in 7,178 for a lifetime. It only matters that insecurity says, "What if I'm the one in seven thousand? I can't handle this!" With your car you don't have these anxieties. Why? Because you're driving. You're in control. You see, it isn't necessarily about dying; it's more about not being in control—you probably wouldn't be as anxious if you were piloting the plane.

The same thing goes for standing in a long line, being in a crowd, stuck in traffic, or too far from home. When you feel you're not in charge of your life, insecurity is. Phobias are specific hooks for your insecurity, and once you experience a panicky feeling while, for example, sitting in a crowded theater, then the die is cast for all similar situations. You tell yourself, "I can't. I just can't do that," as you imagine yourself being trapped, out of control, and panicking.

I recently returned from my son's wedding in Greece. We were at the Santorini Airport waiting for our connecting flight to Athens. The gate consisted of a small room that was quickly becoming overcrowded as our flight was delayed and passengers for a later flight were also filling up the room. Within a half-hour the room was packed. I mean sardines! With inadequate ventilation and no possibility of moving about, the last thing we needed to hear was the voice over the loudspeaker informing us that there would be a further delay. That was the last straw! From the mass of sandwiched people, I began to hear sporadic moans as a wave of panic began to permeate the crowd. Fortunately, at this breaking point, someone finally opened the gate door, allowing the cool breeze to signal that our ordeal was over.

I tell you this because, although I'm not prone to agoraphobia, after two hours of standing shoulder-to-shoulder with a mass of anxious passengers in a hot, airless room, I consciously had to suppress fleeting thoughts of not being able to move, feeling trapped, etc. And when others began to panic, I remember thinking that it was like when someone yawns and you find yourself yawning, you just start to lose your grip. Fortunately for me, I've had enough Self-Coaching experience to know that the last thing you want to do is to allow insecurity to get a foot in the door.

When it comes to any anxiety disorder, insecurity owns your imagination. But unlike other anxiety disorders, for the most part, many phobic situations can be avoided. However, since insecurity is the motor behind phobias, there are usually other psychological issues associated with agoraphobia—like my patient who walked up ten flights of steps each day to go to work. He told everyone he did it to stay in shape. He told me it had nothing to do with wanting to be in shape; it was to avoid riding in an elevator. But that's not what brought him into therapy—it was his growing anxiety, depression, and inexplicable panic attacks.

Substance/Medication-Induced Anxiety Disorder

Although most anxieties are fueled by insecurity and/or compensatory need to overcontrol life, it's important for you to rule out any physical cause related to medication or substances that you take. According to the

DSM-5, anxiety can occur with the intoxication of the following sub-stances: alcohol, caffeine, cannabis, phencyclidine, other hallucinogens, inhalants, stimulants (including cocaine), and other substances. It's also important to note that panic or anxiety can occur with withdrawal from the following: alcohol, opioids, sedatives, hypnotics, anxiolytics, stimu-lants (including cocaine), and other substances. Some prescription medi-cations can also produce anxiety or panic as a possible side effect (especially nose sprays and stimulants to lose weight). Always consult your physician about all the medications you are currently taking.

Along with substances or medications, it's important to rule out any underlying medical condition that may be causing anxiety. Problems with your adrenal gland or thyroid gland, heart disease, respiratory disease, or hypoglycemia, and other conditions can be causing or contributing to your anxieties. If you feel that things are going well in your life and can't identify any significant stressors or reasons to be feeling anxious, it cer-tainly can't hurt to have a thorough physical examination.

Mind-Brain Unlearning Exercise
Exposing Your Child-Reflex

In the exercise that follows, take the time to review any worry-anxiety struggles that you've been dealing with. In a column labeled Child-Reflex, examine what you were saying to yourself (thinking) and your percep-tions. You'll notice (see the example below) the primitive nature of these thoughts because they are the hysterical imprint of a "child" who is vul-nerable, helpless, and often a victim. In the right-hand column, jot down what would be a more mature, adult, proportionate response to the same challenge.

CHILD-REFLEX

"Oh my god! I can't handle this! I know I'm going to have a panic attack. This is terrible."

MATURE-ADULT RESPONSE

"What makes me think I can't handle this? I've handled thousands of challenges in the past. What makes me think I won't handle this one? I've got to stop thinking like a helpless child."

CHILD-REFLEX

"Please, God, don't let him call on me. I want to hide! I've got to get out of this classroom."

MATURE ADULT RESPONSE

"I know I lack confidence, but I also know I have to stop running away from challenges. I have to be strong. I'm tired of hiding. I refuse to avoid life any longer."

CHILD-REFLEX

_____

_____

_____

_____

_____

_____

_____

MATURE ADULT RESPONSE

_____

_____

_____

_____

_____

_____

_____

Mind-Brain Unlearning Training

How to Survive a Panic Attack

In Part III of this book you will be using the four steps of Mind-Talk to unlearn and defuse the habit-loops that underlie anxiety and panic. For now, if you've been experiencing panic attacks, here's a strategy for coping:

You may be familiar with a phenomenon known as a rip current, which is a powerful ocean current that flows away from shore. If you're an unsuspecting swimmer caught in a rip current, the absolute worst thing you can do is fight it. The force of the current will defy all attempts, leaving you exhausted and fatigued. In order to survive a rip current, a swimmer needs to relax and conserve energy by floating along with the current until he or she is finally released.

In a similar fashion, if a current of panic overtakes you, the worst thing you can do is allow your thoughts to flail about, physically and emotionally exhausting you while inadvertently feeding the panic. Instead, try to recognize that when you're panicking, this isn't the time to figure out what's going on, or even to fight back. It's just a time to float along until the rip current of anxiety lets you go. Just as any rip current will eventually exhaust itself and release a swimmer, panic will ultimately dissipate and let you go. The more you fight it and contribute to your agitation, fears, and insecurity, the more you will become victimized by panic.

Self-Coaching can eventually build your capacity to eliminate the triggers that produce panic, but until that happens, keep in mind the simple wisdom that when it comes to panic, less is more. While in a panic, most people will think, Oh, my God, what's happening to me?! This is terrible! This is bad! I can't handle this! I need help. *When you give in to these thoughts, you're no different from the panicked, thrashing swimmer caught in a rip current. Don't be seduced by panicky feelings trying to convince you that you have to do something in order to survive (control) the situation.*

The next time you get swept up by a panic attack, try to picture a calm and knowledgeable swimmer—one who knows that floating rather than fighting makes more sense. Self-Coaching is going to help you build trust and eliminate panic from your life, but until this happens, be willing to ride out any rip current of panic you encounter. And do keep in mind that panic attacks, although associated with our worst fears, are time limited.

7

The Inner and Outer Faces of Anxiety and Depression

As mentioned in the last chapter, wanting to be in control (or less out of control) appears to be a fundamental biological/psychological instinct. If you suffer from anxiety or depression, you will inadvertently employ various controlling strategies to help you feel less insecure and less vulnerable. And when it comes to controlling strategies, there are two types: *inner,* thinking strategies and *outer,* behavioral strategies, each designed to help you deflect your emotional pain. Since an understanding of the nature of controlling strategies is such a critical point in unlearning anxiety and depression, allow me to illustrate this important point.

Perhaps the most iconic of all American coins is the Buffalo nickel. The Buffalo nickel came about as a result of President Theodore Roosevelt's dissatisfaction with the artistic value of American coinage. If you've never seen a Buffalo nickel, Google it; it's truly beautiful. On one side is the majestic head of a Native American chief, and on the other side, a truly magnificent buffalo. Both images, taken together, are a profound expression of our Native American cultural history. Two very different images, yet very much associated with each other. My point is that all controlling strategies—inner and outer—are like two sides of the same coin, both very much associated, not to our cultural history, but to our neurotic history of attempting to ward off insecurity.

For our purposes, let's ascribe our *inner*, thinking strategies to the side of the coin with the Native American chief's head (since the head is the seat of the brain/mind), allowing the brute buffalo, poised on an expanse of grassland, to represent the external, worldly expression(s) of control. Whereas the Buffalo nickel is composed of copper-nickel metal, your psychological "coin" is composed exclusively of insecurity. This happens to be a crucial point—all controlling strategies, inner and outer, are manifestations of insecurity.

Inner and Outer Expressions of Control

The inner strategies of control—those occurring in our mind—have many expressions, such as anticipation, hostility, lying, avoidance, guilt, manipulation, rationalization, procrastination, and so on. But, without doubt, the single most destructive inner controlling strategy is worrying. And that's with a capital W (more on this in a moment). The outer strategies—those that involve compulsive behavior—also come in many different varieties, such as gambling, hoarding, sex, overeating, nail biting, pulling out hair (trichotillomania), cleaning, various addictions, and so on. Although any of the inner or outer strategies of control can generate significant stress, without doubt, I would say the most prevalent contributor to anxiety and depression would be the controlling strategy worry.

Why are controlling strategies so important? Because your anxiety and depression are fueled and reinforced by both your inner and your outer expressions of control. And you need to become familiar with both sides of your insecurity coin in order to end your struggles.

The Control Juggle

Readers of my previous Self-Coaching book will recognize my concept of the control juggle. A control juggle is usually acquired early in life, where various controlling strategies become consolidated into your unique array of strategies, which together comprise your Child-Reflex. This is illustrated by the juggler below (Figure 7.1). You can see in the illustration that our juggler has quite an assortment of balls in the air, each representing an inner or outer controlling strategy.

Figure 7.1
The Juggler

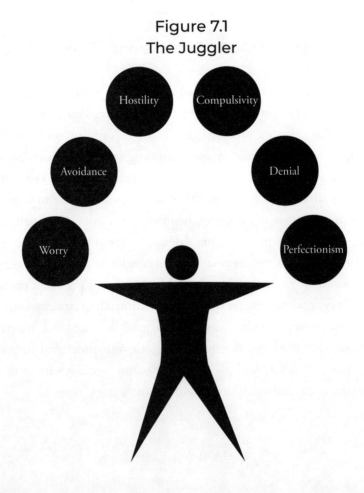

Just as a juggler's muscles become fatigued from a lactic acid buildup in the muscles eventually causing a collapse of the juggle, in time, you too will become fatigued, not by the lactic acid in your muscles, but by the strain and effort (a kind of emotional "lactic acid") required to maintain your control juggle. The point where your juggle begins to crash is the point where you begin to feel the first symptoms of anxiety and depression. This happens because a life dependent on controlling strategies to stave off insecurity is unsustainable, primarily because of the stress that gets generated. Let's face it: trying to control life requires ongoing effort and vigilance, whereas a life of self-trust is lived effortlessly. Why? Because neurotically trying to overcontrol life isn't natural; it requires an output of energy, i.e., stress.

Mind-Brain Unlearning Note

Learning to live more spontaneously from a place of self-trust is natural and doesn't result in emotional or chemical depletion.

The Origins of Your Personal Juggle

As mentioned previously, insecurity is an inescapable byproduct of growing up in a challenging world. A defenseless child spurred on by an instinctual need to feel more in control and less vulnerable will begin to acquire various controlling strategies intended to reduce feelings of vulnerability. "Intended" may be misleading; more often than not, this is a trial-and-error process where a child will stumble onto various controlling strategies quite accidentally. Crying or sulking, for example, might get a sympathetic response from a mom or dad. Having a tantrum might work at home, but not at school with a teacher. Bullying other kids on the playground might provide a sense of power and control—it's a form of natural selection where what works will be repeated and what doesn't will be abandoned. Let's take a look at Sally, whose struggle illustrates how the commingling of inner and outer controlling strategies can have life-altering consequences.

Sally, a college senior who came into therapy complaining of intense anxiety, chronic worry, and frequent panic attacks, described herself as a lifelong "nervous Nelly" whose only solace came from compulsively doing everything right. She, quite literally, *had to* do everything right. Everything! Her efforts were invariably reinforced by the sense of security and safety she derived from her controlling efforts, until her juggle began to crash.

Sally was a perfectionist whose life had become a compulsive, black and white world of chronic anticipatory, worrisome anxiety. The epicenter of her anxiety was that she was absolutely fanatical about not upsetting her mother. From her earliest memories, if her mother even looked at her wrong, or sounded annoyed, intense anxiety, worry, and guilt would be generated, and more recently, two full-blown panic attacks had even been generated.

All her life Sally relied on her mother. She had no memories of her father, who was killed in the Iraq war when she was three years old. Her mom was a hypersensitive, overcontrolling helicopter parent who was there for every emergency, stumble, boo-boo, and upset. Sally, a shy, insecure, reclusive child, wasn't very popular in school, and without much of a social life she became increasingly more dependent on her mother as the years went on. Although she would tell me she only wanted to please her mother, what was apparent was that there was absolutely no wiggle room; Sally *had* to please her mother. She was terrorized by the notion that if she didn't do *everything* right, her mom would get upset. And if her mom was upset, Sally's world stopped spinning on its axis. Even when discussing this with me her eyes would well up in tears, which were followed by an anxious need to change the subject.

As we explored her history, it became apparent that at a very young age, Sally came to believe that she actually controlled her mother's love by being the perfect child. This was the key controlling strategy that reinforced and "fed" her habit-loop of insecurity, which kept everything from unraveling. And now as a teenager, nothing had changed, except that her anxiety had reached critical mass. Her distorted perceptions gave rise to an array of controlling strategies orchestrated by her worrisome fear of losing her mother's love. What's unfortunate is that for the most part, Sally's strategies did work. Her mom couldn't have been prouder of her "star" daughter. As for Sally, she loved being the apple of her mom's eyes. What she didn't love was the crippling pressure she put on herself to maintain her star-like, "apple" persona.

Postscript

I should mention that for Sally, her successful therapy came about through her Self-Coaching insights, most importantly, realizing that by insisting on "controlling" her mother's love, she was, in fact, not trusting her mother's love. After all, according to Sally's reflexive, insecurity-driven thinking, make one false, imperfect step and you'll wind up not being loved, or worse, abandoned (keep in mind our earlier discussion; the Child-Reflex can be quite primitive and irrational).

Before leaving this section, I would like to remind you that the vast majority of controlling strategies that comprise your Child-Reflex have their roots in early childhood development. But unlike Sally, whose controlling strategies were always a part of her life, sometimes these tendencies become apparent only after maturity. "I never used to worry so much. Not like now." "I don't remember being so neurotic about making mistakes." Our early tendencies and strategies to control insecurity, especially if these strategies were mild to begin with, can remain relatively dormant or inconsequential until chronic stressful circumstances in our adult lives resuscitate them.

Mind-Brain Unlearning Recap

Insecurity, control, and lack of trust—
the trifecta habit-loop of anxiety and depression.

Although Sally's insight regarding not trusting her mother's love was pivotal in our work together, unfortunately it did little to change her perfectionistic, compulsive behavior. Why? Because Sally's personality, composed of her worrisome array of controlling strategies, i.e., her Child-Reflex, was part of an intractable, longstanding habit-loop. And habits, you may recall, don't give a hoot about *why* they were initiated. I don't want to minimize Sally's insights—they were truly catalytic—but her ultimate liberation from her control juggle came from her practice of a technique I call Mind-Talk. So, let's conclude: there's no doubt that personal history helps, but in order to obtain what we might call habit re-formation, it takes a bit more than insight—it takes a Self-Coaching structure along with practice, practice, practice.

I can't tell you how often a patient will tell me, "I know I'm being ridiculous, but...." The *but* refers to the disparity between knowing the truth and yet continuing to be driven by insecurity's fictions. In order to break the stranglehold that historical, reflexive emotional fictions have on your life, you're going to have to neutralize and replace the habit-loops created by insecurity. And as with any habit, or addiction, you're going to meet resistance—habit resistance. But don't let this deter or spook you; Mind-Talk's steps and exercises in the third part of this book are designed to help you to unlearn, neutralize, and replace that which has become programmed.

Mind-Brain Unlearning Note

Thinking that you can control life is a
myth perpetrated by insecurity.

Controlling Strategy: Worry

I mentioned earlier that worry is the single most destructive inner control-ling strategy. And that was with a capital W. Okay, so what's so terrible about worrying, and why is it so much an integral part of anxiety and depression? For most people, worrying now and then is innocent enough, oftentimes driven by legitimate and challenging life circumstances. But if your worrying becomes more chronic, driven by insecurity and a compul-sive attempt to control some aspect of life, then worry progresses from be-ing a rather innocuous irritant to becoming the very fabric of anxiety and depression. And don't think of worrying as a purely psychological phe-nomenon. Our bodies can translate the stress and tension of worry into headaches, stomach distress, hives, insomnia, reduced immune-system response, and even heart attacks. Whether it's a susceptibility to catching a cold, or even cancer, there's no question that our bodies abhor worry. Although our controlling strategies are attempts to eliminate vulnerability, the unfortunate truth, as you're about to see, is that worrying turns out to be the dog biting its own tail, causing more harm than help.

In the last chapter I mentioned that worrying is an anticipation of dan-ger, chaos, or bad things happening. After all, we don't worry about good things happening: "Oh my God! What if I win the lottery?" The operative word is that worry is an *anticipation* of future chaos. And since the future does not exist, by definition worrying deals with fictions, not facts—fic-tions perpetrated by insecurity.

This fact-fiction delineation will be critical when we begin to discuss the Mind-Talk technique in the third part of this book. For now, I will just point out that when it comes to worrying, facts don't seem to matter to a worrywart—the *what-if* future becomes their reality. When you worry, you're no longer living in the physical, here-and-now present; a part of you has been transported by your runaway imagination to an uncertain, threatening future.

You've probably never given much thought as to *why* you worry in the first place, right? You just...well, you just do it. Perhaps you've always done it. But as you're about to see, the reason worrying becomes the quintessential, go-to strategy for handling insecurity is because it gives you the illusion that you're at least doing *something* about that which you feel you won't be able to handle. And when you're feeling out of control and anxious, the illusion that you're doing something about your vulnerabilities becomes the incentive to continue worrying in spite of the fact that you're continuing to feel more and more miserable—and ironically, more out of control. Yup, worrying, which ostensibly is intended to make you feel more in control, inevitably leaves you feeling more out of control.

Janet, a thirty-three-year-old graphic designer and mother of three, came into therapy after reading my book, complaining of chronic anxiety and a deepening depression. It became quite evident that Janet's struggle was being fueled by her incessant, dark, debilitating worrying. Shortly after our first meeting I got a series of emails from her:

I'm writing to ask you something because it's fresh in my mind. I got a reminder call today about a gynecologist appointment coming up this week. As soon as I saw the doctor's office on my caller ID I immediately felt unsettled and queasy. Even though it's just a routine mammogram I immediately started wondering if things are okay, what if they find something, etc., etc. I would like to get to a point where I don't become so petrified, always thinking there's a threat, that something terrible is about to happen.

The next day:

I'm really struggling and feeling out of control. I guess I would describe it as a general physical discomfort and feeling absolutely terrified and afraid about what the mammogram will show. What do I do? It's hard to turn away from the thoughts. My husband didn't help by telling me that if the test shows something, I'd handle it. That just stirred up more fear and a sleepless night.

The next day:

This is what is hard. I start to get tied up in knots with "what-if" thoughts that just keep coming. All I can think about is what if the results show cancer? I worry about what I'll do if it's not a good call. I have this paralyzing thought of the phone ringing after the exam—I see myself just standing there listening to the ringing, unable to pick up the receiver. What do I do? It's hard because it affects my sleep. How do I detach from this? I try different things, reading stuff, praying, but yet I still feel plagued by the fear. And always my thoughts center on, what if they find cancer? It's scary to me. I'm having a hard time taking care of my children; I just don't want to have to be dealing with this.

Three days later:

The test was negative. NO cancer!

So, what do you think? Is worrying simply an unavoidable thing that we do when we're scared and feeling out of control? When I read through Janet's emails, I get an image of a little girl stamping her feet, protesting, "No, no, no! I don't want something to be wrong!" She was feeling out of control, and on some level worrying was her attempt to brace and prepare for an inevitable collision with cancer.

Maybe preparing for the worst doesn't sound so terrible to you. You may even think it's prudent, if not smart. And I wouldn't disagree if it weren't for the compulsive, unrelenting loop of worry that Janet was caught in. If there's one thing certain about worrying, as I mentioned in the last chapter, worry begets worry. So, as you can see, worrying isn't innocently involved with wanting to batten down the hatches and prepare for a potential storm; it's more of a primitive, childlike need to escape life's challenges altogether: *No, no, no!* When, because of insecurity and lack of self-trust, you feel you can't handle some aspect of life, then worry becomes an attempt to figure out how to dodge the bullet. Saying this differently, worry is often an attempt to somehow—if not magically—find a way to figure out how to feel less vulnerable.

There's another aspect to worrying that isn't at all obvious. Worrying can be a superstitious attempt to try to control fate itself. Hey, isn't that why we knock on wood? When, like Janet's cancer worries above ("No, no, no!"), on some primitive level, aren't we trying to control outcomes? My patients often tell me, "I feel that if I were to stop worrying, something bad will happen." If you reread Janet's emails, you do get the feeling that she's trying to "worry away" the problem by anguishing over it. All that hand-wringing anticipation becomes a kind of penance that you're willing to pay in order to influence fate. Knock on wood.

Mind-Brain Unlearning Note

Not all worrying is neurotic. If, for example, worrying is connected to a specific threatening stimulus, and our reaction is proportionate and confined to that threat, then we can say that our worry-anxiety can be considered a normal, instinctive, protective reaction. The operative word is "proportionate." In Janet's case, we can see where her response to her mammogram was anything but proportionate. It was disproportionately hysterical.

The Many Shades of Worry

Worrying tends to be a multifaceted expression capable of expressing itself in many ways:

• Worrying can be an irrational, superstitious attempt to influence fate in order to feel more in control. "I'm afraid to get too optimistic. If I do, something bad will surely happen!"

• Worrying can be an attempt to prepare for an anticipated collision in order to feel more in control. "I'm so frightened to have that procedure. I've got to figure out how to handle it...maybe deep breathing. What if I faint? What if...?"

• Worrying can be an attempt to rehearse in order to feel more fortified and in control. "...and if she asks me why I did that, I'll tell her I was busy, and if she wants to know why I didn't let her know, I'll tell her...." Etc., etc.

• Worrying can be an irrational, primitive attempt not to have to face some aspect of life. "No, I don't want to be losing my hair. No! This can't be happening to me. It's not fair. What am I going to do?"

• Worrying can be a panicky feeling that you won't be able to handle some aspect of life. "I know she wants a divorce. I'm not going to be able to handle that. She can't leave me. I can't let this happen."

Okay, so worrying is a misguided attempt to feel in control when facing an out-of-control challenge. But is there an alternative? Absolutely! For starters, recognize that, as mentioned above, worrying deals with what-if fictions of things going wrong. The alternative is to be concerned with facts. Coincidentally, I have two patients who recently found out they have high blood pressure. The one came into our session worrying and ruminating about a life cut short by a heart attack. The second patient (who was concerned) came into our session telling me about his decision to lose weight, eat more healthfully, and join a gym. The worrisome patient was feeling out of control while the concerned patient was deciding how to take control. From now on, when you find yourself worrying, hit the brake pedal and insist on dealing only with facts. By sticking with the facts you may not eliminate a problem, at least in the short term, but you sure as heck can begin to stop fueling insecurity by recognizing that the only thing worrying accomplishes is...well, nothing!

Mind-Brain Unlearning Note

When challenged and feeling vulnerable, it's okay to be concerned with the facts and what you can actually do to be more in control. It's NOT okay to incessantly worry about the fictions of what may or may not happen in the future.

8

The Why of Compulsivity

Grace, a twenty-eight-year-old, part-time medical billing specialist I was working with, complained, "I have no time. All I do is clean, clean, clean." She was exaggerating, but not by much. All her free time was spent cleaning, vacuuming, polishing, and sorting. She had little time for anything else, including her job. Grace was moderately depressed, anxious (which she described as having constant "butterflies" in her stomach), and phobic about everything from bugs to germs. She had come into therapy wanting to know if there was a way to reduce or get off of the Klonopin she was taking for her anxiety, along with antidepressant medication she had been taking for almost a year. The medication, aside from contributing to her gaining twenty pounds, left her feeling lethargic and tired most of the day, which, as you can imagine, only made her rigorous cleaning regime all the more grueling.

Exploring her compulsive lifestyle, I asked her what would happen if she didn't clean. With a pained expression on her face, she told me, "It's the only time I'm not upset. As long as I'm busy cleaning or sorting, I don't feel anxious or depressed." There was no question that when feeling out of control, cleaning, straightening out, sorting, and so on, are all tasks that can produce a sense of order and control. Or as Grace puts it, "At least something in my life isn't crazy." Her closet, for example (which she was more than proud to show me a picture of on her phone), was sorted according to color, style, size (a result of yo-yo dieting), and season. Each garment, meticulously covered with a plastic bag and uniformly spaced, was indeed a picture of order and precision. In a very real sense, her closet was an external expression of what she longed for—control.

Mind-Brain Healing Note

Most compulsive habits offer solace mainly by providing distraction from, or compensation for, the turmoil of insecurity.

If you simply try to force yourself to stop a compulsive habit without an adequate foundation of awareness, confidence, and self-trust, you will undoubtedly begin to feel more anxious, out of control, and perhaps even panicky. It's like trying to put out a fire that you're simultaneously fueling with gasoline (insecurity). In order for Grace not to be a slave to her compulsions (which she did admit was happening more and more), she had to first remove the knee-jerk, insecurity-driven thinking (emotional gasoline) that for most of her life had her convinced that she was no match for handling life's emotional challenges (her Child-Reflex). Without going into the specifics of Grace's therapy, suffice it to say that she was able to accomplish this by ambitiously applying Mind-Talk to build her self-trust muscle. Once she had a new, self-trusting perspective, her internal struggle with insecurity began to weaken, at which point she was legitimately in a position to challenge and conquer her compulsions.

Grace was a willing, albeit frustrated, slave to her home, but nonetheless, she was a slave. She felt she had no choice—clean or feel "crazy." Of course, there was another choice that Grace had not yet become aware of: liberating herself from the source—insecurity. Once armed with understanding, insight, and a newly reconstituted self-trust muscle, Grace was able to stand up to her compulsivity and say, "No more!" The bottom line as stated throughout this book: all habits are learned, and all habits can be broken—even compulsive ones.

Mind-Brain Unlearning Note

All controlling strategies are coping strategies, not healing strategies.

The Efficiency of the Brain

To a greater or lesser degree, all controlling strategies become compulsive habits the more and more we rely on them, whether it's the worrywart who compulsively engages in ruminative worrying, the socially anxious person who compulsively avoids making eye contact, or the compulsive shopper who spends hours buying shoes, only to return them all the next day. What is it about the human psyche that seems to rely on repetitive, go-to behaviors when feeling out of control? Part of it has to do with the biological imperative mentioned in Chapter Three: *avoid pain, seek pleasure.* When you suffer from anxiety and depression, your emotional life feels painfully out of control, which given the opportunity, we would love to avoid or escape. Anything that reduces this suffering will give you a sense of feeling more in control and will therefore be experienced as relatively pleasurable. When it comes to the creation of compulsive habits of control, avoiding pain and seeking pleasure is only 50 percent of the story; our brain's proclivity to create habit-loops based on repetitive behavior is the other 50 percent.

Our Programmable Brain

This tendency of the brain to form habit-loops is what makes us efficient. Take, for example, parallel parking. If every time you parked your car you had to mentally break down each of the steps involved—aligning your car properly, turning the wheel, looking over your shoulder, releasing the brake, giving just enough gas, turning the wheel in the opposite direction just at the right moment, and so on—you would quickly abandon your car in favor of mass transit. But what happens is that after many initially frustrating attempts, a habit-loop is formed, eliminating the need to think or calculate, allowing you to continue your Bluetooth conversation with your mother as you effortlessly slip your car into the spot. Speaking of Bluetooth, just this morning I had to call my wife on her cell. Mind you, this is a number I've dialed countless times. If you were to ask me the number, I'd have to stop and think, reflect, and then retrieve it from memory. But if you handed me a phone, my fingers would rapidly poke at the number sequence, without *any* hesitation. It's called muscle memory—or, the magic of habit.

Through repeated actions (including repeated emotional reactions such as worrying), various habit-loops are created, and with persistent practice, they become stronger and stronger, eventually rewiring your brain (somewhere in my brain is the embedded sequence of my finger movements to call my wife's cell). Whether it's parallel parking, dialing a phone (do we still call it dialing?), blow drying your hair, or using chopsticks, in order to ensure this efficiency, our brains were designed to be quite programmable. Unfortunately, our brains were *not* designed to differentiate between constructive or destructive habit formations—that's *your* job.

Habit Resistance

And once a habit is formed, it's very hard to neutralize it. I installed a new light switch in my house a few years ago. Unfortunately, I installed it upside down, so instead of flipping the switch up to turn on the light, which is customary, you have to flip it down. Rather than changing the switch, I told myself that I would eventually remember that, for this one switch, down, in a sense, was up. That was three years ago and I still keep forgetting. The problem was that this light-switch habit just didn't feel normal; it went against all the other "correct" switches in my house, and therefore, my brain was constantly being reinforced by the old, established loop: switch up, light on.

If your brain is being fed information that supports one particular habit-loop (switch up, light on) and then a contradictory challenge comes along, especially an isolated one like my reversed wall switch, it just can't compete. With anxiety and depression, if insecurity is overwhelming your thoughts with a constant stream of doubt, fear, or negativity, then your isolated attempts to feel more secure don't have a chance. This is why, in Part III of this book, you're going to engage in a systematic process of extinguishing the faulty thinking "switches" that reinforce and perpetuate your habit-loops of anxiety and depression.

Question: What do you think would happen if I changed all the light switches in my house to conform to my upside-down switch? What would happen is that there would be no interference with my learning a new habit, i.e., switch down, light on, and with the now constant reinforcement of all the switches working in unison, a new habit-loop would be formed. Self-Coaching, using my technique Mind-Talk, is going to teach you the steps and exercises necessary to retrain your brain to eliminate insecurity's "switches" one by one, allowing you to begin to neutralize the habit-loops of anxiety and depression by replacing them with another habit-loop—self-trust.

What You Need to Know About Operant Conditioning

When I was an undergraduate, I worked in what we euphemistically called the "rat lab," where learning experiments with white lab rats were taking place. In one experiment where avoidance learning was taking place, a rat was taught to press a lever in order to escape a mild electric shock. Unfortunately for the rat, the lever was calibrated to eliminate the shock on a variable ratio schedule (like a slot machine, you don't know how many pulls it will take before getting a reward). I will never forget the image of a rat frantically pressing the lever over and over again in order to escape getting that anticipated shock.

When humans are trying to escape the adverse experiences associated with the stress of anxiety and depression, we also find "levers" to press. Human levers can take the form of any repetitive behavior (controlling strategies) such as worrying, shopping, gambling, masturbating, hoarding, having sex, overeating or bingeing, lying, nail biting, twisting or pulling out hair, skin picking, watching pornography, cleaning, working, and various drug and food addictions. Sharon, a woman I worked with, complained that her retired, compulsive workaholic husband was driving her crazy:

> Harry never stops. He's constantly fixing, mowing, raking...it doesn't matter. He only stops to eat and sleep. We have absolutely no life together. He tells me he "has to" do these things and that I should be more appreciative. He doesn't get it. The other night he was up until two in the morning trying to figure out how to put the snow blower—that he just "had to" fix—back together. It's August! Why is he fixing it now? God forbid he can't find a project, he walks around like a zombie, sulking, depressed, agitated.... I know *I'm* here talking to you, but I really think he's the one that should be here. I suggested that he come with me today and all he said was, "Don't you know how busy I am? I have to...."

According to what's called *operant conditioning*, any behavior or activity that is reinforced is likely to be repeated. With Sharon's husband, I suspect that his compulsive behavior offered him some form of a reinforcement in the form of a distraction from...let me guess: it could be boredom, which can cause anxiety, especially for a compulsive person; unhappiness; marital issues; or perhaps loss of his previous work identity. Compulsive distractions typically provide some degree of separation from the underlying insecurity issues that fuel a need to not have to think too much. Distractions distract. And this is reinforcing.

Although certain behaviors, especially substance addictions including food compulsions, do offer a transient, reinforcing reward that can significantly alleviate the stress of an anxious or depressed emotional struggle, these same behaviors can become the source of additional problems. We may suffer from hangovers or have more serious consequences of obesity like diabetes or hypertension. So why, even when we know that our compulsive behaviors are hurting us, do we go on repeating them? Two reasons: one, because a habit-loop that offers some reward—pleasure, escape, distraction, etc.—has been wired in our brain, and we have become conditioned; and two, because we've taken a back seat to the reflexive nature of our habits. When this happens, we resist, if not refuse—consciously or unconsciously—to acknowledge that our habit-behavior may be harmful. This is called denial.

When our need to feel more in control at any given moment is more pressing than avoiding future consequences such as cirrhosis, skin infections, bleeding fingernails, and worse, then compulsions will win out every time. And to the extent that you are in denial, there is little if any conscious competition to the compulsive behavior. When the pain associated with compulsivity is something abstract (something that will happen "later"), then escape in the moment becomes an irresistible, if not pleasurable, force—even if we know better! When I was in graduate school, I asked a friend if he was concerned that his smoking might lead to lung cancer. He assured me, "I know that in twenty years or so, I'm going to get cancer, but by that time there will be a cure." That was forty-eight years ago. No cure in sight!

Denial, which can be unconscious, can take many forms. Most people with substance abuse will tell you, "I know it's wrong, but...." There's always that "but" rationalization, which ensures that the compulsive "lever" will get pressed again and again. Have you ever heard the expression "kicking the can down the road"? When you're in denial, whether intentionally convincing (deceiving) yourself or whether you've become unconsciously oblivious to the truth, you're nevertheless kicking the can of responsibility down the road.

Is All Compulsive Behavior Neurotic?

Some degree of compulsivity is probably a normal part of everyone's make-up. Take my jogging. I've been going for a daily jog since I started running in 1977. I've run four marathons and have now settled into a more modest goal of a few miles a day. Do I run compulsively? I would have to say *yes* and *no*. If, because of life's demands, illness, weather, or injury, I decide to skip a run, it's not that big of a deal. Although, I must admit, when I do miss a run, my day isn't the same. I just feel out of sync. I'm sure part of this is physical in that my body responds to the workout, but, more to the point, I feel emotionally out of sync, and wanting to feel in sync is a reinforcing form of control—normal control.

Whether it's your bedtime ritual each night, your shower in the morning, or brushing your teeth, we all have repetitive habits that we might loosely call "compulsive." These habits simply make our world feel more in sync—in control. Just try to skip taking that shower or not brushing your teeth and see if you find yourself fidgeting a bit. We are, after all, creatures of habit. Unfortunately, as stated above, our inherent nature to form habits is indiscriminate, as habits can be positive contributors to our lives, or they can be the fuel for anxiety or depression.

For our purpose of Self-Coaching, what's important is to differentiate normal from neurotic compulsive behavior. You do this by asking what's *driving* your behavior. When your bedtime ritual, shower, jog, or brushing your teeth are driven by positive desire and a sense of well-being, that's healthy, and that's normal. But when compulsivity is driven by insecurity, then the driving force isn't positive—it's destructive. Insecurity, which leaves us feeling vulnerable and helpless, looks to gain control by ritualistically repeating any behavior that quells the gnawing discomfort within.

Mind-Brain Unlearning Note

Compulsive behavior that is driven by desire and a sense of well-being is normal. Compulsive behavior that is driven by insecurity is neurotic.

You may feel that distracting yourself from your anxieties by biting your nails to the nub is a good thing because it takes your mind off of the stress, or that compulsively washing your hands reduces your anxiety about germs, and this would essentially be true. Compulsive behaviors do give us a bit of relief, especially when life becomes too much of a struggle. But remember, from a Self-Coaching perspective it's what *drives* the behavior, not the behavior itself, that determines whether it's normal or neurotic. And this—insecurity—should be your focus. Remove the source of insecurity and the compulsive behavior can be extinguished directly. People said that my going for a five-hour training run before a marathon was not only neurotically compulsive, but downright crazy. But what drove my run wasn't a desire to escape insecurity—it was a desire for self-actualization. Big difference.

Compulsive Personalities

We typically think of compulsivity primarily as it pertains to specific compulsions such as gambling, cleaning, spending, perfectionism, pulling out hair, and so on. But more often, rather than one specific compulsive behavior, compulsivity will often manifest itself more generically in what we might call a "compulsive personality." Someone with a compulsive personality has a compulsive, neurotic need to control life. You've learned that trying to control life is the quintessential stressor that fuels anxiety and depression, but for someone with a compulsive personality, the need for control takes on a whole new meaning. Not only are they trying to feel more psychologically in control, but they are compulsively trying to control the world around them. Why? Because having mastery and control over their external world gives them a compensatory sense of inner control. Recalling Grace's story at the beginning of this chapter, "When I'm busy cleaning or sorting, I don't feel anxious or depressed." The rub is that the real problem—insecurity and feelings of vulnerability—will never be healed vicariously through external compulsivity.

You probably know many such compulsive people. They're the ones who have to read every incoming text regardless of where they are or the company they're with. They can't leave dishes in the sink. They have to finish reading a book or watching a movie (no matter how boring). They just can't stop talking, or eating, or fidgeting, and when it comes to the internet with games, phone apps, Facebook, Instagram, Snapchat, and so on, there just isn't enough time in the day as they get compulsively swallowed up by technology.

Someone with a compulsive personality will often be seen as being "quirky" rather than neurotic. But keep in mind that like worrying, which is an almost universal aspect of anxiety and depression, living a life of *have-tos* rather than *want-tos,* while chronically beating yourself up with *shoulds*, will inevitably wind up making your struggles worse. As you begin the process of neutralizing the habit-loops associated with anxiety and depression, so too will you be simultaneously rewiring the compulsive habit-loops that have become the external face of insecurity-driven thinking.

It's All About...You Guessed It—Control

All compulsivity begins with the reinforcing effect of controlling some aspect of life. Take for example a man who, suffering from depression, decides to check out Amazon's deals of the day. While searching, he comes across a *must-have*, stainless steel cigar cutter, which he immediately adds to his shopping cart. While clicking the "Place your order" button, he realizes that not only is he not feeling as depressed, but he happens to be feeling somewhat elated. This association will now be logged into his memory. He may recall this—consciously or unconsciously—a few days later when he feels particularly agitated, and he may decide to do a bit of browsing on Amazon. Since his behavior is now being associated with the solace and pleasure of escaping his chronic, depressed mood, and since, while shopping, he feels distracted and released from his mood (which is highly reinforcing), there's a very good chance that this association (shopping equals feeling less anxious) will begin the process of rewiring a new neural habit-loop in his brain. Thus, a compulsive habit is about to be born as the deliveries begin to pile up.

As alluded to above, not all compulsive habits are mindless. Compulsive habits may be consciously pursued, as we tell ourselves, "I need to get to the casino tonight before I go crazy," or they may be reflexively (mindlessly) pursued, like nail biting, skin picking, hand washing, and so on. Although both mindful and mindless neurotic compulsive behaviors are instigated by insecurity, once insecurity is removed from the equation and replaced with self-trust, there's still work to be done—the actual habit-behavior has to be dealt with. This is somewhat more difficult with reflexive, mindless, or addictive habits that seem to have a life of their own, but with awareness and persistence, any habit can be broken. Even with stubborn habits and addictions, once they're no longer responding to insecurity's need for escape, deflection, or the comfort associated with distraction, they can systematically be challenged by our healthier, conscious intentions.

Mind-Brain Unlearning Note

When you decide to engage or not engage in a certain behavior, you're making a conscious choice. If that behavior happens to be a compulsion, you're still making a choice, but your ultimate decision is dependent on the strength of your habit-loop.

The Compulsivity Continuum

In his book *The Art of War*, Sun Tzu tells us, "Know the enemy and know yourself." When it comes to anxiety and depression, in order to know *yourself*, you must understand how insecurity sets in motion your relentless need for control. When it comes to compulsivity, in order to know your *enemies*, Mind-Talk is going to help you scrutinize and then neutralize your compulsive controlling habits.

As noted above, not all compulsivity is neurotic; it depends on whether or not insecurity is driving it. I live in suburbia where on any given summer morning you'll find many a neighbor on hands and knees, meticulously pinching out every weed on their manicured lawns. You might be tempted to say, "That guy's pretty neurotic," but take it from me, that guy, although *acting* compulsively, may be driven by something much more positive than insecurity—a deeply satisfying feeling that comes from having something in life reflect a pristine sense of order and control. Whoa! You might say, "Isn't that what insecurity-driven compulsivity is all about—control?" The answer is *yes*, but again, for the guy pinching the weeds, it's not about *escaping* emotional struggle; it's about expressing an innate desire for the joy that comes from mastery over some aspect of life.

Mind-Brain Unlearning Note

Not all compulsivity is neurotic.

Have-to Living versus Want-to Living

So, how do you determine if, for example, your desire to walk or jog that extra mile, meticulously wax your car, or sort your sock drawer, is driven by a neurotic compulsion or desire? Essentially it all comes down to whether you feel you have a choice or not.

• *Want-tos* are driven by a desire for self-satisfaction, not insecurity. Want-tos are optional choices.

• *Have-tos* are driven by insecurity. These are compulsive, rigid attempts to do whatever you have to do in order to feel less anxious and more in control, either by avoiding, escaping, or deflecting the stress of emotional struggle. With have-tos you feel you have no choice.

When life becomes filled with have-tos instead of want-tos, you're being driven by an inordinate need to maintain control of insecurity. You may hear a compulsive person tell you, "Oh, yes, I always wash the dishes after every meal. It makes me feel good." This may, in fact, be true; seeing that clean sink may give you a glow of satisfaction. But you have to be careful that this isn't a ruse for, "I feel good *only* when I have a clean sink." Perhaps a more factually honest way of saying this would be, "I just *can't* leave dishes in the sink." With compulsive have-tos, there's no choice—at least this is how it feels. If you don't do it, you begin to feel more out of control—more anxious. A life driven by controlling strategies of compulsivity is an attempt to compensate for the helter-skelter, out-of-control feelings of insecurity that continue to drive it.

Assessing Your Compulsive Habit

From a Self-Coaching perspective, understanding the true motive of your "compulsive" habits (your enemies) is an essential first step in your liberation. To this end, it's important to view compulsive habits—the neurotic type (have-tos rather than want-tos)—on a continuum ranging from mild attempts to control/escape life, to severe, life-altering compulsivity. Do keep in mind that sometimes there's a very thin line between normal and mild neurotic compulsivity. (In Part III, you're going to be learning more specifically how to separate facts from emotional fictions.)

The following list represents some of the more common compulsive behaviors. Take a look at these traits and decide which apply to you. Put an X on the continuum where you find yourself. If you recognize some mild compulsive behaviors, these are probably not significantly contributing to your anxiety or depression. A few mild, *have-to* compulsions, although not causing significant duress in your life, are still worth addressing. You need to be mindful of any behavior that reinforces the insecurity that drives your anxiety or depression.

Note: As the intensity of a compulsion moves along the continuum from *mild* to *severe*, the probability that these specific behaviors are worsening your anxiety or depression increases.

• I *have to* be in control, e.g., I have to be driving the car, deciding how to load the dishwasher, steering the direction of a conversation, etc.
MILD . . . . MODERATE . . . . SEVERE
. . . .

• I feel overly concerned/compulsive about my appearance. A "bad hair day," a stain on my shirt or blouse, or a zit can ruin my day.
MILD . . . . MODERATE . . . . SEVERE
. . . .

• I might describe myself as being too fastidious.
MILD . . . . MODERATE . . . . SEVERE
. . . .

• I'm either very late or very early. I like to set the time when I arrive and not have someone else dictate this.
MILD . . . . MODERATE . . . . SEVERE
. . . .

• I have specific compulsions that have caused significant complications in my life, such as gambling, drinking, spending, etc.
MILD . . . . MODERATE . . . . SEVERE
. . . .

• I have specific compulsions that are either embarrassing or personally disruptive to my life, such as hair pulling, nail biting, hoarding, etc.
MILD . . . . MODERATE . . . . SEVERE
. . . .

• I'm a perfectionist.
MILD . . . . MODERATE . . . . SEVERE
. . . .

• I have substance or food addictions.
MILD . . . . MODERATE . . . . SEVERE
. . . .

• I'm generally inflexible. Once I decide something, that's it.
MILD . . . . MODERATE . . . . SEVERE
. . . .

• It bothers me too much if my room/house/apartment is untidy.
MILD . . . . MODERATE . . . . SEVERE
. . . .

• I worry all the time.
MILD . . . . MODERATE . . . . SEVERE
. . . .

• I need to be the center of attention.
MILD . . . . MODERATE . . . . SEVERE
. . . .

• I compulsively avoid attention.
MILD . . . . MODERATE . . . . SEVERE

. . . .

• I tend to lie about things even when I don't have to.
MILD . . . . MODERATE . . . . SEVERE

. . . .

• I'm obsessed with pornography, masturbation, or sex.
MILD . . . . MODERATE . . . . SEVERE

. . . .

• I would call myself (or others have called me) a "control freak."
MILD . . . . MODERATE . . . . SEVERE

. . . .

• I think I'm addicted to the internet (phone, texting, Facebook, etc.)
MILD . . . . MODERATE . . . . SEVERE

. . . .

Hold on One Minute!

In spite of what was discussed in this chapter, you may still be thinking that having a compulsive personality isn't such a terrible thing. After all, a person with a mildly compulsive personality (neurotic or normal) who always get the job done, has that perfect attendance record, and lives in a showcase house, will often be rewarded with accolades from friends, family, and employers. On the surface this may sound rather appealing, as long as you're able to ignore the inescapable price tag for trying to control life—stress! Recall the control juggle from the last chapter? Just as a juggler's lactic acid will eventually build up in the muscles and cause a crash of the juggle, your efforts to compulsively keep trying to control life cause psychological lactic acid (stress) to build up, eroding your emotions as well as your chemistry, making you more susceptible to a crash. And when your controlling strategies are no longer able to protect you from insecurity's relentless barrage of doubt, fear, and negativity, eventually anxiety and depression will come knocking.

Other than a crash of your compulsive strategies, there's another reason why a compulsive lifestyle will invariably generate the stress that fuels anxiety or depression. This has to do with what I call compulsivity's "shelf life." Just as the products you buy at the grocery store are stamped with an expiration date (shelf life), so too will compulsively trying to control life begin to falter in time. What initially provided you with emotional distraction, deflection, or escape begins to weaken, requiring more and more compulsivity to compensate.

A prime example of this phenomenon would be physical addiction. What typically defines an addiction is compulsive behavior combined with tolerance, requiring more and more of the drug of choice to achieve the same satisfaction you once felt. With compulsive behaviors, there isn't a "drug" per se; there is instead what we might call a kind of *behavioral tolerance*. There is a need for more and more rigid adherence to certain *have-to* behaviors in order to achieve the same sense of control (relief) you once felt. One reason to equate compulsive behavior with physical addiction is because, whether it's gambling, sex, shopping, binge eating, or cleaning—like Grace's meticulously organized closet from the beginning of this chapter—these activities activate pleasure-reward centers in our brain, giving us a pleasurable dopamine high. At first blush this may not seem like such a bad thing. Unfortunately, it's precisely because of this chemical release in our brain that some compulsions can actually become addictive, especially if you're anxious or depressed, where the release of pleasure chemicals can become a form of self-medication.

In time, as you become more dependent on trying to control life, self-medicating through compulsivity, you find yourself becoming even more compulsive, more perfectionistic, and more rigid. Yet, in spite of your efforts, you begin to feel more vulnerable. And as you begin to feel more vulnerable your inclination is to lean even more heavily on your compulsivity to assuage your insecurity and growing discomfort. Eventually, as with all controlling strategies, the stress required to maintain your equilibrium begins to accumulate, leaving you feeling more frantic and defenseless. It's at this stage of diminishing returns that anxiety and depression begin to become more apparent.

Dust if You Must

I would like to conclude this chapter with a warning. All controlling strategies are attempts to protect you from insecurity, but as you proceed with your Self-Coaching unlearning process it's imperative that you recognize how your precious life is being snatched away from you day by day, bit by bit. I understand it may frustrate and even depress you to recognize this. You may say, "I know, I know, I just can't stop...." But you need to take that frustration and turn it into an incentive. This is your life, and insecurity is the enemy of life. In Part III of this book, unlearning and breaking destructive habit-loops will become the foundation of your liberation, but starting right now, you can begin the process of reclaiming the life you deserve by simply realizing what's at stake. Nothing is more important than fighting to take your life back from insecurity. Nothing!

Before moving on to Part II of this book, I'd like to conclude this chapter with a poem by Rose Milligan. Read through this poem and when you're done, see if what's at "stake" (have-tos versus want-tos) seems a bit more obvious.

Dust if You Must
by Rose Milligan

Dust if you must, but wouldn't it be better
To paint a picture or write a letter,
Bake a cake or plant a seed,
Ponder the difference between want and need?

Dust if you must, but there's not much time,
With rivers to swim and mountains to climb,
Music to hear and books to read,
Friends to cherish and life to lead.

Dust if you must, but the world's out there,
With the sun in your eyes, the wind in your hair,
A flutter of snow, a shower of rain.
This day will not come around again.

Dust if you must, but bear in mind,
Old age will come and it's not kind.
And when you go—and go you must—
You, yourself, will make more dust.

PART II

Preparing for Mind-Talk

9

Demystifying How We Think

The next time you have a chance to go out and observe the night sky, take a look at the stars. Of course, depending on the light pollution of your viewing site, your position on earth, and so on, you're seeing only a mere handful of the one hundred billion stars in our Milky Way galaxy. The starry sky contains about the same number of stars as the neurons in your brain—one hundred billion! Neurons are specialized cells designed to transmit electrical-chemical information to and from the brain. Just how powerful is your galaxy of neurons? Researchers in Japan and Germany found that it took forty minutes using the combined muscle of 82,944 processors using the fourth fastest supercomputer in the world to mimic just one second of your brain's processing ability. Yup, the brain is truly an amazing organ.

Okay, so why is this important, and what does it have to do with anxiety and depression? After all, it's not a brain problem; it's a *mind* problem. And we know it's the insecurity-driven thinking that takes place in our mind that fuels and sustains emotional struggle. For some reason most people continue to think of the mind and brain as being separate rather than being symbiotically related. Hey, the ancient Egyptians were convinced that the heart was the seat of the mind. This may seem incredulous to you because you've always been taught that thinking is a brain thing, but just the other day I heard my wife on the phone telling her girlfriend, "Why don't you do what your *heart* tells you?" Some ideas just seem to persist. For now, it will be helpful to think in terms of mind-brain, rather than mind and brain. But when we take this a bit further and begin to explore the nature of thinking, well, that's where things begin to get really fuzzy. For you to enhance your Mind-Talk efforts to unlearn destructive habit-loops, you're going to have to rethink how you think about thinking. Phew!

On the Nature of Thinking

When we think of the brain, we think of a physical organ. When we think of the mind, especially our thoughts, we think of…well, what? And herein lies the rub: what exactly are *thoughts?* Clearly, we don't think of thoughts as having a physical presence in the body; as a patient recently assured me, "They're *just* thoughts." Unfortunately, when it comes to understanding the nature of thoughts, neuroscience still remains in the dark. One thing we do know through brain imaging research is that thoughts correspond to the activity of neurons, but *exactly* how this happens or what the biology is behind it, well, as my patient might say, *it just happens.* We simply don't have the answers—yet.

If nothing else, insecurity-driven thoughts are the "substance" of anxiety and depression. Although most patients I've worked with would have heartily agreed that their thoughts were what drove them crazy, they nevertheless felt helpless to do anything substantial to stop them. They remained passive victims to doubts, fears, and negative thinking that spun unimpeded through their minds. What they needed was a tool—something that would allow them to stop identifying with these paralyzing thoughts. I needed to create a separation that would allow my patients to treat thoughts in a more objective, less personally contaminated way. What I came up with was to give thoughts a *corporeal* makeover. Let me explain.

The word corporeal comes from the Latin root corpus, or body, refer-ring to something having a physical, material body that exists in the real world. We don't usually think of thoughts as having substance, since we can't physically touch a thought or observe one under a microscope. But what if you were to treat thoughts *as-if* they were physical, *corporeal* enti-ties? You'll find that this as-if approach allows you to work with your in-ner, undirected mental chatter in a more straightforward, less abstract way.

Why is this important? It's a lot like trying to lose weight. As any dieter will tell you, the bottom line of weight loss has to do with being mind-ful of calories, which, in fact, we treat as *things*, saying, "I've got to watch my calories today." We tend to think of a chocolate bar as having two-hundred calories, as if the calories are part of the chocolate itself. Or when we read the ingredient list on a package, we're assessing that food's dietetic value by checking out the number of calories it contains. We do this in spite of the fact that a calorie is nothing more than a unit of energy—not a real thing. It is simply easier for us to grapple with something if we treat it as tangible—even if we don't completely understand it—instead of something abstract.

Just as dieters recognize the impact that every calorie has on their weight-loss efforts, you too need to recognize the cumulative impact that insecurity-driven thoughts have on your habit re-formation. I realize that monitoring your thoughts sounds a bit compulsive, but as with calories, careless thinking adds up. And, for the record, we're not talking about all your thoughts—just the ones that produce that familiar stressful response related to doubts, fears, and negativity...you know, the thoughts that make you feel out of control and stressed. Whenever you start to experience a subjective feeling of distress, whether anxiety or depression, this is the time to check out what's rolling through your mind.

In Part III of this book you'll learn that Mind-Talk will provide you with specific steps for addressing insecurity-driven thinking, but for now it's important to understand that the more you're involved in actively pruning these thoughts, the more you'll begin to unlearn your destructive habits while retraining your brain. You'll find that treating thoughts as things allows you to grapple with them in a more direct, focused way. And once you realize the price you pay for being passively victimized by these destructive thoughts, you'll be more incentivized to actively challenge them—one thought at a time. Most importantly, thoughts, in spite of how you may have felt for years, do not have a life of their own. You have the ability to decide which thoughts you listen to and which ones you reject. But, that's all ahead.

Getting back to my patient's declaration mentioned above that thoughts are *just thoughts*, we don't want to accept this reductionist point of view. When it comes to anxiety and depression, your insecurity-driven thoughts are anything but *just thoughts*—they become both the fuel and the motor of why you suffer. For this reason, it's essential that you learn to treat thoughts *as-if* they are, for lack of a better word, physical "things." Despite the fact that we may never view a thought under a microscope (at least in the foreseeable future), treating thoughts as material things isn't as far-fetched as you may think. Since we are capable of observing thoughts indirectly not only through brain imaging, but, as you may recall from Penfield's research in Chapter Six, where specific childhood memories were accessed through stimulation of that part of the brain, then it doesn't have to be that much of a leap for you to begin to think of thoughts as... things.

By treating *thoughts-as-things*, not only do we demystify them, but even more importantly, we depersonalize them (more on this in Chapter Twelve). You depersonalize your insecurity-driven thinking by understanding that these aren't *your* thoughts (i.e., consciously intended thinking); they are nothing more than iterations of the same-old-same-old promptings of your insecure habit-loop. Insecurity, not you, is instigating, promoting, and delivering these neurotic thoughts to you. And as long as you remain a passive receiver of these thoughts, you will be affected and you will suffer.

I realize it sounds rather bizarre to suggest that *you* aren't feeding yourself neurotic thoughts, but how could this be otherwise when you hear people saying, "I know my thoughts are crazy, but I just can't stop them," or, "I have everything to live for. I'm so blessed. Why do I have these dark thoughts?" The reason is because your habit of insecurity is feeding these thoughts to your conscious mind, and you're reacting to them as if they're your thoughts. They're not! One reason for this confusion is that we inadvertently allow our conscious selves to be swept into an insecurity maelstrom by these spontaneous, neurotic thoughts. At this point we have unwittingly joined the enemy to the extent that the line between *your* thinking and insecurity-driven thinking becomes blurred.

Spontaneous Thoughts

What adds to our confusion is that spontaneous thoughts often just seem to pop into our head, uninvited by our conscious mind: "I was just doing my housework, when out of the blue I began to ruminate about dying. Everything is fine; I just had a physical and all my test results were good. It makes no sense." The reason thoughts do seem to have a life of their own is because insecurity's habit-loop can operate in your brain with or without your awareness. Think of it as background noise.

Occasionally a thought from this loop will percolate to the surface, often instigated by a somewhat less-than-conscious stimulus. The person mentioned above, while cleaning the house may have been only subliminally aware of a commercial that was playing on her radio talking about a cancer-treating hospital. Although she was busy and only paying casual attention to the radio, just hearing the word *cancer* may have been enough of a stimulus to trip off her neurotic fears.

The point is that insecurity-driven thoughts often have a semiautonomous nature and can erupt into consciousness at any time, giving us the impression that these thoughts are truly "alien" to our general state of consciousness. The reason I say that thoughts don't have a life of their own is because you determine whether or not a thought lives or dies. And when it comes to neurotically spinning thoughts, you don't have to feel too bad about killing them.

Make no mistake, unchecked insecurity-driven thoughts, whether spontaneous eruptions into consciousness or part of conscious ruminations, are powerful—they change chemistry, change brain anatomy, and change the quality of your life. By learning to recognize the truly alien nature of insecurity's rants (alien to your healthy, uncontaminated perspective), you're more likely to challenge them rather than allow them to run rampant. Why? Because once you become convinced that thoughts matter, and that you have a choice, you're going to be much more aggressive about taking responsibility for ending your enslavement to insecurity's faulty perceptions. You'll finally come to realize that your disturbed thoughts, which are trying to overcontrol your life, aren't the product of anxiety and depression; they're the precursor to them.

Mind-Brain Unlearning Note

Habit re-formation is the process of neutralizing old, destructive habit-loops and replacing them with more adaptive, healthy habit-loops.

What We Can Learn from Schizophrenia

Schizophrenia has nothing to do with your insecurity-driven habits of anxiety or depression, but there is an analogous concept that needs to be emphasized—it's the importance of learning how to take *active, mental responsibility* for your struggles. In order to empower and overcome that in you which would ruin your life, you will find the practice of active, mental responsibility to be an indispensable component of your liberation.

A Beautiful Mind

The 2001 movie *A Beautiful Mind* somewhat loosely portrays the life of John Nash, a senior research mathematician at Princeton University who won the Nobel Memorial Prize in Economic Sciences in 1994 for his work in game theory. The movie depicts John Nash as a paranoid schizophrenic whose delusions led him to believe that in order to thwart a Soviet plot, he had to decode messages from the "enemy." His entire life became consumed with his "mission" to decode the hidden messages he delusionally felt were hidden in various newspapers and magazines.

In the movie John struggles with both auditory and visual hallucinations (although in real life John Nash did not have visual hallucinations). After a horrendous experience in a psychiatric hospital where he received insulin shock therapy, he decides, with the support of his wife and friends, to force his will to ignore the hallucinations. There is a dramatic moment in the movie where he decides to consciously say goodbye to the three hallucinatory figures that have plagued him for years: the government secret agent, his roommate Charles, and Charles's niece Marcee, whom he adores. At the end of the movie, before turning away from them forever, he thanks Charles for being his best friend and tearfully says goodbye to Marcee, stroking her hair and telling the three of them that he won't be speaking to them anymore.

And this is my point. John Nash (both in the movie and real life) knew that if he wanted to be free of his demons he had to willfully turn away and ignore them. He had to actively take mental responsibility for his sanity. I realize there's a difference between saying no to hallucinations (things that you actually see or hear) and saying no to the neurotic thoughts perpetrated by insecurity, but not as much as you might think.

John Nash went on to live a productive life at Princeton, recognizing that he couldn't afford to lapse into a passivity that would allow his sanity to be hijacked by his psychosis. You, too, are going to have to willfully turn your back on the reflexive nature of your insecurity-driven thoughts.

But for you, unlike with schizophrenia, there will come a point where your active mental responsibility will no longer be necessary, because once you neutralize insecurity's habit-loop and begin to replace it with healthier perceptions and thinking, you will have unlearned your anxiety or depression. This is what we can call habit re-formation.

Clearly, the delusional voices of schizophrenia are different from the "voices" of insecurity that we've been discussing. And yet, there are vague similarities. Of course, *you* don't actually hear insecurity's thoughts—your mind does. But, nevertheless, some insecurity-driven thoughts can be quite riveting, disruptive, and disorienting. *I don't want to live. I feel that everyone is judging me. I can't stand it. Don't ask me how I know it, but I just know I have cancer.* Yet if schizophrenics like John Nash can willfully take their lives back from the depths of psychosis, then you certainly can take your life back from a habit of insecurity. And that's the good news! And in case you've forgotten my refrain: all habits are learned, and all habits can be broken! Even habits of anxiety and depression.

The Danger of Identifying with Insecurity

Once you realize that insecurity is the thread that weaves through all your struggles, you begin to see that thoughts driven by insecurity serve only one master, and it's not you! It's insecurity's never-ending need for control. And it's the habit-loop of insecurity that never tires of holding you (your healthy potential) hostage. The only path to freedom from an insecurity invasion is to recognize that when it comes to depression or anxiety, you are *not* your thoughts; ergo, you are not your anxiety or depression.

I'd like to share with you an email I sent to Martha, a single, middle-aged woman suffering from chronic, ruminative anxiety. It highlights the need to distinguish between thoughts untainted by insecurity and those that are twisted by insecurity's Child Reflex.

Martha was hopelessly identified with her insecurity-driven thinking. She said, "I worry about everything—my car breaking down, my health, my job...I'm even worried what you think of me. I'm really driving myself crazy." Martha couldn't grasp the fact that *she* wasn't driving herself crazy; her insecure Child-Reflex was. I was having no luck getting this concept across to her in our sessions, which were always underscored by "yes-buts." We seemed to be going around in circles. She would say, "*Yes*, I know it's my insecurity, *but* I can't stop worrying." She would often send me emails hysterically asking me to tell her how to stop worrying. I would respond, only to have her reply with, "Yes, what you say makes perfect sense, but...."

One morning, the day after a session where Martha continually abandoned her rational thinking, allowing herself to be dominated by hysterical fears, I received an email demonstrating that her Child-Reflex was once again firmly in charge. The email was typical Martha, asking, *Why, why, why?* Although I kept explaining "why," it was obvious that my words weren't penetrating, since she was so identified with her insecurity and unable to make any effort to resist and try to separate herself from her Child-Reflex. So I decided to try a different approach. Perhaps I should respond not to Martha, but to her "Child."

My note to Martha was an attempt to treat her Child-Reflex habit-loop as a separate *corporeal* entity in order to emphasize the autonomous nature of habits in general, and Martha's steadfast identification with her Child-Reflex in particular:

Dear Martha's Child,

Since you, rather than Martha, appear to be writing to me, I thought I'd address this directly to you. When you worry about something going wrong, of course *you* panic. After all, for you there is no safety. For you the world is held precariously in place by a very thin thread that is always in danger of being snipped by one of life's "what-ifs." I realize that you will never see the world as a safe place because your habit is to only see through the eyes of the frightened child that you are. I know there can never be any peace for you since your world is filled with danger, leaving you chronically feeling vulnerable and out of control.

It's no sense my trying to calm *you* down because this is, after all, who you are and who you will always be (i.e., a conditioned habit-loop). I know you like to dominate Martha's thinking because you think this will somehow make *you* feel safer. But you and I both know that you will never feel safe enough because your habit—your reason for existing—is based on fear and faulty perceptions of vulnerability. So, yes, unfortunately there isn't much I can say to make *you* feel better or safer.

It's a shame that Martha doesn't realize that she isn't you! It's a pity that Martha allows your perceptions and thinking to become *her* perceptions and thinking. As long as she, Martha, does this, she too will be doomed to your view of life—a life of fear and worry.

If only Martha could depersonalize you and see you, not as herself (her own thoughts), but as a separate, reflexive voice, born out of historical habits of insecurity. When Martha allows your thinking to get a foot in the door of her rational mind, she unfortunately abandons her more mature, objective thinking and only sees the world through your eyes. What a pity!

Perhaps one day Martha will grasp the notion that your hysterical nature can never be reasoned with; it can only be seen for what it is—an alien voice of insecurity that, if allowed, will always override and bully a weak ego. Nevertheless, you'd better be careful, because one day Martha might surprise you by realizing that your "voice" isn't her voice! When this happens, you will no longer control Martha's mind.

Recap

In Martha's email I wanted to emphasize how the Child's "voice" not only contaminates our rational thinking, but at times will totally hijack it. Hopefully by now you realize that I'm talking about insecurity's powerful domination and sway over our thinking, not psychosis. To this end let me reassure you that it's normal and healthy to have different levels of conscious awareness (i.e., "voices"). If you monitor your inner mind "talking" you'll notice that most of your thoughts seem to be quite normal and responsive to life circumstances: "Should I call Linda or should I wait?" Or, "Now who can that be at the door?" Or, "Remember to put bananas on the shopping list." Other thoughts aren't as innocuous. These are the doubts, fears, and negatives perpetrated by insecurity: "Oh my God! I'll never be able to pass that exam!" Or, "What if I get cancer?"

What's going through your mind right now as you read these words? Can you "hear" your inner talk? If you were to say, for example, *I'm reading right now, but I'd better put the book down and get to work,* you're actually talking to yourself, not, of course, with your mouth, but with your mind. In order for your thoughts to affect you, two things have to happen: First, you—a part of you—must listen to what you're saying. And second, you must either accept or reject what you're hearing. There is a third alternative, where your thoughts may be slightly less than conscious and are affecting your mood, but even these thoughts can be brought to full consciousness with a determined attitude of self-scrutiny.

A part of you talks and a part of you listens. This may seem strange at first, but with some reflection, you can see how obvious it is. If, for example, I say to myself, *I never have any luck*, and then I find myself feeling somewhat depressed, then not only have I listened to this negative thought, but I have also embraced it. I could just as easily have responded to my lack of luck with a bit of optimistic relativity, saying, "It's just a bad day. I'll be fine," and not have experienced any depressive reaction.

Here's another example: Let's say I have been learning the clarinet for two years. One day my practicing is terrible; every other note squeaks. I say to myself, *Why am I wasting my time? I'm never going to be any good at this.* I then feel like a failure and think I should give up entirely. I have listened to my negative thought and believed it. Instead, I might react by saying, *Guess I'm having an off day. Everybody has them. It's my turn. Tomorrow will be better.*

But, of course, in order to offer these rebuttals, I would have to be aware of my need to take my life back from insecurity. I would have to embrace the duality inherent in my thought process, i.e., healthy, rational thinking versus reflexive, insecurity-driven thinking. Understanding this duality is a crucial step in separating yourself from your struggles.

10

Saying Hello to Your Unconscious

From what you've read thus far, you may have concluded that Self-Coaching is fundamentally a cognitive-behavioral approach to anxiety and depression. And this would be correct. However, in order for you to employ the liberating technique of Mind-Talk, you're going to need more than a program to consciously reframe your destructive thoughts or change your compulsive behaviors. You're going to need to develop a working rapport with your unconscious mind, which is where your habit-loops reside. Don't worry; we aren't going to get lost in the theoretical woods of the unconscious, which by its very nature is unknowable. We're just going to give it a kind of facelift. Actually, to be more accurate, we're going to give it a face!

Giving Insecurity a Face

When it comes down to it, we know so very little about our mind, and even less about our unconscious mind. Dreams, which are the very voice of the unconscious, are a good example of this confusion. Who hasn't scratched their head pondering a vivid dream that seems to defy any logic or common sense? For our purpose of Self-Coaching, it won't be necessary to interpret dreams; it will only be necessary to understand how dreams offer a unique unconscious view of insecurity.

Aside from interpreting dreams, there is an even more important Self-Coaching reason why I've included this chapter on dreams and your unconscious. As you're about to read, it's to help you understand the need to give your habit-loop of insecurity a recognizable "face." Although dreams aren't necessary for Self-Coaching, occasionally a dream comes along offering vivid insights into your struggles, and it can wind up complementing your hard work. But if you're one of those who say, "I never dream," not to worry, your Self-Coaching will in no way be less effective.

Sigmund Freud referred to dreams as "the royal road to the unconscious." C.G. Jung felt that "the dream is a little hidden door in the innermost and most secret recesses of the psyche. "And from a Self-Coaching perspective, *dreams symbolically reflect what we know and what we don't know about ourselves.* Although there is consensus that dreams represent the unconscious, do you know how many different psychological approaches there are to dream interpretation? Freudians might tell you they're wish fulfillments, Jungians may suggest they are archetypal manifestations of the collective unconscious, Adlerians see them as attempts to address our inferiorities, and even I have a Joe Luciani theory. My theory is that dreams represent the symbolic, emotional depictions of what we bring with us to bed; our day-to-day unresolved, conscious or unconscious struggles.

Mind-Brain Unlearning Note

The Biology of Dreaming

Before going on, you should know that everyone dreams—every night. This is a biological fact. We know from dream research that during the course of the night there are periods of rapid eye movement (REM sleep) that occur when the sleeper is vividly dreaming. The only reason someone will tell you they don't dream is because they don't recall their dreams. Although there is much controversy as to the effects of dreaming on our waking lives, there does seem to be ample evidence that dreaming is involved in psychological "maintenance," and emotional stability.

No doubt dreams are fascinating, and patients are always eager to focus on a particularly "weird" dream. Although dreams can be helpful at times, for the most part they remain difficult to interpret and, at best, are *always* speculative. You may recall my bug-on-the-back-of-my-knee dream that was discussed in Chapter Two. Unless you're able to make an immediate and obvious connection between your dream and your life and struggles, your Self-Coaching energy will be better spent practicing and focusing on your Mind-Talk efforts. That's not to say that every once in a while a dream may come along with the potential to accelerate your unlearning efforts by offering you a different perspective on what you've been struggling with. This type of dream, though, is usually the exception, not the rule.

This was the case for Peter, a forty-nine-year-old high school teacher suffering from anxiety and depression. His lifelong Child-Reflex of low self-esteem and insecurity dominated his life, leaving him feeling victimized by his symptoms. He was eager to tell me about a rather exceptional dream:

> *I remember this dream where I was a very young child, wearing only a diaper. I was seated next to a giant spider. It was at least four feet tall. In my hand I had a small hammer. Somehow, I knew that my job was to crack open the spider. I kept pounding and pounding. I must have succeeded because I saw a crack with green ooze flowing out of the crack. In that moment I knew I killed the spider. I don't recall having any emotion. I wasn't happy or sad; this was just my job.*

As you might imagine, there are probably many psychologists who would have a field day interpreting this dream. For me the interpretation was a fairly straightforward recapitulation of the work Peter and I were doing. Peter was the son of a rather menacing, codependent, web-weaving mother. As long as she (i.e., the giant spider) dominated his life, he was reduced to a relatively powerless child. I say "relatively" powerless because the dream *child* demonstrates that with persistent hammering, the spider can be mortally wounded.

The dream reflected a recent discussion we'd had about how controlling his mother was. As he put it, "When I was growing up, no matter what I did, she would intrude, zipping my coat, fixing my hair. I especially hated it whenever we went to visit someone. She would lick her handkerchief and then use it to clean my face. She treated me like a baby!" (The diapered child in the dream.) Peter grew up controlled, never in control. Since he depended on his mother to swoop down and protect him from every challenge or struggle, Peter never developed the self-confidence to handle life independently. (This is the scourge of codependency.) What controlled him now as an adult was no longer his dominating mother, who, incidentally, had passed away years ago; it was his perception of powerlessness and lack of self-reliance that had tracked him through his life.

You might conclude, as I did, that the giant spider was an obvious symbol of his symbiotic, devouring mother. And you wouldn't be wrong. But for Peter, the spider lends itself to an even larger interpretation. You see, no spider in the world grows to be four feet tall—none that I've ever heard of. This suggests that Peter's spider was an exaggeration of what his insecurity had grown into.

Yes, the spider was representative of his mother's dominance over him during his developmental years, but now it had morphed into something much larger and more pervasive in Peter's life—something that had to be cracked and killed. Take a look at Peter's sketch in Figure 10.1. What's striking is the contrast in size between child-Peter and the spider. This imbalance in potency—gigantic spider versus diapered child—is a vivid, visual example of how insecurity can get represented by the unconscious.

It's what I mean by giving your habit-loop a face.

Figure 10.1
Peter's Sketch of Spider and Child

As it turned out in our sessions following this dream, it wasn't so much the spider image that motivated Peter to fight the good fight; it was his realization—and disgust—at seeing himself (his psyche) as a small, insignificant, diapered child! This image was truly catalytic in encouraging his Mind-Talk "hammering" efforts and eventual liberation from his spider world.

Peter's Self-Coaching Treatment Plan

Peter had to free himself from the unconscious habit-loop that insisted he was a powerless child in a menacing world.

From a Self-Coaching perspective, Peter's dream gave us a tool to work more directly with his unconscious. Now his neurotic habit-loop had a face—the face of that powerless, diapered child. No longer were we referring to an abstract concept such as "insecurity," "habit-loops," or even the "Child-Reflex." Now we could bring up an image of that small, intrepid child killing the spider. And for Peter, this helped focus his Self-Coaching challenge—to hammer away at his reflexive doubts, fears, and negatives. Additionally, the dream infused Peter with a sense of hope. It demonstrated that with persistent work, he could begin to free himself from the spider and the psychological web he had found himself trapped in. For the first time that Peter could remember, he felt a bourgeoning sense of empowerment—all instigated by a dream. So, what do you think? Was this dream valuable?

Mind-Brain Unlearning Note

A point that will be discussed more fully in the next chapter is that whenever we can take an abstract concept, like a habit-loop, and think about it in a more objective way, as a tangible "thing" (as with Peter's spider-child image) rather than a concept, it makes the process of dealing with the unconscious more direct and accessible.

On the Nature of the Unconscious

Could Peter and I have progressed without this dream? Of course we could have, but nevertheless, dreams (whether or not we remember or interpret them), according to many researchers, appear to have a homeostatic function of maintaining emotional balance in our lives. Aside from the anecdotal nature of dream interpretation, many scientists believe that dreaming is a rehearsal for the struggles and emotional challenges we currently face in our lives. Perhaps we will never know the true nature of why we dream, but as Einstein put it, "God does not throw dice," meaning, we dream because in some necessary and fundamental way, it has proven adaptive to our survival.

So, whether you remember your dreams or not, I believe it's safe to say that when you go to sleep at night your unconscious mind is doing the best it can to regulate your emotional stability. Unfortunately, if your conscious mind has been seized by your habit of insecurity, then your unconscious attempts to compensate (or rehearse) will fall short of achieving emotional balance as you go on suffering with anxiety or depression. You may recall our bucket analogy from Chapter One. When insecurity pokes too many holes in the bottom of the bucket, your balancing chemicals just can't replenish the loss fast enough, creating the chemical imbalances associated with anxiety and depression.

Clearly, not all dreams lend themselves to such immediate and obvious interpretation as Peter's spider dream. As I said, dream interpretation can be quite speculative at best. The takeaway from this discussion is that occasionally dreams, by offering a visual representation of your inner self—a depiction of your neurotic habit-loop of insecurity—can give you an opportunity to work more directly with your unconscious. And as you'll see with Mind-Talk, this direct work will make it much easier for you to separate the facts from the emotional fictions of your life. It's worth repeating that if you aren't a dreamer or can't remember any significant and obvious dreams, you don't need to be at all concerned, as you're going to be learning about other Self-Coaching tools for adding a face to your unconscious.

Don't Kill the Messenger

Traditionally, because of our inexplicable moods and anxieties, the unconscious often gets a bad rap: "I have no idea why I was so mean to her; I guess I was harboring unconscious resentment." Although the habit-loop we've been referring to as insecurity (which typically gets expressed through the Child-Reflex) can cause all sorts of mayhem in our lives, this represents only one aspect of the unconscious—just as other nonpsychological habit-loops, such as the coordinated moves necessary to drive a car, the complexity of mindlessly tying your shoe, or even the way you laugh at a joke, represent other unconscious, reflexive components that have been imprinted on your unconscious mind.

My point is that although our moods, fears, worries, and so on may emanate from the unconscious, the unconscious is only the "messenger." If you're going to point a finger, point it at your specific habit of insecurity. In other words, it's not your unconscious that's out to harm you; it's your acquired habit-loop of insecurity. And this is what sets in motion a compensatory need for control, both consciously *as well as* unconsciously. And it's our controlling strategies that generate the stress that in turn depletes our chemistry.

If you recall our circuit-breaker analogy in Chapter Five, the controlling strategies designed to stave off insecurity are merely reflecting our instinct for protecting us from further loss of control, real or imagined. This may be a bit confusing, but if, for example, you smelled a natural gas leak in your home, you would reflexively do whatever was necessary to protect you and your family—open windows, vacate the premises, call the gas company. And if it turns out there was no gas leak at all, simply a sulfur odor coming from your drain pipe, you wouldn't criticize yourself for taking precautions. The same goes for insecurity. Like a false sulfur alarm, insecurity is simply sending you the faulty message that *you are in danger of losing control and becoming more vulnerable.*

Since we are instinctual survival machines, it only makes sense that our conscious as well as our unconscious mind would work in tandem to achieve—or attempt to achieve—physical as well as emotional control over our "perceived" vulnerabilities. Unfortunately, for the developing child whose misinterpretations and distortions have led to neurotic controlling strategies, then, rather than achieving psychological balance, we wind up with psychological imbalance, which invariably paves the way for anxiety and depression to take root.

Mind-Brain Unlearning Note

Your unconscious isn't out to get you; it's just following the orders of a misguided, imprinted, insecurity habit-loop—a habit that you need to consciously begin to neutralize.

The Face of Your Unconscious

You're going to find one other aspect of dreaming to be useful with Mind-Talk. Dreams allow you to recognize that your conscious mind has some competition. Let me explain. I had a dream the other night where someone was taunting me with a riddle. I tried and tried to figure out the riddle to no avail. Finally, the riddle teller in the dream gave me the punch line. And, let me tell you, it was good punch line—one I would not, could not, have known. My point is that in my dream there was me, my conscious familiar self, and there was the riddle teller—also me.

Whether it's your familiar self in a dream or someone quite different from you, when it comes to the unconscious expressing itself, there certainly appears to be more than just a "you" who's doing the dreaming. So, when I suggest that we have a conscious mind (that which we are identified with) and an insecurity-driven, *independent,* unconscious mind that contains various habit-loops that may be antagonistic to our conscious mind, you *should* take this quite literally.[14]

---

14. Clearly, not all unconscious content is antagonistic. Aside from insecurity-driven, "antagonistic" habits that may or may not be unconscious, your unconscious is the repository of all attempts to maintain a healthy, homeostatic balance.

What Was I Thinking?

If you accept the notion that insecurity has a voice of its own, and if insecurity can twist your healthy intentions and thinking, then we can begin to understand why there might be confusion as to what's healthy and what's neurotic. A recent example was told to me by a woman who thought she was offering a bit of innocent advice to her friend: "I thought I was being helpful when I told her that if she lost a few pounds she would look terrific. What was I thinking? I've always been jealous of her good looks, but now I realize that the truth was that I was being passive-aggressive. You know, trying to bring her down a few notches. I really should have known better. I do know better! Especially knowing how sensitive my friend is. How could I have said that?"

Yup, sometimes what seems to be inexplicable behavior (or thinking) on our part turns out to be the neurotic overlap of insecurity. By subtracting the influence of insecurity (Mind-Talk will teach you how), what's left is a healthy desire to pursue happiness, love, and solace—all of which have become muted by the warping forces of insecurity that have robbed you of your natural potential.

11

Gearing Up for Mind-Talk

What you are about to learn is a progressive 4-step program designed to neutralize and replace the habit-loop of insecurity and liberate you from a life of anxiety and depression. Using the Self-Coaching technique of Mind-Talk, you're going to learn how to:

- Develop critical awareness of your inner neurotic dialogue.
- Differentiate between facts and insecurity-driven, emotional fictions.
- Depersonalize your identification with insecurity's Child-Reflex.
- Stop and neutralize the progression of insecure, ruminative thinking.
- Reject neurotic thinking while redirecting a more adaptive, mature thinking.
- Stop anticipating and controlling life.
- Start living more responsively with self-trust.

And, most importantly:
- Reprogram your brain.

In order to eliminate confusion and provide a foundation for the Mind-Talk steps that follow, I'd like to provide more background into the nature of the "Self" part of Self-Coaching. After all, it's the Self (capital *S*) that does the talking in Mind-Talk. As you're about to see, when it comes to the chatter that roils through your mind, as you saw in the last chapter, there's often more than one "chatterer" influencing us at any given moment. Three, to be exact.

Cogito, Ergo Sum (I think, therefore I am)

René Descartes (1596 – 1650), the French philosopher often credited as being the father of modern philosophy, is perhaps most well known for his postulation, Cogito, ergo sum, "I think, therefore I am." Descartes was the first to formulate the mind-body (brain) problem as it exists today and associate the mind with consciousness and self-awareness. All in all, Descartes' views are quite compatible with Self-Coaching, especially his assertion that our senses can deceive us, for example, in a Self-Coaching sense, when we are *deceived* by insecurity.

The "mind"—what exactly is the mind? Most would probably consider it to be an independent, standalone kind of ethereal..."thing." What say you? Perhaps trying to pin down a static definition of the mind should be left to the philosophers, but that doesn't mean we can't throw our psychological two cents into the debate. Think of a stream with tributaries flowing into it, creating a larger stream. From a Self-Coaching perspective, I like to think of the mind as consisting of three main "tributaries" all merging into one stream that we can collectively refer to as the *mind.*[15] And like a stream, the mind isn't a static entity; it's an ever-flowing, ever-changing, dynamic, unfolding process consisting of:

• Consciousness: that which we are aware of or can become aware of.

---

15. In general, where applicable, I will use the term "mind" to connote the conjoint concept of mind-brain. But at times, for the sake of clarity, a distinction will be made. For example, when talking about the brain's circuitry, we would specifically refer to the brain rather than mind. For our purposes of Mind-Talk, think of the brain as the physical place where the mind resides.

- Unconsciousness: that which we can access only indirectly through dreams, reveries, and other spontaneous influences.
- Reflexive habit-loops, which are stimulus-response driven thoughts and perceptions that can occur without any conscious or unconscious deliberation.

Depending on your life circumstances, each of these aspects of the mind can influence your behavior and emotions. Typically, when it comes to anxiety or depression, it's the reflexive habit-loops in conjunction with unconscious, past associations that will dominate the picture while consciousness may impotently try to resist—I call this *passive-mind*. Let's, for example, say that Trish is a worrywart who's been dreading an upcoming job interview. For days she might experience a heightened state of anxious arousal, fidgeting, snapping at others, not sleeping, worrying, and so on. Most of these reactions are reflexive and unconsciously driven. Trish, for example, didn't decide to feel anxious; she just did. Well, let's just say that her anxiety wasn't *consciously* intended.

Reflexive habit-loops of insecurity are typically joined by historical, most often unconscious, associations. What happens is that the doubts, fears, and negative thoughts and perceptions of insecurity begin to create a feeling of vulnerability or loss of control, sending up distress flairs in your brain. The brain, which has the capacity to store almost unlimited amounts of information indefinitely, begins to scour its memory banks, seeking all associations that are relevant to assist you in the fight to regain control (these associations occur spontaneously and are mostly unconscious). This is part of your brain's protective, survival makeup.

In Trish's case, her past associations might include the job she applied for a few years ago where she started sweating profusely in the interview, embarrassing herself and not getting hired, or the time in fifth grade when she didn't get picked to be a hall monitor because she froze when the principal asked her to explain why she wanted the job. These, along with perhaps dozens of other similar, relevant memory-associations, might all be called up to contribute to her frantic efforts to feel less vulnerable.

Think of this automatic, cherry-picking process of past memory-associations as your brain's attempt to assist you with your present challenge (real or imagined)—it's your brain's Google. If, for example, you're pulled over by a state trooper for speeding, you, your unconscious, within a nanosecond might begin Googling your brain's past associations: *best behavior for speaking with police officer, what not to say to a traffic cop, your last encounter with an authority figure,* and so on. Your brain, at the speed of light, condenses all this information, making it available for...what? Ostensibly, to better equip you to handle any further loss of control. You can see where this would be an invaluable asset when confronted with real danger. Or, in an evolutionary sense, a saber-toothed tiger.

Like, for example, the time I was caught in a quicksand-like marl at a fossil dig and was sinking fast. Without any conscious deliberation, my amygdala, located deep in an evolutionary part of our "old" brain, instantaneously began Googling various strategies that allowed me to extricate myself and slither toward the dry bank. Only in retrospect do I fully appreciate that if I allowed my conscious mind to ponder the question, "Hm, let me think about this...," I probably wouldn't be here writing this book today. When it comes to the fictional dangers served up by your Child-Reflex, oftentimes these past associations, rather than extricating you from the quicksand of anxiety and depression, will only contribute to your sinking further and further into your struggles. Remember what was said in the last chapter: the brain is only the messenger; it can't moralize or evaluate the information that it looks for. Just like Google.

From an evolutionary standpoint, our brains evolved in such a way that we became a walking repository of potentially useful and protective information (quicksand notwithstanding). Remember, your brain, first and foremost, is genetically programmed for survival, and when, because of insecurity, you begin to feel a loss of control, then anything that seems to be protective (e.g., your controlling strategies, worry, compulsivity, etc.) will become part of your amygdala's survival reaction. Unfortunately, as discussed, since your brain doesn't engage in moralizing or evaluating a given situation or challenge (that's what your mind does), it's also unable to differentiate real from imagined or perceived danger.

This is why a phobic person having a panic attack while sitting in a crowded theater might have the same reaction as someone caught in a burning building: *I'm going to die! I can't breathe!* Your brain has no alternative but to take these distorted thoughts literally and react accordingly with a whatever-it-takes survival response, which can lead to some rather embarrassing reactions as you start plowing your way out of the theater to the nearest exit. Typically, you would have little if any awareness of these unconscious influences that have hijacked your consciousness.

And What About Consciousness?

Okay, we have the reflexive habit-loop of insecurity and the unconscious associations that glom onto it, but what about consciousness? What role does it play? And herein lies the crux not only to understanding the *why* of your suffering, but also the key to unlearning anxiety and depression. Our theater patron mentioned above, prior to losing it, might have anxiously asked, "What am I doing to myself? This is ridiculous! I've got to calm down!" And this would be his conscious mind desperately attempting to rebut the frantic tsunami waves of panic that are quickly escalating from below. What determines the outcome—panic or not—is whether or not this person's consciousness is imbued with adequate self-trust to ward off the emotional fictions of insecurity: "I'm going to die!" This is a critical point. Let me explain.

Self-trust, which is the goal of Mind-Talk, also happens to be the sine qua non, bottom-line solution to unlearning anxiety and depression. Simply put, self-trust is the ability to believe that you have the wherewithal to handle and endure life's challenges. Contrast this with the doubt, fear, and negativity inherent in insecurity's self-*distrust*.

Mind-Brain Unlearning Note

Self-trust neutralizes the old habit-loop of insecurity.
Self-DIStrust reinforces the habit-loop of insecurity.

Self-trust is the difference between feeling adrift and out of control versus feeling in control—regardless of the challenge. I often tell my anxious patients who insist on telling me they can't handle or survive a particular challenge, "How many problems have you solved in your life? Hundreds? Thousands? And every time, without exception, you've somehow managed to get through and survive. You wouldn't be here with me if it were otherwise. What makes you think this challenge is any different?" To which, unfortunately, I often get the self-distrust rebuttal, "Yes, but this time might be different!" Inadequate self-trust will invariably leave you conceding to despair or what-iffing as you find yourself sinking deeper and deeper into insecurity's vortex. The sequence could be expressed as follows:

habit-loop of insecurity + unconscious reinforcing associations + ineffective conscious rebuttal (lack of self-trust, mental passivity) = anxiety or depression

You may feel powerless and victimized by anxiety or depression's strangle-hold on your emotions, but do keep in mind that it's your conscious mind that ultimately has the greatest potential power to neutralize your struggle. This is worth restating: with self-trust your conscious mind ultimately wields the greatest power over your psychological fate.

Mind-Brain Unlearning Note

By empowering your conscious mind, Self-Coaching's Mind-Talk is more powerful than anything that currently holds you back from the life you want and the life you deserve.

Understandably, you may still have difficulty believing (especially if you're a worrywart) that *you* can actually learn to interrupt the flow of destructive, insecurity-driven thinking by something as simple sounding as Mind-Talk. After all, you're probably reading this and thinking, *I've tried to talk myself out of these feelings for years.* Or maybe you fear getting your hopes up, only to be disappointed. Whatever your trepidation, recognize that you now have a solid understanding of the simple mechanics of how insecurity, combined with your human tendency to form habit-loops in the brain, has set in motion a compensatory life of control, stress, chemical depletion, and suffering. With this foundation I assure you that you are now well equipped to institute the action steps of Mind-Talk in order to put an end to your mindless, reflexive servitude to insecurity, which, as you'll see in the next section, is called *passive-mind*.

Mind-Brain Unlearning Note

Anxiety and depression have an Achilles Heel—
it's called Mind-Talk.

Active-Mind, Passive-Mind: Awakening Your Sleeping Giant

As a prelude to the Mind-Talk steps ahead, remember that the reason you struggle with anxiety or depression is because you have become a passive victim of old, insecurity-driven habits. And make no mistake, a passive-mind will always be susceptible to manipulation by insecurity.[16] An *active-mind*, though, can learn to overcome passivity and begin the important process of rewiring your brain's circuitry. Your passive-mind is only doing what it's conditioned to do, and in the case of anxiety or depression, that's to worry, ruminate, and so on. But your active, conscious mind can inter-

---

16. Essentially a passive-mind is one that capitulates to the doubt, fear, and negativity of insecurity as if these disturbances are unavoidable.

rupt this sequence and hit the brake, questioning, "Wait a second, what am I doing to myself?" When I work with someone who is passively being hammered by anxiety or depression, I'm quick to let them know that their active-mind has inadvertently become a *sleeping giant.* Mind-Talk will show you how to wake your giant! Okay, I realize that you're probably chomping at the bit to get started with Mind-Talk. Still, this section on active-mind versus passive-mind is absolutely crucial to set the stage for what's ahead, so, patience please.

Waking the Giant

A while back I was getting a root canal. During the procedure I happened to notice that my body was completely tense. I asked myself if this tension was unavoidable. The answer was *no*! I then made a conscious effort to relax my body (and my mind). I actually felt my body sinking back into the dental chair. I also recognized, once I examined my somewhat less-than-conscious thinking, that I had been allowing tension, anticipation, and expectation of pain to dominate my passive mind. So, what were the facts? The facts were that the pain was not only manageable—at that moment it was nonexistent! But my mind—at least my reflexive habit-loop along with a few unconscious, negative historical associations—was interpreting things quite differently! Allow me to explain.

Past Associations

We all have shaping experiences that not only have molded who and what we've become but persist and contaminate our present lives. When I was a child (come on, just let me tell one more Joe Luciani story), I was given sulfa drugs for an infection, and these drugs had a deleterious effect on my emerging baby teeth. According to my mother, she was told by the dentist that he had to pull out all my baby teeth because they had been compromised. She was also told by the dentist that it wasn't a big deal and that I wouldn't need any anesthesia, as these were "only baby teeth." While my parents waited in the waiting room, I have a vague, but nevertheless, unforgettable memory of the dentist and his assistant holding me down, as my teeth, one by one, were extracted. I can't exactly tell you how much pain I felt, but it was traumatic.

I remember being toothless for much of my early childhood. By the time I reached kindergarten, my gums had solidified from chewing (gumming) without teeth and were so strong, my adult teeth couldn't erupt. I never smiled. By first or second grade, I was told that my adult teeth could only come out if my gums were cut to expose and allow my teeth to grow. My next rather traumatic visit was at least aided by the dentist administering ether. To this day, more than sixty-five years later, I still remember that nauseating smell and the room spinning as a cloth doused in ether covered my nose and mouth allowing me to mercifully slip into unconsciousness. My adult teeth finally were able to be released.

I tell you all this because of the psychological after effects. Whenever I saw an ambiguous stimulus, for example, seeing kids crying on the first day of kindergarten, I automatically assumed we were all about to go, not into a classroom, but to the dentist. After all, why else would so many children be crying? I remember being taken by my mother to a movie theater and noticing a dimly lit staircase going up to the balcony. Since I couldn't read the sign that said *BALCONY*, I assumed it said, you guessed it, *DENTIST*! Such was the post-traumatic picture of my dental "sensitivity."

Okay, so now you know my knee-jerk reason for my body rising three inches above the dental chair during my root canal. And for our discussion, here's what's significant: My reaction happened despite the fact that *I* wasn't consciously afraid, but my body was! My mind seemed to be relatively relaxed as I listened to the dentist tell me about his recent vacation, but on a different, less-than-conscious, passive level, my body was literally lifted out of the chair! I was fortunate enough to have the Self-Coaching wherewithal to recognize the discrepancy between my mind and body's reaction, as I willfully and *actively* relaxed my muscles, feeling myself sink back into the chair. This was quite a revelation to me, as if someone other than me had tensed my muscles, and I had passively, somewhat unconsciously, levitated out of the chair. I now know it wasn't "someone" levitating me; it was a reflexive, traumatic habit-loop imprinted long, long ago.

I use this example of a rather traumatic imprint so you can see that ultimately, it's consciousness that has the final say as to whether or not the past needs to repeat itself in the present. Sure, it's possible that going forward I may have to do a "body-check" each time I visit the dentist, but with a modicum of awareness I don't ever have to be the unwitting victim of the unconscious manipulations of my passive mind.

If you've been suffering from anxiety or depression, then you need to guard against being passively manipulated like I was during my recent root canal, perhaps not by traumatic imprints, but by any and all of your Child-Reflexes. And like me, you're going to need to wake up your sleeping giant and actively Mind-Talk yourself into a position where you have a choice. Unlike the imprint of traumatic events that will often decay and fade over time if not continually strengthened by continued exposure (such as my routine dental visits), insecurity won't fade or decay—it actually strengthens over time because of the ongoing, incessant reinforcement of doubt, fear, and negativity. The good news is that with reflexive habits of insecurity, you don't have to wait for decay or fading to happen—not once you actively begin to unlearn them.

Mind-Brain Unlearning Note

By becoming an active participant in your thinking, you will no longer be a victim of your own neurotic thoughts. Victims are powerless— you are not powerless!

Habits Are Stubborn Things

If you never played the piano, but nevertheless had a burning desire to learn to play Tchaikovsky's Piano Concerto No. 1, what do you think would happen? Well, probably one of two things: You would one day play the concerto or you'd put an ad on Craigslist to sell a slightly used baby grand piano. So, what was the variable that led to either giving a concert or trying to unload the piano? Answer: practice. Fortunately, learning Mind-Talk is actually less complicated than learning Tchaikovsky, but it nevertheless will require practice, practice, and more practice.

If nothing else, I hope that at this point in your reading you don't need to be convinced that habits are indeed, stubborn things. Habit-loops exist in your brain's structural anatomy, and in order to neutralize any habit, you are required to stop reinforcing the neuro-circuitry that feeds that habit. With anxiety and depression, we are of course talking about a habit-loop of insecurity that underwrites a life of control. And just as a habit of insecurity was learned over time—sometimes for an entire lifetime—the only way to neutralize it is to recognize the importance of consistently reframing your thinking over time.

So, whether it's playing Tchaikovsky, riding a bicycle, or learning a foreign language, the bottom line is that habit re-formation requires consistent...you guessed it—practice! Mind-Talk needs to be approached with this purposeful, determined mindset.

Mind-Brain Unlearning Note

Fact: you are not going to rid yourself of anxiety or depression by reading this book (or any book for that matter)—not unless you translate what you read into repeated, ongoing action.

Since you can't "read" yourself out of emotional struggle, then it's up to you to learn exactly what you're going to have to do and then *do* it. Every day! For you to achieve habit re-formation using Mind-Talk, you have to be realistic from the start. Half-hearted efforts will only, at best, bring half-hearted results and not the change you're hoping for. But if you approach your Mind-Talk with a tenacious commitment to practice, practice, practice, then, circuit by circuit, you will begin a process of rewiring your brain, releasing yourself from insecurity's dominance.

Okay, so let's assume that you're highly motivated to practice Mind-Talk every day, which would be great. But aside from practicing, we need to emphasize a critical component of practice—it must be practice *over time*. It's the *over time* aspect that trips many people up. Typically, most people start off with a flurry of enthusiasm and excitement as they start practicing every day and then...slowly begin to drift away from their efforts, especially if progress is slow or inconsistent. This is why Mind-Talk relies on the *coaching* part of Self-Coaching—the motivational part. And for this reason, the final Mind-Talk step deals with motivation.

The reason motivation is so important is because it's the psychological fuel that keeps you going. If, for example, your goal were to drive from New York to Los Angeles, you would have no problem understanding the need to have your GPS coordinates logged into your car's computer and your car's fuel tank topped up. You would expect to refill the gas tank many times before reaching Los Angeles. Motivation, along with a resolute "GPS" understanding of the path ahead, will become your high-octane brain fuel ensuring that you will go the liberation distance.

As you progress with your Mind-Talk efforts, you'll sense a growing optimism and clarity as you begin to develop your self-discipline muscle. It's this muscle that will increase your confidence and motivation to sustain your training efforts over time. Insecurity's end game will come about when you're ready to take one last leap of faith and risk trusting yourself and your life. At this point you'll be in a position to start living more responsively to life, which means you'll be living your life more in the present rather than in the worrisome, what-if future of anxiety thinking or looking back over your shoulder with past regrets and guilt. You will be in a position to spontaneously experience life rather than trying to neuroti-cally control it.

All this is what Mind-Talk is going to teach you. Tall order? No! Not if we break this process down into manageable, daily exercises and drills. Like any other life habit, whether it's driving a car, playing the guitar, or learning another language, if you are taught the basics and you're willing to commit yourself to daily, active-mind practice, you can be assured of incremental shifts in your mood and struggles, and you will additionally begin to notice a growing sense of optimism. Optimism is the wind in your sails—the belief that you can and will prevail.

You now know that the brain only does what it is programmed to do. So, don't blame your brain for your emotional struggles; blame the faulty programming that results from insecurity's insistence that you need to overcontrol life. And make no mistake: insecurity relies on the passivity of your conscious mind to remain viable. Neuron by neuron, circuit by circuit, when you turn away from passivity and begin to use active-mind to train yourself to live according to life's facts rather than emotional fic-tions, you are literally beginning the process of reprogramming your brain to go from struggle to solace.

Ready to Take the Leap?

If at this point you're willing to take a leap of faith and risk believing that you can—and will—do whatever it takes to succeed, well, then let's just say that you'll be giving yourself a tremendous psychological jumpstart. A willingness to believe is like a free lunch; it will accelerate your efforts and foster an optimism that will see you through rough times. So, perhaps you can take a moment to reflect. See if you're willing to take a leap of faith and risk trusting and believing that *you*—your conscious, healthy self—are up and ready for the challenge ahead. If it turns out you're just a bit too pessimistic to take this leap, that's completely understandable. Just understand that as you begin to progress with your training (and you will progress), there will come a point where even the skeptical part of your mind will realize that, *Maybe, just maybe, I can do this!* And this will be the point where your pessimism is beginning to bend. Or as I like to say, the beginning of the end of your suffering. Now it's time to take some action—Mind-Talk action.

PART III

The Four Steps of Mind-Talk

12

Mind-Talk Step One
Becoming a Critical Observer:
Separating Facts from Fictions

Thoughts flow through our minds continually. Some thoughts—like *What was her address?* Or, *Who will I invite to the party?* —are quite conscious, deliberate, and practical. But much of our thinking isn't as purposeful, operating just at or below the threshold of consciousness as we go about the everyday tasks of daily living. Although we aren't particularly paying attention to these thoughts, they are, more or less, retrievable upon reflection. You might, for example, be sitting at a traffic light on your way to work, staring blankly at the red light as you drift off in a pleasant reverie, when the car behind you blows its horn to let you know the light has turned green. Startled, you snap back into reality. For that brief minute, even though you were enjoying this mindless escape—perhaps revisiting your previous vacation—it wasn't *you,* well, not the conscious you, who was manufacturing these thoughts, creating the vacation movie in your mind. Your daydream just seemed to unfold on its own, spontaneously. Daydreams, much like nighttime dreams, do seem to have a life of their own.

I bring up daydreams and nighttime dreams because as was discussed in the last chapter, conscious intentions—in fact, consciousness itself—can easily be contaminated if not hijacked by less-than-conscious influences. Let me expand. For years I've been curious about a phenomenon psychologists call the "hypnagogic state." This is that fuzzy, transitional experience that occurs when we slide from being awake to being asleep. It's the transition point where your normal, intentional thinking is taken over and controlled by your unconscious.

Just the other night, I was reading a passage from Michael Shaara's wonderful book, *The Killer Angels*, about the Battle of Gettysburg. One moment I was reading about Pickett's charge of the Union soldiers on Cemetery Ridge, and the next I was dodging bullets as I too was charging the ridge! It was as if, at some critical tipping point, my conscious thoughts were replaced by an unconscious battlefield reality. This "transition" has always fascinated me. But just *who* in us is creating these movies in our minds?

Whether it's daydreaming or nighttime dreaming, it's important for you to know that you—your consciously directed thoughts—can, at times, be influenced, if not taken over, by the meanderings of the unconscious. A similar hypnagogic state happens where your normal, rational consciousness is at risk of being seized by a reflexive habit of insecurity-driven thinking, which, if you suffer from anxiety or depression, I'm sure you will agree, has a mind of its own.

What's critical is for you to understand that when it comes to your awareness, your conscious thoughts are not alone. With conscious awareness, you can, for example, be totally conscious and aware of your compulsive, worrisome ruminations—*What if I get sick? What will happen to my job? What if I lose my job? What if...?*—but equally unconscious of the reflexive habit-loop of insecurity that's spawning these thoughts, feelings, and perceptions. So, the question remains, with all this cross-fertilization—conscious-unconscious melding—how in the world do we separate truth from untruth, facts from emotionally driven fictions? In order to answer this, we need to begin the process of Mind-Talk. But before proceeding, I'd like you to put this book down for a minute and just observe what goes through your mind, and then come back to this section.

You probably were aware of an inner dialogue, perhaps something like this:

Oops! I forgot to make that call.
Guess I'll call for that appointment today.
I know they're going to be mad at me!
Why am I so afraid to make the call? It's not like it matters what they think of me. This is crazy!
The heck with it, in only two more weeks I'll be lying on the beach, listening to the waves...seagulls darting about...ah!

In the above sequence of thinking, *who* exactly in you is having this discussion? And with whom? Exactly who are you talking to in the first place? Let's take a closer look. First, we see there's a spontaneous, maintenance kind of thinking—*Oops! I forgot to make that call*—which just seems to pop into your head unexpectedly. This is followed by a conscious, deliberate thought—*Guess I'll call for that appointment today*—but then there's another, qualitatively different kind of voice of insecurity that, as you read in the last chapter, has a mind of its own: *I know they're going to be mad at me!* This is the reflexive worrisome voice of insecurity, which, if you were observant, you may have noticed brought some physiological changes, perhaps an increase in stress, a "knot" in your stomach, or a faint hint of panic. And, if you thought that they were going to be mad at you, you might begin feeling a bit out of control (and afraid). As we've discussed in Chapter Two, whenever we sense a loss of control, consciously or unconsciously, our biochemical survival instincts kick in.

Mind-Brain Unlearning Note

Insecurity-driven thinking invariably will
create some degree of physical discomfort.

For the sake of simplicity, let's designate the three levels of thinking:

1. Spontaneous thoughts. Unprovoked thoughts that erupt spontaneously into consciousness: *Oops, I forgot to make that call.* These are thoughts, triggered by the unconscious, that emerge into consciousness from the unconscious.

2. Conscious, intentional thinking. In the above example, it was the decision to call for the appointment.

3. Insecurity-Driven thoughts, for example, *I'm so afraid!* Thoughts that evoke doubts, fear, or negativity. These thoughts are not consciously driven (you become aware of your fear after you feel it).

What about the Unconscious?

The reason the unconscious has been excluded from the list above is because, other than triggering spontaneous thoughts that erupt into consciousness, the unconscious remains unknowable. Essentially, the unconscious indirectly influences conscious thinking and can be thought of as a vast storehouse of memories, experiences, and associations that augment our conscious experience and perceptions (for better or worse). Reverie or daydreaming, like imagining yourself lying on the beach, listening to the waves, *Ah...,* can loosely be considered a form of thinking, generated, triggered, and sustained by the unconscious. But since we can become aware (conscious) of our daydreams, then technically they are no longer unconscious. Or, if you prefer, semiconscious.

For our Self-Coaching purposes, reverie and daydreaming are a form of semiconscious escape and not critical to your Mind-Talk efforts. Your major Mind-Talk concerns will be specifically with insecurity-driven thoughts. There can be some confusion with spontaneous thoughts that become contaminated by insecurity. In the above example, *Oops! I forgot to make that call* is an emotionally neutral, spontaneous thought. You may question why this is emotionally neutral, especially if it leads to an uneasy or anxious feeling. The critical point here is that forgetting to make the call isn't what elicits an anxious feeling; it's your reaction to the thought that does. And if insecurity is allowed to take this thought and run with it— "Oh, my God! I forgot! That's terrible!"—then what was neutral becomes neurotic. Therefore, you can see where a neutral spontaneous thought can morph into an insecurity-driven thought.

neutral spontaneous thought + contamination by insecurity
= insecurity-driven thinking

This is a crucial point worth expanding. Let's say we were to interview ten people who received an IRS audit notice. Perhaps five of the ten would be mildly upset, which we might expect would be a normal response. Two of the ten might become quite anxious, another two might become hysterical, nauseated, and unable to eat or sleep, and the tenth person might simply shrug it off with a, "Whatever!" As discussed previously, life circumstances don't dictate our fate; how we react to these circumstances does. In order to not be victimized by your knee-jerk, neurotic "reactivity" to insecurity, you will first need to develop the critical awareness necessary to actively become involved in your thought process. And this is what Mind-Talk's first step is designed to teach you.

Becoming a Critical Observer

Most people are aware of their stream of consciousness—those thoughts that seem to flow willy-nilly through our minds moment to moment. But being *casually* aware of your thoughts is very different from being *critically* aware of them. Before I discuss critical awareness, there is one important prerequisite. In order to maximize your efforts, you must first learn to detach and depersonalize yourself from your thoughts.

Mind-Brain Unlearning Note

If you do nothing about your thinking, nothing will change. If you do something about your thinking, you will change

Detaching and Depersonalizing

In order to detach and depersonalize from your thinking, you need to learn to observe your thoughts from a more neutral, nonemotional vantage point. Rather than being unwittingly manipulated by your thoughts, you must learn to observe these thoughts without your usual bias, which is the result of personalizing them. For example, someone manipulated by neurotic emotional thoughts might think, *Life is too hard. I can't go on.* Whereas someone with detached awareness might apply a little Self-Coaching and ask, '*Who' is it in me that's saying I can't go on? Is it me telling myself I can't go on, or is it my insecurity?* This is the essence of Step One—determining where the thoughts that influence you originate. This may not seem like a big deal, but trust me, it's the first nail in the coffin of passive-mind thinking.

Without detached awareness, when you say you can't go on, you, in a Zen sense, become one with your insecurity. There is no separation. End result: you're depressed or anxious. If instead you detach and observe, you can begin to recognize a distinction between *you*, your healthy, detached "voice" and the contaminated voice that comes from the habit-loop of insecurity. By making this distinction—healthy voice versus insecurity-driven voice—you put yourself in a position of having a choice. You can either passively listen to insecurity (and be negatively affected), or you can resist.

Figure 12.1 illustrates a healthy detachment and depersonalization. In this scenario the habit-loop of insecurity is having no noticeable effect on normal functioning. Referring to our example at the beginning of this chapter, it would be, *Oops! I forgot to make that call. Guess I'll call for that appointment today.* Figure 12.2 illustrates some contamination of normal, healthy thinking by insecurity. This might be expressed by, *I know they're going to be mad at me!* This would be especially true if there were some ambivalence: *Why am I making such a big deal out of this? It's not the end of the world.* This kind of confusion is typical of worrisome ruminations, the what-ifs. Figure 12.3 shows insecurity dominating your thinking. This would be where your emotions kick into high gear: *I'm so afraid!* And this would be especially true if you were experiencing panic, depression, or both.

You might find the detachment depicted in Figure 12.1 to be somewhat unnatural, especially if you have chronically been contaminated by insecurity. But once you get the hang of detachment, it becomes effortless.

Figure 12.1
Healthy Detachment from Habit of Insecurity

Figure 12.2
Contamination by Insecurity

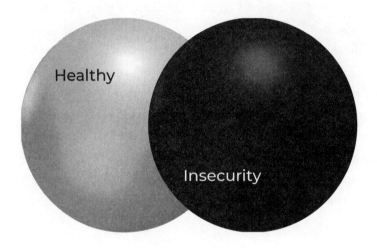

Figure 12.3
No Separation

Let's Get Started

Here are two exercises that will prepare you to begin separating facts from emotional fictions:

- Detached Mind-Checking
- Critically Observing (separating facts from emotional fictions)

Exercise 1: Detached Mind-Checking

The first technique, detached mind-checking, is a crucial, preliminary step in eventually learning to separate yourself from the habit-loop of destructive, neurotic thinking.[17] You can begin your practice of mind-checking by randomly observing, without any judgment, thoughts that come and go. Although your Mind-Talk will eventually be focusing on thoughts of insecurity—thoughts that typically cause distress (doubts, fears, or negativity)—for this exercise it's important to simply practice observing all thoughts as dispassionately as possible.

Think of yourself as a court stenographer whose job is to accurately record what is being said in the courtroom, not interpreting or reacting, just recording. Let's say, for example, you're driving home from work and you decide to do a mind-check: *Okay, what's going through my mind…let's see…. I've got to get home and pay some bills…. I need to stop and get gas…. What should I eat for supper?* You don't need to be concerned with the content of your thoughts—just the observation of them. Don't judge or evaluate these thoughts; just make note of them. That's it. Simple, right?

The goal of this exercise is just to familiarize yourself with becoming a detached observer, *not* a participant. By seeing yourself as an observer rather than a participant (a participant reacts; you're only recording), you

---

17. I expect you'll find this exercise to be familiar; no doubt you've been aware of your mind's inner chatter all your life. The difference now is that we're going to formalize your awareness and add a kind of mindful observing of your thought flow.

begin the very important process of depersonalizing—not emotionally identifying with your thoughts. It's not necessary or possible for you to observe every thought, but every time you decide to do a detached mind-check, insist on observing with focused attention, whether it's for a few seconds or a few minutes. Try this repeatedly throughout the day. Once you're comfortable with your detached mind-checking practice, it's time to move on to becoming a critical observer.

Exercise 2: Critically Observing: Separating Facts from Emotional Fictions

Critically observing is observing with the specific intention of separating facts from emotional fictions. Similar to mind-checking, critical observing is also done dispassionately as an observer rather than as a participant, but rather than randomly observing, now your focus is exclusively on thoughts that are driven by insecurity. Typically, these are your doubts, fears, and negative thoughts. You're not going to have to look too far to find these thoughts; they're the thoughts that invariably churn up distressful feelings and reactions.

Mind-Brain Unlearning Note

Anytime you find yourself experiencing emotional distress, if you critically observe your thoughts, you will find insecurity-driven thinking running amuck.

Take a Memo

In my practice, I give each new patient a three-by-five-inch spiral memo pad, one that you can purchase online or at any stationery store—one that fits easily in one's pocket or purse. My instructions are as follows:

Throughout the day, whenever you become aware of any emotional stress or struggle, do a mind-check. Ask yourself whether what you're feeling is associated with a doubt, fear, or negative thought. If so, jot this down in your memo pad at your first opportunity.

Although it would be helpful to describe the thought(s), for our purpose of developing critical awareness, it's not essential, especially since you'll be making a lot of entries initially as you begin to increase your awareness of your destructive habituated thinking. Quick shorthand notes will do. For example:

1:35 PM Anxiety about losing job/Doubt
3:45 PM Anxious worrying/Fear

The only thing we're concerned with in this exercise is awareness. Recognizing insecurity-driven thinking is where retraining your brain formally begins.

As you progress with the Mind-Talk steps ahead, you will find that mind-checking and critically observing will increase your awareness of how you "mindlessly" reinforce your habit of anxiety or depression throughout the day. When you remain passive, you allow insecurity-driven thinking to go unchecked. The key is understanding that your brain doesn't learn habits on its own—you teach it!

Mind-Brain Unlearning Note

You're allowed to be concerned with facts, but you're not allowed to let emotional fictions be treated as if they're facts.

Rather than identifying with these habituated destructive thoughts, feelings, and perceptions, when you critically observe them, you're attempting to separate and categorize these thoughts as either facts or emotional fictions. I'm sure you've noticed by now my frequent reminder that doubts, fears, and negative thinking are reliable tip-offs when it comes to calling out insecurity. By making this differentiation—facts versus fictions—you're empowering your rational mind to take a step back and scrutinize the validity of what you most likely, and passively, accepted simply out of habit. This critical first step of separating facts from emotional fictions lays the groundwork for what's ahead—putting an end to insecurity's carte blanche dominance over your emotions and perceptions. Let me illustrate this fact versus fiction concept by telling you about a bogeyman named Clarence.

Clarence

Bogeyman: An imaginary evil character of supernatural powers,
supposed to carry off naughty children

When I was young, probably around four or five, I was told there was a bogeyman named Clarence living in our attic who, if you didn't behave, would do God knows what to you—I never wanted to know "what." I have no idea why I was told this or why parents would want to scare the bejesus out of their children, but nevertheless, that's what I was told.

Here's my point: Clarence, like all bogeymen, wasn't real; he was a fiction, but the impact he had on me was very real. I was terrified of Clarence and the attic. Then at some point in my young life I did what any adventurous kid would do—I wandered, very, very cautiously, up into the attic to peek into Clarence's lair. No Clarence! After a few more cautious excursions into the attic, I began to wrestle with two competing perceptions: Clarence was either real or Clarence was fake. I may not have resolved my fears in that moment of clarity, but I certainly was on my way to extinguishing them.

This is why separating facts from emotional fictions is so important for you. Listening to and allowing yourself to be needlessly compromised by the distortions of insecurity is no different from my being afraid of

Clarence. But once you recognize there is no "Clarence," no factual basis for insecurity's doubts, fears, or negatives, then you begin to reinforce your conscious, uncontaminated perceptions. This is the point mentioned above where you begin to realize that you have a choice. You'll have a choice to decide if Clarence (insecurity's distortions) is real or if Clarence is fiction. Anxiety and depression rely on the distortions of a Clarence-like stranglehold on your feelings and perceptions.

As a postscript to Clarence, I should point out that many of my fondest, post-Clarence memories took place playing in that old attic. I had my Lionel trains set up, a workbench for making models, and it was a refuge on rainy days. You see, this is what happens when you dispel the toxic fictions in your life; it opens up opportunities for untold riches—in your case, the life you've been denied and the life you deserve.

Dealing with Resistance

If you suffer from anxiety or depression, you're well aware that your thoughts are often highly charged. You tell yourself, "I can't go on. This is too much to handle," or, "I'm driving myself crazy. I'm so afraid of making the wrong choice. What if I'm wrong?" No doubt you may feel like you *can't* go on or that you *can't* stop driving yourself crazy with fear. And when it comes to being anxious or depressed, perception is indeed reality. In order to dismantle the habit-loop of insecurity, you're going to have to first differentiate it from your normal healthy thinking. At first, since strong emotions are usually a component of the fictions of insecurity, this process is going to require effort; your habit-loop of insecurity will resist you every which way to Tuesday. Your most potent weapon is to use critical awareness to objectively determine the truth. Let me give two examples of how easy it is to become confused about the "facts" of your life.

Getting Off the Hamster Wheel

A good example of the process involved with differentiating facts from emotional fictions occurred recently while I was working with Tom, a dyed-in-the-wool worrywart, who kept insisting, "I can't stop worrying." I understood that Tom *felt* like he would never be able to stop worrying, but when I asked him whether he thought that he was truly unable to stop or if he simply *felt* that he couldn't, he insisted, "No, I really feel like I can't stop. I definitely can't."

Explaining to Tom that feelings aren't (necessarily) facts, I asked him, "Have you ever seen a hamster on one of those spinning wheels? The faster he goes, the faster the wheel turns. You're on kind of an insecurity-driven hamster wheel, spinning worry-thoughts on and on. Is it possible that, like a real hamster, you don't realize you can step off the wheel?" Cautiously, Tom responded, "Okay, but do you think I haven't tried to stop worrying? So how do I get off the wheel?" And this is where I felt an opening. I said, "You only feel like you can't stop worrying because you're stuck in a negative habit-loop. It's your insecurity, not you, that has you convinced you can't stop. If, hypothetically, one day you were to learn to stop worrying and get off the wheel, then your perception that you can't stop worrying wouldn't be a fact at all—it would be a fiction. Right?"

Not to be easily convinced, Tom responded, "Okay, I understand what you're saying, but it really feels like a fact." And this semi-acknowledgement was the beginning of his loosening the grip of his insecurity loop. It was the point where, rather than reflexively (and passively) accepting that he was powerless, he was beginning to realize that maybe, just maybe, there was another explanation. This is why separating facts from fictions is such an important first step in your Mind-Talk, because in order to unlearn anxiety and depression, you must first, as Sun Tzu wrote in his book *The Art of War*, *know your enemy*. And your enemy is the habit-loop of insecurity. Unless you get to "know" and become conscious of your enemy (insecurity), then you, like Tom, will assume you simply "can't" do anything to stop your suffering.

The bottom line in knowing your enemy is determining whether *your* thoughts are, in fact, your rational thoughts, or thoughts that have been tainted and manipulated by insecurity. This is what becoming a detached, critical observer is all about: facts overriding fictions. By separating your thoughts from insecurity's thoughts, you, as the critical observer, are in a position to decide whether or not what you're thinking needs to be embraced or rejected. But as is often the case, especially at first, differentiating facts from fictions may be quite challenging. Why? Because the emotionally distorted logic of insecurity can seem quite compelling.

Carl

Expanding this discussion, let me introduce you to Carl, whose distorted logic was just as entrenched as Tom's. A recent college dropout, Carl came into therapy moderately depressed, telling me, "I'm such a failure." I asked him to tell me why he *felt* that he was a failure. He told me, "I couldn't cut it in school, so I just gave up. To me that's the definition of a failure." I'm sure Carl would get no argument from his friends or parents on his logic; after all, he did in fact fail out of college. But I had a different interpretation, so I asked him to speculate with me, "What if a year from now you decide to go back to school? Let's say you've matured some, become more determined, and are just emotionally in a better place. And what if you were to get A's in all your classes and wind up graduating with honors? Would you still be a failure?" Carl struggled with this and finally responded, "No, of course not. In that case I guess I would have succeeded." I went on, "So, if you wind up succeeding, would that wipe out the fact that you were a failure? Which would you be: a success or a failure?"

I was trying to help Carl realize that his insecurity-driven pronouncement that *he* was a failure was an emotional dead end as well as an exaggeration of the facts. And it was simply not accurate. Our discussion didn't end there; Carl wanted to challenge my perceptions. He said, "You have to agree that I failed out of school, right?" I agreed, but added, "Yes, you failed out of school, but in order for *you* to be a failure we would have to extrapolate your experience in college to you the person. And that is just not accurate; it is an emotional fiction. You tried something, and it didn't work out. *You* are not a failure!"

I mention my exchange with Carl to help you understand how insecurity-driven logic will often seem, well, quite logical. Once Carl accepted (and became identified with) the faulty notion that *he* was a failure, a part of him began to give up, creating a fertile environment for his depression to grow. You may recall from Chapter Five how depression is an attempt to minimize further damage—shutting down the circuit breaker—caused by an emotional loss of control. As Carl's brain "circuits" began to get emotionally overloaded by his identification with being a failure, he began to feel more and more out of control. And in order to prevent further meltdown he began to shut down his circuits, becoming more withdrawn and dysfunctional as he retreated to the basement of his parents' home to play video games and more than occasionally smoke marijuana. He was trying to feel less vulnerable by avoiding life and further experiences of "failure." If it were true (and from a Self-Coaching perspective, it can't be) that Carl was, in fact, a failure, then we can see where retreating from life would make a kind of neurotic-sense.[18] It's all about control. Protecting himself from further rejection, loss, chaos, and failure was Carl's way (well, to be clear, "insecurity's" way) of trying to feel less out of control.

As you might guess, our discussion did give Carl something to wrestle with, which he did. His mood slowly began to improve as he began to open up about the *real* reason why he dropped out of college. Plain and simple, he dropped out because his studies didn't fit in with his social life. Now, with the critical observation that insecurity had been steering his faulty conclusions, he was able to work with his real problems—the

––––––––––––––

18. Although we fail from time to time with the challenges of our lives, we do not become our failures. Thus, Carl, the person, could never be a failure. With anxiety and depression, there is always a danger of identifying with insecurity-driven thinking.

fact that he failed because of his lack of self-discipline and poor choices, specifically, getting high and socializing rather than studying. As it turned out, Carl found it easier to leap to the conclusion that he was simply a failure than to take responsibility for the poor choices he had made. His personal character assassination was insecurity's way to sidestep the real issues by flipping the depression circuit breaker to the off position.

Polarized Thinking

Tom and Carl were both caught up in one of insecurity's typical ploys, the black and white world of polarized thinking. Polarized thinking happens to be a particularly stubborn fiction. Essentially, it's designed to protect/excuse you from the ambivalence of your rational mind desperately trying to fend off further loss of control. By capitulating to polarizing words like *always, never, can't, too hard, no way,* and so forth, you're actually squeezing rational thinking out of the picture, allowing insecurity's neurotic perspective to call the shots. (This progression would be illustrated by Figure 11.2 progressing into Figure 11.3 above.) If you suffer from anxiety or depression, you know that giving up only acts as an accelerant to further suffering. And this is that hamster wheel where you know you're making yourself miserable, but you *feel* you just can't stop.

13

Mind-Talk Step Two
Stopping Insecurity-Driven Thinking

Now that you're on your way to separating facts from emotional fictions, the question remains, especially if you're prone to incessant rumination, *how*? How exactly do you stop allowing yourself to be manipulated by your insecurity? The simple answer to this question is best summed up by something my grandmother was fond of saying: *You can't stop a bird from flying into your hair, but you don't have to help it build a nest.* From a habit-loop perspective, you may not be able to stop an insecurity-driven thought from percolating up into consciousness (at least not at the moment), but you don't have to passively allow your conscious mind to become part of the nest-building problem. This is the essence of Mind-Talk's Step Two—stopping the progression of insecurity-driven thinking.

Depending on what works for you, there are three techniques to stopping this progression:

- Engaging—focusing your conscious mind to actively stop the progression of insecurity-driven thinking.
- Active Ignoring—asserting your conscious mind to ignore and disengage from insecurity-driven thinking.

• Envisioning—using visuals to actively engage your conscious mind to shut out insecurity-driven thinking.

Once you understand these terms, you'll have to experiment to find out which technique, or combination of techniques, works best for you. I've found that for many people, depending on the particular struggle of the moment, having all three methods available affords you the best possible advantage to stop ruminative, insecurity-driven thinking in its tracks. Let's begin our discussion with the more direct approach, engaging insecurity head-on.

Engaging: The A-B-C of Suffering

All insecurity-driven thinking starts with what we might call a seed, or an "A" thought: *Maybe I can't trust him.* This may then be followed by a "B" thought: *If I can't trust him, maybe I should get a divorce.* That's followed by a "C" thought: *What if I'm wrong? But what if I'm right?* Got the idea? In order to put a stop to neurotic, insecurity-driven thinking, you must learn to stop the A to B, to C, to Z progression. In the last chapter, you learned about the value of critical awareness, which now becomes your go-to strategy for actively becoming conscious enough to nip the A thought in the bud before it progresses to B, to C, and so on.

We've discussed the dangers of passivity, and now you can see that doing nothing is allowing your passive, conscious mind to run the alphabet (more precisely, it's your insecurity-driven thinking that runs the alphabet; your passive mind sits back and allows this to happen). In Chapter Eleven we also talked about waking the sleeping giant of consciousness, and now it's time for just that to happen. You begin with the realization that although you've felt impotent to stop this runaway progression of toxic thinking in the past, it's not because you can't stop it; it's because you haven't made a focused, empowered conscious effort to do so. Once engaged, your conscious mind is in a position to make the decision as to whether or not emotional fictions are allowed to dictate. Which brings us to a fundamental Self-Coaching principle: in order to stop the A to B to Z progression, it's going to take a firm act of will. So, how in the world, if you've been pummeled for months, if not years, by the neurotic promptings of anxiety or depression, do you dig your heels in and say, STOP IT!

Invariably, the patients I've worked with who suffer from anxiety and depression have come to faulty conclusions that they are weak, ineffective, and victims of their insecurities. They are so identified with their impotence that any suggestion that they need to, for example, *stop worrying*, is scorned. They say, "I've tried, for years, I've tried." The problem goes back to our hamster-wheel metaphor. If what you mean by "trying" is to run faster and faster on the wheel of insecurity-driven thinking, hoping that you can worry or what-if yourself off the wheel, then of course, the only thing that changes is, well, nothing.

It's not a matter of doing the same-old-same-old, it's a matter of doing something different: getting off the wheel altogether. Step Two is designed to stop the wheel spinning (running the alphabet), which will put you in a position for what's ahead in Step Three, where you'll learn that in order to do something different, you're going to have to *be* different. For now, before getting to Step Three, you need to stop the wheel, not with weak or haphazard efforts, but with a consolidated focus that understands the pitfalls and missteps of the past and recognizes the unlimited power of your active conscious mind—the power to employ a very important mantra: STOP IT! DROP IT!

Mind-Brain Unlearning Note

You may not be able to stop that first insecurity thought from popping into your mind, but you sure as heck don't have to add the second thought, third thought, fourth....

Floodlights, Spotlights, and Laser Beams

You may not realize it, but you assert your consciousness all the time. Let's say you have an important meeting in the morning, and as the alarm goes off, you feel like you'd like to hit the snooze button. But recognizing the importance of the meeting, you say *no* to yourself and make yourself get out of bed. Or when you decide to get more exercise and instead of giving in to your habit of lethargy, you make yourself get off of the couch and go for a walk. Sometimes we have the power to take control of our out-of-control lives, and sometimes we don't. How come?

Think of it like the difference between a floodlight and a spotlight. A floodlight casts a wide beam of light, while a spotlight casts a narrow one. If your approach to any personal demand is too wide, too nebulous, or abstract, the energy is dispersed and you'll probably wind up abandoning your intentions. If, instead, you have a spotlight intentionality, then your energy is concentrated, and more focused energy means a higher probability of success. In fact, if you were to go from a spotlight to a laser beam focus, then your energy would become so concentrated that, like a laser, you could cut through just about anything your insecurity throws at you.

Actively Ignoring: Doing Something by Doing Nothing

So, what happens when, in spite of your intended, focused efforts, you wind up actually accelerating the progression of insecurity-driven thinking? "I've tried to stop worrying about my son, but the more I try not to think about him joining the military, the more anxious I become. Nothing is changing! I'm driving myself crazy!" This is not unusual, especially at the beginning when starting your Mind-Talk efforts where your conscious intentions to *stop it, drop it* are no match for the entrenched ruminations of your insecurity. In such cases where all your efforts at engaging only

bring on more suffering, you need to do a one-eighty and try doing…
nothing! I know this sounds not only passive and counterintuitive, but
even absurd, but believe me, under certain circumstances, *actively* ignoring can be just as powerful as a head-on engagement. The operative word
here is *actively* ignoring.

I recall introducing this concept to Alan, an anxious person whose constant and chronic worrying was ruining and ruling his life. Understandably, he was shocked to hear me tell him that instead of fighting so hard
to stop his insecurities, he instead needed to…well, do nothing! "I don't
understand. You're telling me to do nothing? That doesn't make any sense.
You want me to just be anxious? Depressed?" Alan's response, like so many
who suffer from anxiety and depression, wasn't unusual considering that
for most, yielding to (rather than resisting) insecurity's doubts, fears, or
negatives seems to be why they're suffering in the first place.

What kept tripping Alan up was his conviction that there had to be an
answer as to *why* he couldn't stop worrying, stressing, and beating himself up. Seeing how fixated Alan was with finding that abracadabra *why*,
I sensed that the last thing he needed to do was to get deeper into the
never-ending quagmire of his insecurity-driven thinking. His emails began to pour into my inbox, asking, over and over again, why he couldn't
stop worrying, why he was so scared, what he should think or not think,
always asking how others handle such life challenges. For Alan, the only
thing that made sense was that he had to find the hidden key to his suffering—the golden *why*.

If anything, Alan was getting more impatient and agitated about his
inability to talk himself out of his emotional fictions. What became even
more obvious was that by constantly trying to stop his ruminations, he
was inadvertently becoming more devoured by them, to the point where
there was no separation between Alan's healthy, rational mind and insecurity's contamination (refer back to illustration 11.3 in the last chapter).

Unfortunately, Alan just couldn't grasp my concept of actively ignoring. After spending years battling his thoughts, it just felt too risky to stop
fighting. As he told me, "I feel like you're telling me to jump in the ocean

and just allow myself to drown. I can't do that. I've got to do something!" And I totally agreed with Alan on this point. Where we disagreed was on what *something* needed to be.

You too may find *doing nothing* to be a rather confusing concept. After all, how do you stop something from progressing by doing nothing? It just doesn't make common sense. Perhaps not, but as you'll see, it does make psychological sense, especially once you realize that we're not talking about passively ignoring—we're talking about *actively* ignoring. Which, as you're about to see, makes all the difference in the world.

Actively Ignoring the Noise

It wasn't long after my discussion with Alan that I visited my son Justin in Manhattan. Sitting in his apartment listening to the chronic din of traffic, ambulances, and honking horns, I asked him how in the world he was able to sleep at night. He looked puzzled, as if for the first time he was hearing the street noises, and simply told me that he didn't "hear" the noises. Considering the disorienting racket from the streets below, I found that somewhat hard to believe until, driving home that night, I realized that Justin was being quite accurate. His ears heard the noises, but his brain had long ago learned to block them out. Talk about neuroplasticity! His brain learned to filter out extraneous noises, allowing him an uninterrupted sleep. A part of my son's brain had become Manhattanized.

Interestingly, my daughter Lauren had the reverse Manhattan effect. Lauren, who would occasionally come back to the tranquil suburbs of North Jersey from Manhattan for an occasional sleepover and to visit old friends, would typically complain, "I couldn't sleep. First it was too quiet, then the birds wouldn't stop chirping." And, you guessed it, my reaction was, "What birds?" You see, my mind had become suburbanized. I learned to stop listening to the early morning chirping long ago.

From these insights, I had the perfect metaphor to explain active ignoring to Alan—an understanding that when it comes to noxious stimuli, if the brain can be trained to defocus and filter out uncomfortable street noise, then why not train the brain to defocus and filter out uncomfortable psychological noise? In Alan's case, the noise wasn't caused by traffic or birds, but by the incessant noisy "voice" of insecurity.

Alan, because of his intense anxiety, was often unable to recall our discussions afterwards, so he would take copious notes during our sessions. We ultimately decided that it would be more efficient for him to record our sessions. From one such recording, I was therefore able to transcribe a very pivotal session where Alan finally saw the light. As I explained to him:

> *When I go into Manhattan, I'm often distracted by the obnoxious clamor of a bustling city. When I find myself focusing on the noise, it winds up causing a degree of stress. You're like me, only you're not focusing on traffic noises, you're focusing on the neurotic "voice-noises" of your insecurity.*
>
> *Just as the traffic noise of the city wafts up to you from the streets below, your insecurity-noise wafts up from the depths of your habit-loop of insecurity. Like me when visiting my son, if you allow yourself to focus on the noise, your conscious mind will be contaminated by it. If, on the other hand, you actively defocus or distract your mind and teach yourself to ignore the noise, then eventually your brain will learn to stop hearing it. Why? Because instead of listening to the "noise" and fueling the habit-loop of insecurity, you're making the noise irrelevant.*
>
> *I know this won't seem natural at first. In fact, it's going to feel totally unnatural, but that's only because you've convinced yourself of the myth that you need to pay attention to insecurity's distortions so that you can talk yourself out of your struggles. By actively ignoring, you're doing something very important—you're training your brain to no longer reinforce your habit reflex. Understand that when you wrestle with these thoughts you're inadvertently validating, reinforcing, and giving them life. When you dismiss and ignore them, you are nullify-*

ing them.

Alan was quiet when our session ended, but he sent me the following email a few days later:

I know it's early, but I really think I'm getting it. I haven't felt this good in a long time. I just never realized that I don't have to listen.

Envisioning

You've heard it said that a picture is worth a thousand words. When you get caught up in the incessant chatter of insecurity-driven thinking, having a simple picture in your mind can be far more useful than a thousand words of analyzing or trying to understand the *whys* of your suffering. Why are visualizations so powerful? Simply, because the brain likes—even craves—visual images. You can tell yourself to stop worrying, which more often than not requires a tedious effort, but, if you create a visual image in your mind-brain, you will be generating a much deeper awareness and actual experience of solace.

When you participate in a visualization the brain itself reacts the same way as if you're physically performing the action. So, if you saturate your brain with comforting, experiential images, you accomplish two things:

1. You reduce the stress of insecurity-driven thinking.

2. You tune into your parasympathetic nervous system (often referred to as your "rest and digest" system).

In other words, mentally and physiologically, you go from stressful arousal to calm restoration. Yup, don't underestimate the power of a visualization.

So, rather than fatiguing your brain with word-chatter attempts to feel better, draw it a picture. Do this and it will respond with a much deeper interest and attention that will allow you to turn away from the toxic chatter of insecurity.

The visualization I suggested for Kate is a good example of enlisting different parts of your brain in order to loosen insecurity's grip on your consciousness. Kate, an aspiring artist, was having trouble grasping the concept of active ignoring. Recognizing that Kate was a visual person, I eventually came up with the following visualization:

> *Imagine that you live next to some noisy, obnoxious neighbors. Historically you've gone through your life complaining and stressed, but never realizing that the noise is coming through the open windows in your home. I want you to shut out insecurity's chatter by actively visualizing yourself shutting the windows, one-by-one, room-by-room. Whenever you start to spin with toxic thinking, visualize yourself closing those windows, slowly drowning out the noise, window by window.*

Essentially, you're making your conscious mind focus on your visualization, while defocusing your mind away from insecurity-driven thinking. So, the next time you find yourself struggling, take a moment to close your eyes and picture the open windows in your home or apartment, hear the obnoxious insecurity-noise, and then go through all the motions of slowly closing each window one by one and room by room. As each window is lowered, imagine that chatter becoming less and less until it's merely a murmur. When all the windows are closed, visualize yourself in your quiet, tranquil house. The noisy neighbors may still be making a racket, but the noise doesn't reach you. You're closed off from hearing it.

You may want to create a personalized visualization that works just for you (like imagining shutting windows one by one). I've had patients offer up some interesting images, and one of my absolute favorites was told to me by a patient trying to stop her incessant ruminations:

> *Imagine that you're holding the strings of a dozen brightly colored*

helium-filled balloons. Feel your hand gripping the strings. Notice the slight tug of the balloons buoyed up by the helium. Start by releasing the string of a red balloon (you can pick any color) and watch it as it slowly floats up, up, up…diminishing in size until it vanishes. Then go on to another color, separating the string from the others and letting go and watching it float up into the blue sky, doing this over and over until the train of toxic thinking is interrupted.

Finding What Works for You

Whether you choose to engage, ignore, or envision your departure from insecurity-driven thinking depends on a bit of experimentation to find out what is most effective for you. There may be times where a focused, *Stop it! Drop it!* will be all that's necessary to stop the runaway train of doubt, fear, and negativity. Whereas other times where you just can't shake yourself loose from the hamster wheel, you may find that actively ignoring will offer you a more detached capacity for getting on with your outer world, rather than a congested inner one. And there might be times where you need to focus on a very conscientious visualization, capable of absorbing your attention away from the feeling of powerlessness so typical of ruminative struggles.

Whichever techniques you gravitate toward, these are all powerful Self-Coaching tools designed to systematically train your brain to starve the habit of insecurity. (Do keep in mind that Self-Coaching isn't just about symptom removal, although that's important. The larger goal is the more permanent rewiring of your plastic brain.) The problem has been your conscious passivity, which inadvertently allowed insecurity to have its way with your consciousness. That's all going to change with your Step Two efforts as you cut off insecurity's psychological food supply. Always keep in mind that every attempt to actively resist insecurity matters—the effect is cumulative. At this point in your training it doesn't matter whether you succeed, somewhat succeed, or fail; what does matter is that with each effort you prove that you're not a victim. You may recall from Chapter One my assertion that victims are powerless. You are not powerless!

The Goal of Step Two

Stopping the unimpeded flow of insecurity-driven thinking thereby starving the habit-loop of insecurity.

How to Maximize Your Self-Coaching

All emotional struggle has an element of stress. When we're stressed, essentially, two things happen:

> **1.** Stress causes an overactivity of the amygdala—fight-flight—portion of the brain.
> **2.** This overactivity suppresses healthy thinking as you become hijacked by the visceral effects of insecurity-driven thinking.

In order to maximize your Self-Coaching, you'll find it helpful to first quiet down and calm your body.

What's needed are "bottom-up," sensory exercises intended to quiet your overactive, stressed brain. These can include slow, deep breathing, meditation and/or meditation music, "body checking" (looking for pockets of tension in your body), physical exercise, yoga, and so on. Once you begin to calm the amygdala's reflexive response to stress, you'll be in a much better position to apply some critical "top-down," active-mind techniques mentioned in this chapter, e.g., envisioning, active ignoring, engaging—the A-B-C technique, detaching and depersonalizing, and so on.

14

Mind-Talk Step Three
Responsive Living

Here's where things get exciting! As you continue your ongoing practice of becoming a critical observer, separating facts from fictions and then stopping the runaway train of insecurity-driven thinking, you begin to starve your habit-reflex of insecurity. As insecurity begins to weaken and lose its influence over your thoughts and perceptions, you put yourself in a position to finally challenge the fractured life that anxiety and depression have left you with.

I can't overstate the need for practicing Steps One and Two on a daily basis. Every effort, no matter how small or seemingly fruitless, is critical to your ultimate liberation. Since it helps to think of the brain as a muscle that can grow with exercise, it's important that you adopt a patient, realistic approach to your unlearning process. Just as you wouldn't expect that doing one crunch or one pull-up would make a dramatic change in your musculature, the same is true with your brain. Stopping insecurity one thought at a time may not make a noticeable difference in the beginning, but by stopping or thwarting insecurity again and again...and again, you're literally beginning the process of rewiring your brain—circuit by circuit. You're unlearning the neurotic thinking that has prolonged your suffering.

Every thought, positive or negative, has a corresponding physiological impact in your brain. While one thought's impact may be infinitesimal with no detectable change in your mood or behavior, you need to be aware that these thoughts are cumulative. In 1949 the Canadian neuro-psychologist Donald Hebb coined the phrase "neurons that fire together wire together." What this phrase tells us is that every thought, feeling, per-ception, and experience triggers changes in our brain's neurons, and when repeated over and over, these neurons wire together to make up a neural network—a reflexive habit-loop. Hebb's postulate not only tells us that neurons can wire "together," but that they can also "unwire," or according to Self-Coaching, be unlearned.

Until now insecurity was winning the thought battle, tilting the scales in the direction of overcontrolling life and keeping you prisoner. But now you're reversing the process, thought by thought, neuron by neuron, knowing that every effort you make to assert your healthy consciousness is rewiring your brain, balancing your chemistry (homeostasis), and liberat-ing your mind.

From now on, insecurity-driven, shabby thinking will be going up against a new sheriff in town—you! Along with your determination that, rather than accept the life handed to you by insecurity, you're going to awaken the sleeping giant of consciousness and demand the life you want—the life you deserve. The culprit all along has been your conscious passivity, which was inadvertently lulled into allowing insecurity to go unchecked. When we drill a bit deeper into the "why" of your passivity, it all comes down to a lack of self-trust. Insecurity led you to believe that you couldn't trust that you could actually handle life's challenges instinctually and spontaneously—certainly not without anticipating, worrying, or fret-ting about the what-ifs. The only choice seemed to be control. Control with a capital *C*, which makes a kind of neurotic sense because you and I and everyone else are survival machines, and without adequate self-trust, trying to overcontrol life, well, seems like a reasonable alternative—until now!

Self-Trust

Aside from treating the brain as a muscle, you may recall from Chapter One that I also refer to self-trust as a muscle (yup, another muscle metaphor). When your self-trust muscle atrophies and you lose the ability to ward off feelings of vulnerability and insecurity, anxiety and depression become an inevitable last-ditch outcome (recalling our circuit-breaker analogies). As a result, our attempts to overcontrol life through various controlling strategies becomes a crutch intended to prevent further collapse and loss of control. Ironically, rather than preventing collapse, neurotically trying to control life hastens, if not ensures it!

If you were to break your leg, having crutches to lean on would be essential. But, unlike a broken leg, your "leg" (self-trust) was never broken. You don't need a control crutch. You require only a bit of Self-Coaching physical therapy to rehabilitate a bruised and atrophied self-trust muscle. In actual physical therapy, week by week you're given progressive exercises designed to stretch, stimulate, and revitalize your muscles. The same goes for your psychological rehab—you need to stop relying on the crutch of passivity that insists on overcontrolling life and instead begin building, strengthening, and revitalizing your self-trust muscle.

So, what exactly is self-trust? From a Self-Coaching perspective, it's a willingness to risk believing that you can handle life's challenges. That doesn't sound so difficult or complicated, right? It may sound simple, but if I were to tell you to go ahead and stop worrying about your finances, stop ruminating about the fact that you're getting older, or stop thinking that your headache is brain cancer, do you think you could simply stop? Probably not, which is why learning to live more *responsively* is so important. Just imagine allowing life to unfold without trying to anticipate or control it, with the conviction that you can and will handle what comes your way. It's hard to even imagine such an unburdened life, right? That's okay; soon you won't have to imagine it.

For some, the proposition that anyone who suffers from anxiety or depression lacks self-trust may not sit well. You may have tremendous self-confidence in your expertise at work, or an extroverted social life. Don't be insulted, and don't be misled. Just because you do some things well doesn't mean that you can ignore the fact that if you suffer from anxiety or depression, then your *core* self-trust muscle has atrophied. Certain areas of your life may seem secure or confident—your role as mother or father, your skill on the sports field or tennis court, or, if you recall Officer Mike from Chapter Two, your work persona. Speaking of Officer Mike, I originally told you his story in order to introduce you to the concept that insecurity and control are the smoke and fire of anxiety and depression. At this point let me add that a lack of self-trust is the match that starts everything burning.

Learning to Micromanage Self-Trust

Most things seem complicated until they become uncomplicated. I was telling a friend about an old sports car I had many years ago. I told him how my fantasy was to find the same car today, almost fifty years later, and to be able to completely restore it into mint condition. My friend asked me why I just didn't go ahead and do it. I chuckled and said, "I wouldn't know where or how to start. Aside from finding the car, I would need to find a mechanic to teach me each step of the reconstruction, a garage to work on it, my wife not thinking I was crazy…." My friend simply said, "So, why not just do it?" You see, my friend was thinking I was serious, but I wasn't. I was just fantasizing. But afterwards, reflecting back on this conversation, I asked myself, *if* I had the time, the money, the support of my wife, and a dozen other compliant variables, would I actually consider taking on such an overwhelming challenge? The answer was *yes*.

After all, if I had a mechanical mentor who would work with me bolt by bolt, a body restorer who would teach me how to restore and paint the body, an upholsterer who could teach me how to make rugs, seat covers, and so on, and the time and unlimited funds, I see no reason to believe that I couldn't turn that fantasy into a reality—as long as all the steps were taught to me in a way that allowed me to approach my project not from a macro, but from a micro level, one bolt at a time. And if this were the case, what would stop me from realizing my fantasy? Well, nothing.

Obviously you're not interested in restoring a vintage sports car (nor am I, not really), but you are interested in restoring self-trust. And like me, if you don't want to be intimidated by the challenge, then you're going to need to approach this not from a macro level, but from the micro level of Mind-Talk—not bolt by bolt, but thought by thought.

A good example of micromanaging your self-trust restoration can be seen in my exchange with Scott, a forty-four-year-old security guard at a local community college who had come into therapy because of a deepening depression. Scott told me about growing up with his "rejecting" (indifferent) father:

> *"I was always criticized by him. For my looks, the clothes I wore, my friends, my grades. I wanted to go to college and study art, but he said it was a waste of his money and insisted I get a 'real' job. Forget the fact that I didn't think he loved me; I really think he just didn't like me. I grew up afraid to make any decision. It just seemed that I couldn't do anything to please him. It's not like I didn't try; it's just that everything I did always came up short with him."*

Lately, Scott would find himself fantasizing about doing something more creative. "I love to draw. I probably couldn't support myself, but if I could wave a magic wand, I'd love to be an artist. If I wanted to, I could take an oil painting class at the college and I wouldn't even have to pay for it." Like my friend asking me about restoring my sports car, I too asked what was stopping him. He responded, "Oh no, I couldn't do that!" When I asked why, he told me, "I hear this little voice (Child-Reflex) saying, 'What's your father going to say?'" I found it interesting that Scott was well aware of his "little voice" holding him back, but that he never thought of actually resisting it.

I asked Scott how it was that, as an adult, he was still responding to his father as if he were a child. He crunched up his brow and responded, "Good question. I really don't know, but going against my father, even now, just seems to freeze me." I discussed the nature of habit-loops with Scott, telling him, "Growing up, your father's influence created a habit-loop of self-doubt and insecurity. That habit-loop, in spite of your adult awareness, is alive and well and emotionally holding you hostage." Scott replied, "Yes, I can see that, but how do I stop listening to that voice? It's not like I decide to have those thoughts." I responded, "No, you're not deciding to have those thoughts, but you're not doing anything to neutralize and replace them with more mature, appropriate thinking." Perhaps for the first time, Scott was awakening to the concept that there was a mature, present-tense Scott, and there was a reflexive, little boy Scott. Mature Scott was in the backseat and little boy Scott was driving.

I went on to explain to him that as long as he allowed himself—consciously or unconsciously—to be dominated by his Child-Reflex of insecurity, there was no way he could ever begin to trust his decisions, desires, or actions. He had long ago assumed that his perceptions were faulty; after all, this is what his father continually drummed into him. I told Scott a simple truth: "In order to liberate yourself from your depression, you're going to have to separate from your Child-Reflex and begin to build self-trust." "But how?" pleaded Scott again. "By recognizing that every time that little-boy voice wants you to hesitate and back away from your inclinations—because your father might not approve of you—you need to be willing to go to war with these thoughts. Unless you recognize the need to make a conscious stand against your knee-jerk habit of trying to please your father, you will never be rid of your depression."

I concluded with, "You can't expect to neutralize your depression if you inadvertently continue to perpetuate the myth that reinforces and feeds the habit-loop that says you can't know what's best for you. Starting right now, you're not allowed to sit on the sidelines and witness these father-inhibiting thoughts and do nothing; you need to begin to fight back. You need to become a critical observer, and every time you become aware of that familiar self-doubt knot in your stomach, at the very least, I want you to tell yourself in no uncertain terms, 'What am I doing? STOP! That's my insecurity talking. There is absolutely no reason I have to be afraid of my eighty-year-old father!'"—no healthy reason.

As you might imagine, at first it felt risky for Scott to even think about going against his reflexive fears and self-doubt, but by taking this one-thought-at-a-time approach, he conceded that this could be a manageable task. Initially, "going against" his father seemed overwhelming to Scott, but by taking it thought by thought (bolt by bolt), he understood that there was no reason why he couldn't steel himself and begin to wrestle with these sabotaging, guilt-ridden Child-Reflex thoughts. And it was this realization that became the catalyst for Scott to finally realize, "I think I can do this!"

I should mention that prior to this realization, Scott's reaction to do anything liberating (much less taking an oil painting class) was met with a blanket, "I can't!" End of discussion. He was so used to reflexively saying, "I can't," that he never, not once, asked *why* he couldn't. This is the nature of an imbedded habit-loop; it operates in a black-and-white world of absolutes—no grays.

In order for Scott to build self-trust, there was only one way: he had to risk trusting himself, which of course meant handling his reflexive, life-long discomfort of "doing something wrong." He also had to lose the reflexive word *can't*, which he cautiously replaced with *maybe I can*. This was no small accomplishment; in fact, it was a titanic breakthrough! For the first time, he was thinking on his own, separate from insecurity. And once he awakened his consciousness, embracing a pragmatic thought-by-thought approach, he was well on his way of separating from and neutralizing his previously conditioned, little-boy insecurity.

Self-trust is a process of taking your life back from insecurity piece by piece. Done properly and systematically, whether it's a sports car or a life-long self-distrust, everything is possible.

Laying Your Cornerstone

At this point in your reading you might be gratified to know that I've saved the best for last. In order to illustrate the importance of this last critical piece of information, I want to introduce you to the architectural significance of the cornerstone. The cornerstone is the first stone laid in a building's foundation to which all other stones are set in reference to this stone, thereby dictating the eventual structure (Figure 14.1).

Figure 14.1
The Cornerstone

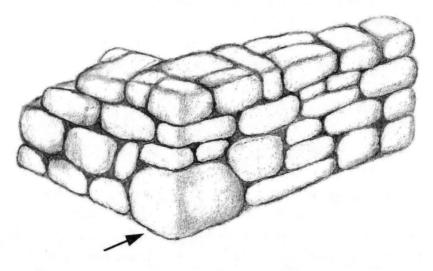

It helps to think of your Self-Coaching program as a building consisting, not of stones, but of an array of interlocking convictions, strategies, and beliefs, each held in place and oriented around the cornerstone. Before defining your cornerstone, let's review all the related psychological "stones" that comprise your habit re-formation efforts. Take a look at the list of stones below. The Self-Coaching structure that you build will consist of your having an adequate grasp of the many stones discussed in this book:

- Neuroplasticity
- Habits
- Reflexive habit-loop
- Control
- Controlling strategies
- Self-trust
- Critical awareness
- Child-Reflex
- Consciousness
- Stress
- Homeostasis
- Neurosis
- Anticipation versus worry versus concern
- Compulsivity
- Habit resistance
- Operant conditioning
- Spontaneous thoughts
- Active mind, passive mind
- Emotional fictions
- Detached observing
- Critical observing
- Mind checking
- Polarized thinking
- Engaging
- Active ignoring
- Envisioning

After reviewing the elements that comprise your habit re-formation structure, you must be quite curious as to what, specifically, is the orientating cornerstone. Ready? It's called Responsive Living. Perhaps the best way to describe Responsive Living would be the Alcoholics Anonymous (AA) phrase I mentioned in Chapter Six: *Let go and let God.* The poignancy of this adage may escape you due to its simplicity, but trust me, it's quite profound. In AA parlance, it has to do with letting go of compulsive destructive thinking and handing yourself over to a higher power. From a secularized, Self-Coaching standpoint, Responsive Living is learning *to let go and let life.* Translation: letting go of trying to control life, and instead learning to risk letting life unfold spontaneously without anticipation, worry, or fear. This is Responsive Living—the cornerstone that dictates your ultimate liberation from emotional struggle.

Responsive Living may be the cornerstone of Self-Coaching, but this is a bit misleading because without self-trust there can be no Responsive Living. Perhaps it would help to expand the cornerstone image. A cornerstone needs to be shaped to just the right shape and dimensions in order to support the construction that grows around it (i.e., emotional liberation). Responsive Living is the result of the shaping forces of self-trust that allow it to function as the embodiment of your Self-Coaching program.

One thing you should know about self-trust: you're never going to self-trust if you cling, on any level, to your doubts, fears, or negative thinking. If you're on a diving board and you're dying to get in the pool, you can't *almost* dive; you either dive or you remain on the diving board. Self-trust ultimately is an all-or-nothing proposition. You either risk going against the voice of your insecurity and let go, or you remain fixed on a diving board of ambivalence. Letting go and letting life unfold is a leap of faith.

The endgame of anxiety and depression begins with the self-trusting proposition that you can and will handle every challenge that comes your way—no *ifs, ands,* or *buts.* Like so many people I've worked with, you probably want a guarantee that letting go won't leave you more vulnerable. I often tell my patients, if you want a guarantee before you take the leap of self-trust, buy a blender. If, however, you're willing to take that leap of faith and risk self-trusting, you will, in fact, be guaranteeing an end to your suffering.

Mind-Brain Unlearning Note

Responsive Living and self-trust are two sides of the same coin called emotional liberation.

Whether on a diving board or with life itself, sometimes it takes a bit of a nudge to take that leap. Aaron, a young man I was working with, came to our session telling me that he'd had his first panic attack. Although we had been making steady progress, a confluence of stressful circumstances brought on a panic attack, which landed him in the emergency room. I asked him whether or not he felt that his panic attack was going to sabotage his recent efforts to let go and trust. He responded, "Hell no! The first thing I did when I got home was take off my Fitbit (which he used to compulsively monitor his heart rate). I refuse to ever let this happen again! All the way to the hospital I was well aware that I had recently been feeding my anxieties, but I just kept feeding and feeding. Stupid, huh? This has been my wake-up call, and from now on I refuse to be such a patsy. No more!"

Aaron, although he knew better, had passively allowed insecurity to creep back into his life. You might think his declaration, "No more!" was Aaron just trying to convince himself that he was going to beat his anxieties. But let me tell you, when someone has a legitimate *aha* moment where they recognize—*really* recognize—the problem along with the solution, and then combine all this with a fierce determination to go to war with insecurity, well, this is usually the point where the fat lady begins to sing. In the weeks that followed, this was indeed the case for Aaron as he steadily reported sleeping better, feeling less anxious, and standing up to and neutralizing his phobic fear of having a heart attack (his father had died of a heart attack at fifty-two years old). In fact, he was proud to announce that he was selling his Fitbit on eBay.

So, how do you nudge yourself to take the self-trust leap of faith? This is different for every person. For some, it's a matter of getting fed up. For others, like Aaron, it's a circumstantial wake-up call. And for yet others it's a gradual process of inching toward that tipping point called *liberation from insecurity*. As long as you have been diligently working your Mind-Talk steps, you will be preparing yourself to let go and take that leap of faith. Think of that *nudge-moment* as a moment of clarity, a moment where you realize—really realize—that the only things stopping you are the distortions of insecurity. Remember Clarence from Chapter Twelve? It's that empowered nudge-moment when you realize there's no bogey-man.

Still unclear about what exactly Responsive Living is? This visual will help:

Imagine that you're going to take a drive in your new Bentley (hey, it's a fantasy). As you pull out of your driveway, the thought occurs to you, *What if a deer runs in front of my car? Should I slam on the brakes perhaps causing me to get rear-ended, or swerve, which may send me into oncoming traffic? What if I can't stop and have to run over the deer?* Okay, got the picture?

Our driver represents living in an anticipatory world of insecurity, vulnerability, and what-ifs. Obviously, our driver, caught up in this neurotic reverie, ignores the beautiful music wafting up from the Bentley's Naim Audio sound system and doesn't notice the stunning roadside scenery. (Shall we say the ocean views along the Pacific Coast Highway?) Our driver is not *present*; she's not enjoying her Bentley, listening to beautiful music, or watching the sunset's long red rays playing on the waves below. Nope. She's in a stressful, fictional future that doesn't exist.

Let's see what changes if we inject some Responsive Living into a second visual. In this updated fantasy, our Responsive Living driver would get behind the wheel of her car, turn on the radio, begin to pull out of the driveway and, although she may have the thought, *Hm, what would I do if a deer runs in front of my car?* her immediate response would be, *Well, if that were to happen, I'm sure that I would react instinctively in that moment.* And that would be it as our driver feels the ocean breeze (of course, her Bentley is a convertible), notices a dolphin leaping in the distance, and begins singing along to her favorite song. Our Responsive Living driver in this case would be present, living in the moment, and most importantly, self-trusting that life can be handled responsively, rather than proactively by neurotically anticipating chaos and a loss of control.

Letting Go

Like most things mentioned in this book, learning to let go and be responsive to life is a nuts-and-bolts, trial-and-error process. Expect challenges. And from the start understand that you're going to come face to face with your insecurities *and* with discomfort. Most change in life entails some discomfort until the change becomes the new normal. No doubt after all this time of trying to overcontrol life, letting go will seem alien to you. Expect to be somewhat confused at first, but nevertheless, be aware that letting go and self-trusting (Responsive Living) is a process where, by turning away from insecurity's doubts, fears, and negatives, you're left with…what? You're left with an opportunity to simply *be.*

Whoa! Let's not get too existential about this. But it is important for you to embrace that *being* is qualitatively different from *thinking* about being. (I doubt the good people at Nike would have embraced the slogan, *Just think about doing it!*) Until now you've been caught up in your compulsive, worrisome world of abstractions: "What if I get cancer?" "What if I get more depressed? What will happen to me? What if I get fired?" When you get caught up in congested, insecurity-driven thinking, you're removing yourself from the possibility of living more spontaneously in the present. You may have one foot in the real, external world, the other in the abstractions of neurotic thinking (refer back to Figure 11.2). Letting go and taking that leap of faith is a process of allowing yourself to become

more and more *responsive* to life rather than proactively trying to anticipate it. Let me elaborate.

Imagine that you're about to start a new job. You're standing outside
the building fretting about whether or not your coworkers are going to
like you, whether the workload will be too much, or whether you'll be
bored to death. As your anxiety begins to rise, you become more and more
panicky. All this happens because your insecurity is trying to figure out
how you can avoid vulnerability and possible chaos.

Okay, now let's say you've been practicing Responsive Living. You
stand outside the building, already feeling a bit tense. Maybe you feel insecurity beginning to percolate, but instead, you notice that thought and
pause. You look around. It's a beautiful day. You take a few long, slow deep
breaths (quelling your amygdala response), recognizing that you were chosen over all the other candidates for this job and it was your decision to
take it. What are you worried about? You open the door, get on the elevator, and walk into the office. That's it. You don't anticipate what you'll do
or how you'll do it—you'll find out in *that* moment, as it unfolds. You're
trusting that you don't have to be rehearsed in order to be safe. You're a
survival machine, and letting go, allowing life to unfold, leaves you calm,
clear, and composed on that first day of work.

Starting today, see if you can be more responsive.[19] It can be simple
things. For example, not rehearsing how you'll tell your neighbor that his
dog is using your yard as a toilet, or not worrying what *might* happen if
you were to get a notice for jury duty. Instead, do nothing! Risk letting
these and other situations come to you rather than you abstractly going to
them. Let life present itself to you. If you do this, you'll begin to find out
something really, really amazing—you'll be able to handle whatever life

---

19. Responsive Living does not mean you can't anticipate, organize, or prepare for life's demands. It's why we have calendars, reminders, and sticky
notes. These anticipations are the emotionally neutral aspects of normal adult
functioning. Responsive Living isn't concerned with your emotionally neutral, organizational life—only with the emotionally charged, insecurity-driv-
en need to overcontrol that which we doubt or fear.

throws at you. You won't let yourself down! You'll handle deer running in front of your car, your first day on the new job, and any other circumstantial challenge. Truth is, you're much more formidable in all matters when you allow yourself to react spontaneously, instinctually, and intuitively to life than when you hobble yourself with self-distrust. I know it will feel risky, which is why I suggest you start with simple things—low impact challenges that begin to demonstrate that, lo and behold, you really can handle life on the fly.

Mind-Brain Unlearning Note

Self-trust and Responsive Living all come down to a willingness to believe in yourself and your resourcefulness to handle life's challenges.

15

Mind-Talk Step Four
Motivation

The Fuel of Emotional Liberation

As you begin to combine your Self-Coaching perspective with your practice of Mind-Talk, there's one last crucial and indispensable step to your liberation from anxiety and depression—motivation. Just how important is motivation? Well, how important are things like the gas in your car, the batteries in your flashlight, or the food that you eat? Sure, you, your car, and your flashlight can last a while without replenishing their fuel sources (well, actually, your flashlight would stop working immediately without batteries). But then what? It's only a matter of time before the engine, flashlight, and your body begin to falter and stop. Without fuel, nothing can be sustained...not even your intentions to liberate yourself from anxiety and depression. Motivation is fuel! And what fuels motivation is optimism.

But first, how do we define motivation? Essentially, it's an extension of an optimistic attitude. Optimism and motivation go hand in hand. Although it's conceivable that you could be an unmotivated optimist, it's hard to imagine being motivated without optimism. The opposite is true for pessimism; it's hard to imagine being motivated if you're pessimistic. When we anticipate positive outcomes, we release positive energy—the psychic fuel of motivation. To be clear, optimism doesn't guarantee success, nor does pessimism guarantee failure. Either attitude can wind up with a successful outcome. But if you're a pessimist trying to liberate yourself from anxiety and depression, not only are you hindering the chances that you will unlearn your insecurities, you may inadvertently wind up feeding them! Optimism, on the other hand, becomes your energy factory, enhancing the probability of your ongoing success and release from suffering. Where optimism generates energy, pessimism drains it.

Whether you're an optimist or a pessimist, you can't know the future. But I think you'll agree with me that if optimism is motivation's gas pedal and pessimism the brake pedal, there's no contest which will serve you better as you ready yourself for the necessary Self-Coaching work ahead. An optimist is buoyed and energized by the belief that they can and will handle what life throws at them. From this belief, positive energy (psychic fuel) is released and transformed into psychological resilience, allowing you to resist neurotic distortions of insecurity without abandoning your Mind-Talk efforts. In contrast, the pessimist wastes valuable psychological energy bogged down by negativity, doubt, and fear, never getting far from insecurity's gravitational pull. And when it comes to battling longstanding neurotic habit-loops, it matters how much energy you have available to fight the good fight and go the distance. How much does psychological motivation matter? A lot!

On the Nature of Pessimism

As discussed previously, whenever adverse circumstances create an atmosphere of vulnerability, we humans instinctively try to regain control. Pessimism, which can be expressed as negativity, doubt, or fear, is an acquired, twisted strategy whose aim is to make us *feel* more in control. However, far from feeling more in control, the pessimist's self-doubt, self-distrust, and lack of confidence only lead to the handwringing anticipation of the many things in life that *could* go awry, the what-ifs and yes-buts of doubt and fear.[20]

This anticipation ostensibly makes a pessimist feel protected from feeling more vulnerable and out of control. Pessimists are wedded to the proposition that: *If I anticipate the worst, I'll be better prepared to minimize the damage. Being braced and ready makes me feel more in control and less vulnerable.* This isn't illogical—after all, anticipating danger isn't necessarily a bad thing. But it is, nevertheless, one of insecurity's ruses. You see, for the pessimist, it's not simply a matter of *anticipating* the worst; it's repeatedly and incessantly anticipating it until the stress and chemical depletion inexorably lead to furthering anxiety and depression. When this happens, you're eliminating the possibility of living mindfully in the present because you're caught up in the abstractions of future disaster.

Identifying with Pessimism

Perhaps one of the most nefarious aspects of pessimism is that we tend to identify with our negativity. People torture themselves mercilessly with labels like failure, has-been, weakling, loser, and so on. Unfortunately, because we passively wind up identifying with these labels, they become what we call a self-fulfilling prophecy. And once you label yourself a failure or loser, you begin to act like a failure or loser, thus perpetuating this deception of insecurity.

Pessimistic identification is an acquired habit driven by insecurity. Unfortunately, your *truth*—who and what you are—often becomes shrouded in self-doubt and emotional fiction. We tell ourselves, "She would never talk to a person like me…I'm such a loser." What's interesting is that, not infrequently, self-loathing often has some justification. Well, kind of.

---

20. There's a subtle difference between pessimism and worrying. Where worry anticipates specific things going wrong, pessimism is a capitulation to negativity in general.

With pessimistic identification, you *become* your pessimism; there's no separation. So, as mentioned above, when you say you're a loser or a failure, this may accurately be describing exactly how you've been acting. Although your negative label may be accurately describing what you've become, it doesn't describe the person that's buried under all the negatives. Jessica's struggle will highlight this point.

Jessica, a twenty-nine-year-old bank employee, believed that no matter what she did, it was only a matter of time before she would mess up. She said, "This is my third job in the past two years. At work I try hard to do a good job, and yet I keep making stupid mistakes. I just get so nervous. It feels like everyone's looking at me, waiting for me to screw up. I just can't concentrate. I'm sure it won't be long before I get fired—again!" Jessica was mired in a lifelong Child-Reflex of pessimistic identification—she expected to mess up because she saw herself as incompetent. Rather than recognizing that the real problem was her anxiety, she instead accepted the notion that she was a flawed human being—incompetent. In order to understand why she accepted such a notion, we need to dig a bit deeper into her childhood.

As a child, she recalls being highly emotional and sensitive. Her parents were young and immature—her mother was just seventeen when she accidentally became pregnant with Jessica. Her father was an immature eighteen-year-old who made it known that he resented being tied down with the responsibilities of a family. They had no time or patience for Jessica's needs and many insecurities. Her attempts to please them were ignored and more often harshly criticized (indifferent, unloving parenting). No matter how hard she tried, invariably she wound up disappointing them. As far back as she could remember, Jessica felt like there was something wrong with her; after all, her parents kept telling her so. She felt alone, unloved, and paralyzed by fear. She said, "I was always walking on eggshells. I just couldn't afford to do anything that would make things worse."

As you might imagine, she began to become anxious and overly cautious. She came to distrust her judgment, not because it was faulty, but because her parents were too preoccupied to ever take the time to listen.

As time went on, she was becoming more and more reclusive, whenever possible avoiding not only her parents but her friends as well. Although this avoidant behavior minimized the emotional friction in her life, it did put in motion a life of insecurity-driven controlling strategies, of which pessimism reigned supreme.

As an adult, Jessica was confused. She said, "No matter what I do nothing works out. I don't want to lose my job at the bank, but it really doesn't look good. Are there people who just have bad luck?" Jessica's conditioning created the insecurity habit-loop that led her to believe that she was destined to a life of failure and rejection. After all, nothing she did seemed to disprove this view. She truly felt cursed. But this all began to shift once she learned to separate herself from this devastating identification.

I've often found that pain and struggle can be a great motivator, and this was certainly true for Jessica. All she needed was a plan. She eagerly embraced Mind-Talk and realized, perhaps for the first time, that she didn't have to plod through life as a perpetual victim. She wasted no time aggressively challenging and dismissing her Reflexive Child insecurities with a tenacity born out of years of pent-up frustration. Feeling the exhilaration that comes from finally being able to see the light at the end of the tunnel, Jessica was soon motivated to take that crucial leap of faith and risk believing that she was about to change her luck! As she put it, "From now on, I make my own luck."

Jessica's Self-Coaching was a process of awakening her sleeping giant of consciousness and becoming aware that her pessimism was setting her up to be distrusting, overly cautious, and controlling. Although she was highly motivated, Jessica did face substantial resistance. After all, her entire life was spent tiptoeing through a minefield fraught with fear and danger. She worked hard to keep her focus on separating here-and-now facts from self-defeating fictions. Once this distinction was clear, the battle lines were drawn…no longer was she anxiously expecting to "mess up." Quite the contrary: she was choosing Reflexive Living, trusting that she could and would handle whatever challenge presented itself. She was absolutely resolute about fighting off her now obsolete, pessimistic identification. Her efforts reminded me of a Dr. Seuss quote, which I shared with her:

I have heard there are troubles of more than one kind.
Some come from ahead and some come from behind.
But I've bought a big bat. I'm all ready, you see.
Now my troubles are going to have troubles with me!

Postscript

Jessica did not lose her job. She was eventually promoted to bank manager.

I have often found that pessimistic patients like Jessica aren't necessarily exaggerating when they report their "bad luck." But what's most interesting to me is that when someone begins to replace pessimism with optimism, their "luck" seems to change! I'm well aware that the optimist simply focuses more on what's positive, but I'm talking about good things beyond their control that seem to happen. Not to sound too New Age, but it's almost as if the universe applauds optimism and punishes pessimism. Go figure!

On the Nature of Optimism

People who are able to embrace an optimistic attitude are able to let life unfold naturally. They have no need to brace and protect themselves from perceived weakness and anticipated chaos. Why? Because optimists are inherently convinced that they'll be okay no matter what life throws at them. Optimists have the habit of self-confidence and self-trust—a *willingness* to believe in yourself and your ability to handle life's challenges spontaneously, in the moment.

When it comes to an optimistic attitude, I'm sure you've heard the saying that it depends on whether you see the glass as half empty or half full. And this is the key to becoming optimistic. For starters, understand that everyone has half-empty aspects of their lives—feeling weak and undisciplined, dealing with problems at work, having relatives who disappoint... or finances, not to mention anxiety and depression. No one, whether it's the happiest, most successful person you know or yourself, no one and no life is without negatives! The key is to start training yourself to focus on the positives that exist in your life. And if you're tempted to say—especially if you're depressed—that there are no positives, then think again. Don't let your insecurity suggest *there are no positives*. Keep looking— they're there. It's just that sometimes our "half-empty" vision is obscuring the truths of our lives.

The Value of Optimism

One patient, who in my estimation embodies the essence of optimism, stands out. Diagnosed with pancreatic cancer and informed that there was a less than 7 percent five-year survival rate, he was told it would be a good idea to get his things in order. Rather than heeding this advice, he quite literally decided to focus on life and having a good time! His profoundly optimistic attitude was, "Cancer? Hey, it is what it is. Now what am I going to do today?"

Although, sadly, the cancer did take his life, he lived for fifteen years after his diagnosis! Fifteen years filled with 5K walks, trips to Mexico and Costa Rica, writing a screenplay, and watching his grandchildren play soccer and Little League. He once told me that when he went back to Columbia Presbyterian Hospital to visit his oncologist and nurses, they actually applauded him as he walked down the halls. A week before he died, we spoke on the phone. Aside from him reminding me, as he often did, "My life has truly been blessed," he told me that he was looking forward to the adventure of discovering what lay on the "other side." He also promised that he would prove it to me by coming back and leaving a message on my desk. That hasn't happened...yet.

Active Denial

If every person has half-full and half-empty aspects to their lives, then we can define the optimist as a person who focuses on what's half full while ignoring what's half empty. Now, you may be tempted to think that this is a form of denial, and in a sense, you would be right, since denial is ignoring negatives. However, this form of denial, unlike neurotic denial, is consciously intended—you are actively ignoring that which traditionally has tripped you up. We can call this a form of "active denial," and when it comes to maintaining an optimistic attitude, active denial is not only healthy, it's essential to your well-being. Perhaps the best example of active denial I can think of is my pancreatic cancer patient's reaction to his diagnosis mentioned above: "Cancer? Hey, it is what it is. Now what am I going to do today?"

Most people caught up in pessimistic negativity don't realize their perceptions are, in fact, habits that are continually being reinforced by insecurity-driven thinking. And they don't realize that they have a choice! If—I should say *when*—you choose to become more optimistic, you're going to have to practice active denial. You do this by consciously turning away from the negatives, and focusing on what's good in your life and with yourself. You're not denying that there are negatives and shortcomings in your life; you're simply focusing on what's positive. Lest I forget to mention, active denial, like all aspects of Self-Coaching, is something that needs to be practiced, practiced, and practiced until it becomes natural.

Mind-Brain Unlearning Exercise

You can expect to meet some resistance as you insist on the critical awareness necessary to catch your knee-jerk pessimism and then willfully steer it toward the positive. In spite of the resistance, do this for a week and you'll be truly amazed at how different you feel.

Take a look at Bill, an aspiring Broadway actor I was working with, who told me in one of our sessions, "My girlfriend says that all I do is complain. She's right, but she doesn't understand the politics and back-stabbing involved in the theater. There really isn't any security, especially as everyone trips over each other trying to kiss up to the director. It's nauseating! On top of all this my girlfriend tells me that she's thinking of moving back home to her parents' house in Jersey. I think I have a right to complain. Right?"

Sensing Bill's entrenched pessimistic view of his career along with his habit of complaining incessantly to his girlfriend about his plight, I asked if he would try a little experiment. I said, "I want you to go home, and no matter how difficult or frustrating your day was, you're not allowed to complain! You have enough awareness to know that you've been passively allowing yourself to bludgeon your girlfriend with your negativity, and now you will refuse to utter one negative comment. Not one!" Bill was game.

The next week Bill came to our session with an interesting report. He said, "I did it. I didn't complain for the entire week! It wasn't as difficult as I thought. I realized that it was just a stupid habit that only made me feel worse. By not complaining, I found that I was actually feeling bet-ter, less anxious, and more relaxed. I can't say I'll never complain about anything ever again, but I've got to tell you, not complaining sure makes more sense." Bill initially thought that complaining was a good way to get things off his chest. Well, perhaps he didn't actually *think* it was a good thing—he just mindlessly did it because complaining had become his habit. What he came to realize was that his pessimistic negativity was, in fact, perpetuating his stress, feeding his insecurities, and making him feel worse.

Mind-Brain Unlearning Note

The Chicken or the Egg of Pessimism

It doesn't matter whether pessimistic negativity generates anxiety and depression or whether anxiety and depression generate pessimism. Either way, you lose.

I should mention that pessimism (like optimism) isn't necessarily a black-and-white phenomenon; there are many intermediate shades of gray. For example, you don't have to be a complete pessimist to be a worrier, complainer, or moaner. Everyone is prone to doubt, fear, and negativity from time to time. But if you recall from our previous discussions, much of what constitutes a neurotic, pessimistic attitude is the disproportionate and excessive extent to which our lives are affected. What differentiates pessimism from worrying, complaining, and moaning is that pessimism is a pervasive attitude about life itself, not necessarily connected to a specific worry-thought or a bad day. But you don't have to be a card-carrying pessimist to be tripped up by pessimistic tendencies (like Bill's complaining above). Any amount of doubt, fear, or negativity can conspire to hold you back from your goals while making your life miserable.

Taking the Leap

Whether it's negativity, worry, unease, or simply fear, no matter how you define it, a pessimistic attitude will always hurt your efforts and fuel your emotional struggles. In order to maximize your Self-Coaching and Mind-Talk efforts, you'll need to eliminate the friction caused by a pessimistic attitude. To do this, you're going to learn to take a *leap of faith*, releasing your innate potential for optimism. And of course, here's where many run into an impasse—taking that leap.

You may already be telling yourself that you're going to be more positive, that you're going to turn away from negatives. This is the right place to start. But how exactly do you get to the point where you're willing to abandon the pseudo-safety of overcontrolling life by throwing yourself to the wolves of Responsive Living? Of course, there are no wolves, but when you begin to entertain the notion of letting go of control, this is exactly how it might feel.

I recall seeing a BBC interview with the Swiss psychiatrist C.G. Jung, shortly before his death. In the interview, Jung was asked whether or not he believed in God. Jung almost fell out of his chair as he responded in no uncertain terms, "I don't believe! I know!" And this is the attitude you want to strive for. You want to go beyond *believing*, which to me connotes a kind of hopeful anticipation of things to come, to a *knowing*, which suggests that you have already arrived! Once you *know* something to be true, you're free to embrace it without hesitation, debate, or further scrutiny. And this is where motivation plays such a vital role in developing a *knowing* attitude.

Leaping

When it comes to habit re-formation, your Self-Coaching efforts will put you in a position to take that leap of faith, opening the door to an optimism that heretofore has been absent in your life. The main reason optimism is so important is because an optimistic attitude releases ongoing positive energy, which sustains that rather elusive phenomenon we refer to as motivation. From a Self-Coaching perspective, motivation isn't a static thing—it's an ongoing process, fueled by optimism, that solidifies your energy, desire, and commitment to change.

Motivation is that intangible *thing* that coaches, teachers, and psychologists try to instill in their players, students, and patients. It's that psychological *something* that enables human beings to do extraordinary things. Although unlearning anxiety and depression may feel like an extraordinary challenge, once the process is demystified and approached from a micro, step-by-step perspective, you can do it using *ordinary*, disciplined Mind-Talk efforts. This is not to say that you won't be challenged. Let's be realistic; insecurity has polluted the waters of consciousness for a long time. As you begin to apply Mind-Talk, you're going to have to handle habit resistance, and this is where motivation becomes indispensable.

Initially, you can expect insecurity to battle you every inch of the way. If you're not motivated enough to fight that good fight, you may falter. But if you've taken that leap of faith and have begun to recognize a bourgeoning self-trust and optimism along with a motivational fire burning within you, then the question I would pose to you is, *Why in the world would you not succeed?*

Mind-Brain Unlearning Note

What you say and what you believe is what you become.

I often tell my patients that psychology isn't rocket science. Once you understand the nature of insecurity, the need to overcontrol life, and the nature of habit-loops, then only two questions remain: *What am I doing that feeds my insecurity? What am I doing that starves it?* I guess I'm trying to tell you that psychology is, when you look at it through a Self-Coaching lens, essentially common sense. Going all the way back to our discussion in Chapter One, the grand unifying theme of this book is that we are all creatures of habit. And the one thing you should be completely convinced of at this point in your reading is my refrain that habits—all habits—are learned, and all habits can be unlearned. Even the habit-loops that sustain anxiety and depression!

This concept of whether you're feeding or starving insecurity is eloquently portrayed in an old Native American story that has been passed down for generations:

> *An old grandfather, sitting by the fire one day, wanted to teach his grandson about the difference between good and evil, and so he said, "Inside each of us there are two wolves struggling with each other. One wolf is anger, resentment, self-pity, indulgence, doubt, and fear. The other wolf is contentment, strength, happiness, hope, truth, and love." The grandson sat, deep in thought, then asked, "Which wolf wins, Grandfather?" The grandfather replied, "The one you feed."*

"The one you feed" is an apt analogy for our purposes. There is no question that pessimism is a bad wolf, and considering that you've been struggling with anxiety and depression, a rather overfed, frightening wolf at that. And that's okay, because with active denial in conjunction with your ongoing Mind-Talk efforts, you're not going to get caught up with focusing on the bad wolf of pessimism; you're going to be conscientiously feeding the good wolves of optimism and self-trust. In time, if you're not feeding the bad wolf, what do you think happens? Bye bye, bad wolf!

EPILOGUE

16

How Long Before
I Start Feeling Better?

My daughter Lauren was born with a condition called amblyopia, commonly referred to as "lazy eye." Lazy eye is a neurological condition in which the brain develops a preference for the stronger eye. This is a serious condition that, if left untreated, can result in permanent blindness of the weaker eye. In a sense, the brain *learns* to ignore the vision from the lazy eye. The remedy was, as my daughter would later call it, "wearing the pirate patch." An adhesive patch was applied to her "good" (stronger) eye, forcing the brain to work with her weaker eye.

You probably know enough about neuroplasticity at this point in your reading to guess what happened after months of patching. Yup, the weaker eye became stronger and eventually caught up with the strong eye. Well, this isn't exactly what happened. You see, this wasn't about the weak *eye* becoming stronger—there was nothing wrong with the eye itself—it was about the "plastic" brain being forced to work with the weaker eye to form new neural circuitry. End result: perfect binocular vision.

Neuroplasticity, the brain's ability to learn (or unlearn), isn't a myth—it's an anatomical reality. Throughout your life, your brain is not only capable of forming new habit-loops, but is also capable of reversing them.

With anxiety and depression, you need to neutralize the habit-loop of insecurity by applying a different kind of "pirate patch"—one that forces your weak, atrophied self-trust muscle to begin to gain strength by forming new neural circuitry (habit re-formation). The pirate patch I refer to is your critical awareness that comes from your Mind-Talk efforts that, similar to my daughter's patch, enables you to ignore the input from the dominant, neurotic habit-loop of insecurity (doubts, fears, and negativity), forcing your atrophied self-trust muscle to grow and flourish.

If you understand how my daughter's brain was forced to change, then you should have no problem embracing how Mind-Talk will force your brain to change. Mind-Talk will force your brain to see things differently and think things differently, and it will force you to behave differently. For the record, don't make the mistake of thinking that your brain is conspiring against you; that's not the case. The brain does not think for itself; it is the repository of all our experiences, emotions, and thoughts that have been fed to it. Your brain does not want you to suffer. It only wants one thing: to remain true to its biological imperative—survival.

If because of insecurity you've come to perceive danger in safe places, and have convinced yourself that without a strong sense of security you'd best be served by trying to overcontrol life, then the circuitry in your brain will reflect this misguided "survival" perception. Unfortunately, as we've seen, overcontrolling life leads to a life of stress, which invariably depletes us chemically, emotionally, and physically. In time, our chemistry shifts and becomes imbalanced (which is why medication works), and emotionally we respond with symptoms of anxiety and depression. Both, as we've discussed previously, are neurotic attempts to quell further loss of control. All this follows from the reflexive perception that you can't trust yourself to handle life's challenges spontaneously—certainly not without worrisome, compulsive strategies of control.

My daughter had to wear her patch for more than a year, followed by special glasses with one opaque lens, and she had to complete various eye-strengthening exercises, all designed to force her brain to rewire itself. Your brain isn't going to object to your process of rewiring, but don't think your habit of insecurity is going to take this lying down. Unfortunately, habit resistance is a real obstacle when it comes to unlearning neurotic habit-loops. My daughter's patch forced her brain to comply, but we can't literally patch insecurity. So you're going to have to force your brain to comply using Mind-Talk to awaken your sleeping giant of consciousness in order to change. I fully understand that anxiety and depression have eroded your confidence and stamina, and that you're feeling a bit like David about to encounter Goliath.

As the biblical story goes, David, armed only with a sling, brought down the giant with one well-placed blow. Michelangelo's David is not shown *after* the battle, as most previous artists had done, but at that expectant moment *prior* to hurling the stone—that archetypal moment of absolute fearlessness and conviction. David waits...waits for Goliath. Try Googling the statue of David and you'll see a visual of the exact, defiant, empowered attitude you need to embrace in order to slay your Goliath of insecurity. Your Goliath won't be slain by one stone, but by the many stones of Mind-Talk.

Okay, But How Long?

I do hope you're ready to get started with your Self-Coaching training—if you haven't already. As enthusiastic as you may feel, it's important to approach your training in a sober, realistic manner. Patients and other visitors to my website (www.selfcoaching.net) always want to know how long it takes to break a habit of anxiety or depression. As much as I'd like to use Maxwell Maltz's 21 days to break a habit (from his book *Psycho-Cybernetics*), the truth is no one really knows how long it takes to break a habit—your habit.

I suspect there's nothing more dangerous when writing a self-help book than to offer arbitrary timelines as to the very understandable question, "How long?" Like most things in life, some people progress more rapidly than others. If you go to a gym and ask a trainer how long it will take to get those six-pack abs, assuming your trainer is honest, you'll probably get the same answer I would offer: "It depends."

The reason for my vagueness is because it depends on you, your history, the degree of self-distrust that has accumulated over the years, your capacity for handling some frustration, your willingness to practice every single day, your level of optimism, pessimism, and so on. Okay, get the point? Breaking a habit depends on many variables, the most important of which is your persistence. Self-Coaching works, and the only variable you need to concern yourself with is staying motivated enough to go the distance—period!

One last piece of advice: focus on the process, not the goals of Self-Coaching. This is one sure way to keep insecurity from creeping back into the picture and whining, "It's taking too long." "I'm not feeling better." Make no mistake, take your eye off your day-to-day Mind-Talk *process* and you leave yourself open to just such insecurity gobbledygook. That said, here's a better sense of what you can expect going forward:

Mind-Brain Unlearning Note
Beware Infatuation

As when starting most things, we have a tendency to think that our initial wave of enthusiasm and motivation will last. Unfortunately, this typically isn't the case. Whether it's playing a musical instrument, deciding to learn a foreign language, or running a marathon, when you start out, your motivation soars as you eat, sleep, and breathe your passionate desire to accomplish these goals. And as motivated as you may feel right now, this form of "infatuated" motivation is short-lived; you can't count on it to carry you through the period of habit resistance. It's nice to come out of the blocks in a sprint, but it's the steady pace of the long-distance runner that will serve you best.

Your goal from the beginning has been to liberate yourself from anxiety and depression. The good news is you won't have to reach your ultimate goal(s) before you start to feel better. This will begin to happen along the way. You'll find yourself worrying less, feeling more confident and optimistic, feeling less depressed and anxious, and, although you'll know you're not quite there yet, you'll also know that you possess the Self-Coaching means of fully liberating yourself from insecurity. It's no longer a matter of *if* you'll succeed—it's only a matter of *when*. As I've said before, it's not rocket science. It will happen!

Mind-Brain Unlearning Note

Self-Coaching and Mind-Talk are part of a process, an ongoing daily effort to rewire your brain.

Self-Coaching Daily Pep-Talk

It's time. Time to begin. As a coach, you're going to need to motivate, encourage, and light a can-do fire of optimism into your efforts every day. The days ahead are critical to your process of liberation as you acquire proficiency using Mind-Talk. In order to help your coaching efforts, I suggest that you start each day with an inspirational, Self-Coaching pep talk. Understand that positive thinking along with positive visualization can begin to rewire your brain's neurocircuitry.

Throughout the day, as you continue to work your Mind-Talk, reflect on your daily pep talk. The pep talks that follow are all reiterations of themes that you've been introduced to throughout this book—themes that will help keep you focused and determined to go the distance. You'll find an inspirational pep talk for each of forty-four days. I'm not exactly sure why I stopped at forty-four, but I just did. I felt that, by Day Forty-Four, you'll be well on your way to your personal liberation from emotional struggle. Out of curiosity, I Googled the number forty-four and found the following numerological quote: "Forty-four builds for both the present and the future. It wants rewards for its work in the present and wants to have a large positive effect on the future." So, there you go! Forty-four it is!

Good Luck Coach

I'm going to be signing off; your coaching is now in your hands. You have all the tools you need, and as you progress, it's always a good idea to revisit various sections of the book to refresh your understanding and renew your confidence. And now, I wish you godspeed with your liberation from anxiety and depression as you begin to approach the life you've wanted and the life you so richly deserve.

Forty-Four Daily Inspirational Pep Talks

Day 1
Prescription for having a great day

See if you can resist the temptation of overthinking your life today, and instead allow the day to unfold naturally and spontaneously. Be responsive rather than neurotically proactive. You might be surprised how effortless life can become. The late mythologist Joseph Campbell once said that we must be willing to relinquish the life we've planned, so as to have the life that is waiting for us. Lose the self-doubt, be courageous to let go of your chronic fears, and by all means recognize that negativity is a habit that you don't have to indulge. Do this and you'll find the life that's waiting for you.

Day 2
Injecting hope into your day

"I can't do this; it's too hard." Thus speaks the voice of insecurity, which is the voice of despair and defeat. When everything in you is telling you to give up and quit, you have only one ally—hope. Granted, when you're feeling hopeless, it seems impossible to reverse the tide of pessimism, but just because it seems impossible doesn't mean it is. Hope is nothing more than a leap of faith. Regardless of your circumstances, if you take the leap, at the very least your struggles will no longer own you.

Day 3
Stop making mountains out of molehills

Ever notice how silly someone else's worry seems to you? How many times have you told someone to stop making mountains out of molehills? Unfortunately, if worry has become your knee-jerk reflexive response to life challenges, then mountain-making is what you do best. And when you're making mountains out of molehills, the strangest things can seem very real. Insecurity, aside from making emotional fictions seem like facts, is opportunistic. Give it an opening and it will take you for a ride.

Day 4
Changing your perspective

Starting today, remind yourself of the countless problems and worries that have come and gone in your life. How many problems do you think you've solved to date? One thousand? Fifty thousand? Somehow, you've managed to survive, figure out, solve, get around, under, or over every obstacle, right? You wouldn't be reading this if it weren't true. Every crisis eventually becomes history, and you move on. What makes you think that today's worries are any different? The next time you come across a molehill, insist on *not* calling it a mountain!

Day 5
Take a lesson from a bumble bee

Bumble bees are not supposed to fly. Their bodies weigh too much and their wingspans are too short. Thank goodness the bumble bee doesn't know these facts. What are the supposed "facts" that are holding you back? Sure, there are challenging circumstances in your life, but it's not life circumstances that are holding you back or making you feel anxious or depressed—it's your reaction to these circumstances.

Day 6
Finding today's opportunities

Every challenge, no matter how small, is an opportunity to grow in self-respect, confidence, and self-trust. Every setback, no matter how significant, is an opportunity to grow in self-respect, confidence, and self-trust. In the grand scheme of life, there should be no regrets—only appreciation for the opportunities to grow toward our full potential. Be clear about this: no setback has to set you back! Not if you refuse to let it.

Day 7
Realizing your intentions

What stops you from achieving your goals? What exactly is the resistance that keeps you from taking charge of your life and realizing your intentions? As complex and multifaceted as the answer to this query may be, one way or another it all boils down to self-discipline. And from a Self-Coaching perspective, self-discipline is the ability to willfully endure the transient discomfort of changing who and what you are. You weren't born with self-discipline—you acquired it. Like a muscle, you need to develop your self-discipline muscle, one challenge at a time.

Day 8
Expanding your repertoire

Charles Schulz, the creator of Peanuts, once quipped, "Life is like a ten-speed bicycle. Most of us have gears we never use." Sometimes when circumstances challenge us to respond in extraordinary ways, we look back and marvel, "I didn't know I had it in me!" Surprise yourself. Try out some new gears today.

Day 9
What's holding you back?

If you're persistent and patient, you can only be held back from reaching your goals for so long. Steel yourself against the tide of frustrations, setbacks, and problems. These challenges don't determine success—you do! Your mindset needs to be, "If not the front door, then the side door, the back door, the rear door, the window...." There's always a way. Sometimes you have to be patient, but mostly you have to be persistent! Do not allow sabotaging emotional fictions to tell you otherwise. If you think you can't go on—then think again. And again. And again, until you can!

Day 10
When it comes to clinging to habits of insecurity, familiarity breeds contempt

Beware of the saying: "Better the devil you know than the devil you don't." All too often we cling to the shortsighted safety of our controlling strategies. Overcontrolling life may feel like a better option than risking self-trust, but if you truly want to live a more passionate, liberated, enjoyable life, then it's time to realize that there's only one devil: refusing to risk trusting self and life. Risk believing that you can let life unfold today without your usual anticipatory ruminations. It's the only way to prove to yourself that you actually will survive. You will! I guarantee it. Don't let insecurity tell you otherwise.

Day 11
Losing the word "can't"

Ever hear yourself saying, "I can't"? "I just can't be more positive." Or, "I simply can't stop worrying." No doubt that buying into the "can't" ploy will get you off the hook by excusing you from action. If you're able to convince yourself that you can't, then you get to feel somewhat blameless. According to Self-Coaching, lose the word *can't*. Those who can't are those who won't! The only time you can use the word *can't* is in this sentence: "I can't say can't."

Day 12
No digging today!

Will Rogers once quipped, "When you find yourself in a hole, stop digging." When facing any life challenge, allowing worrisome doubts, fears, or negatives to spin endlessly is a surefire way of digging your way into an anxiety attack or even a depression. Maybe you can't figure out how to get out of your hole, but you sure as hell don't have to make matters worse. How do you stop digging? By using your Mind-Talk to stop the runaway train of insecurity-driven thinking.

Day 13
Making today matter

I was working with a patient recently who lamented, "Nothing I do matters." What about you? Do you feel like your days are a meaningless shuffle without merit or purpose? And yet, who's to say that washing dishes is any less important than building a bridge or writing a book? From a Self-Coaching perspective, it's not *what* you do that matters, it's how you feel and what you think about what you do that does. Want to have a great day today? Try living your life as if everything you do matters. Building self-esteem—that's today's challenge.

Day 14
Making today more simple

There's a wonderful Zen adage that sums up the essence and simplicity of life: *chop wood, carry water*. Finding serenity, happiness, and meaning in your life doesn't have to be complicated—not if you just do everything with your full attention and your full heart. Do this and you'll never need to ask, "What's the meaning of life?" Keep in mind that it's impossible to feel anxious or depressed if you are fully and completely involved in the external world in front of you rather than the congested, insecurity-driven inner world swirling within you. Distractions can be helpful in teaching you that it's possible to step apart from your struggles. And if you can do it sometimes, why not all the time? With practice you can, and will.

Day 15
Realizing your resourcefulness

For someone caught up in a spiraling habit-loop of insecurity, anticipating and figuring life out (essentially worrying or ruminating)—before it happens—seems much safer than living unrehearsed. In fact, if you've been trying to overcontrol life, then living more spontaneously may feel downright reckless. Fact is, it's not reckless—it just *feels* that way. You have six million years of instinctual, survival hardwiring that's not going to let you down—not once you learn to trust your innate, unlimited resourcefulness. Only with self-trust will you be willing to risk living your life more naturally, more spontaneously, and less rehearsed. And when you do, it will be without anxiety and depression.

Day 16
Choosing to believe

The optimist says, "I can." The pessimist says, "I can't." The doubter says, "I'm not sure." The optimist will find a way to succeed, the pessimist a way to fail, while the doubter finds a nice fence to sit on. No one knows the future, but how you frame the future will determine your present. Optimism, pessimism, and self-doubt are all choices we make, consciously or unconsciously. Today, with critical awareness, choose to believe. Choose optimism. And if you can't quite get to optimism, then at the very least, be neutral. Anything but pessimism.

Day 17
Today, try being more like a child

Remember when you were a child. Everything seemed possible. Why is it that we grow up and ignore life's wonder and magic? The answer is rather straightforward: The unencumbered child knows how to simply *be*, while adults suffering from anxiety or depression are overwhelmed by swirling doubts, fears, and negative fictions. They're too absorbed just trying to keep their psychological heads above the waters of chaos to simply *be*. Is it possible to go beyond struggle and experience life's wonder and magic again? Yes—once you realize the extraordinary power of simply being in the moment rather than mindlessly allowing yourself to become victimized by your insecurities.

Starting today, with critical awareness, do not allow emotionally driven fictions to go unchallenged. Liberate yourself—one thought at a time. Do this and you'll be giving yourself a chance to once again experience not only relief from suffering, but perhaps a bit of life's magic too. Bottom line: let go, let life.

Day 18
Today, see if you can rethink your negativity
Caterpillars are compelled to laboriously crawl through life, inch by inch. If caterpillars could feel, perhaps they would be quite depressed. How different the caterpillar's life would be if they could know about the liberated, butterfly life that lies ahead. How different your life will be if you live with optimistic expectations that one day you too will fly. Think about flying!

Day 19
You won't need a magic wand today
What if you had a magic wand? Want to stop ruminating? Done! Want to find lasting happiness? Done! Success? Done! Alas, there are no magic wands in life, but that doesn't stop some people from becoming mired in wishful, magical thinking. If you're tired of waiting for happiness, abandon wishful thinking and replace it with something better than a magic wand: purposeful Mind-Talk action.

Day 20
Today, it's all up to you
Starting today, regardless of what goes on around you, recognize that you and you alone make the decision as to what kind of day it will be. Focus on what's right with your life rather than on what's wrong. Some say, "If your glass is half empty, fill it up." Self-Coaching says, "Forget waiting

to fill up your glass; it's quicker to just ignore the half-empty aspects of your life while actively focusing on the half-full aspects." In other words: optimism now!

Day 21
Reclaiming your power today

Victims accept the faulty proposition that they are powerless. Maybe you can't prevent bad things from happening, but you can decide how these circumstances will impact your life. When it comes to your emotions, you are never powerless. Repeat: NEVER powerless! As the poem by Richard Lovelace goes: "Stone walls do not a prison make, Nor iron bars a cage."

Day 22
Going with the current today

Life is like a stream with a swift current running through it. With pessimism, we plod against the force of the current, feeling the strong resistance of the water pushing against us. With optimism, we flow with the current, feeling the endless energy and buoyancy of the water. In a stream, why would anyone choose to go against the current? In life, why would you choose to go against life's current? Instead, simply let life unfold... without doubts, fears, and negatives. Why indeed!

Day 23
Figuring out what will make a difference today

Human beings hate being out of control. You've read throughout this book how overcontrolling life is the precursor to anxiety and depression. To avoid confusion, you need to understand that overcontrolling life isn't the same as taking control of life. You take control of life when you pay the bills, get some exercise, lose weight, resolve conflicts, and so on. This type of control makes us feel great. The opposite is also true. Postponing our chores, harboring resentments, and ignoring our health make us feel out of control, often contributing to ongoing stress, anxiety and even depression. Taking legitimate responsibility for controlling our lives doesn't guarantee happiness, but it sure helps!

Day 24
It's time!

Why do you think we spend so much time procrastinating? One reason is because living effectively in the present requires responsible, here-and-now action. It's a lot easier—and effortless—to imagine taking responsible action tomorrow. Truth is, there will never be a better *now* for purposeful action. In fact, there will never be anything other than now. When the future does come, it will only be your new now. Therefore, if not now, when?

Day 25
Focusing on what's right with your life

The key to genuine, sustainable happiness is to stop putting your life on hold. A good life free of reflexive insecurity-driven thinking doesn't start tomorrow; it starts now—right now! So stop wasting time focusing on what's wrong with your life, and instead begin focusing on what's right in your life. And if you can't find something right, how about this: you are now engaged in your Self-Coaching program, and you're going to beat anxiety and depression! And why not? You're tough, you're tenacious, and you're tired of suffering. Starting today, live alongside your challenges, not immersed, drowning in them. Having a better life really is a here-and-now choice. What have you got to lose, other than your negativity?

Day 26
Connect rather than disconnect

When you work, whatever your job, whatever the task, make everything you do become an expression of you. My father used to tell me, "If you're going to be a bean counter, be the best bean counter you can be." Regardless of the task or job, connect rather than disconnect, but most importantly, value and embrace your efforts rather than holding out for an anticipated outcome. Do this and you won't have to ask what the meaning of life is. Take, for example, Saint Francis of Assisi, who, one day while hoeing his garden, was asked, "If you were to die at sunset today, what would you do now?" Saint Francis replied, "I'd finish hoeing my garden." Saint Francis was connected.

Day 27
Living less compulsively

When I was young, I had a job in construction. One of the truck drivers was a know-it-all. No matter what you said to him, he *knew* it! "Sam, your truck's leaking oil." Sam: "I know it!" One day, while Tom was driving home intoxicated, a state trooper stopped him. Sam was told he was driving with his headlights off. Sam's response: "I know it. I see better with them out!" How about you? Do you always have to "know it"? If so, recognize that it's okay not to have all the answers. Sometimes the answers have to find you. Years ago I thought, like Sam, that I knew all the answers. Now that I'm older I realize I don't even know the questions! It's really okay to live without crossing every *t* or dotting every *i*. It's truly liberating!

Day 28
Stop feeling there's anything wrong with you

"What's wrong with me? Why can't I be happy?" For starters, there's nothing wrong with you—nothing that you can't fix. According to an old proverb, "It's not the horse that draws the cart, but the oats." When it comes to a happy, successful life, what draws you forward is what you feed your mind. What do you think happens when you feed your mind a constant diet of doubts, fears, and negatives? What happens is that, rather than being drawn forward, you become paralyzed by insecurity's inertia.

If you truly want to be happy, then you need to become more responsible for what you feed your mind—your "oats!" It all begins with critical awareness as you start to neutralize insecurity's chatter and then, one thought at a time, gradually begin cultivating a more positive outlook. And just because embracing a more optimistic outlook may feel unnatural, this doesn't mean it can't become natural. Why? Because feelings aren't facts! Want another fact? You weren't made to be miserable! And that's a fact!

Day 29
Don't worry about the "stumbles"

According to a Portuguese proverb, "Stumbling is not falling." As you strive each day to reach your goals, keep in mind it's likely that you'll stumble on the way. Don't let setbacks, miscues, or delays derail your efforts. And even if you do happen to fall now and then, there's another worthwhile Japanese proverb: "Seven times down, eight times up."

Day 30
Make today a *good* day

Do you ever say, "Today's not a good day"? Or, "I have to go to work"? Or, "I have to pay the bills"? Life sounds like drudgery, doesn't it? Before you resign yourself to just "getting through" another day, recognize what you're doing. For starters, you're conceding that today won't be an opportunity for anything worthwhile. We call this a self-fulfilling prophecy. That is, what you tell yourself and what you believe are what you and your life become.

Stop prejudicing yourself with a shortsighted, pessimistic attitude. Instead, open yourself up to the awareness that every day—in spite of your whining—is an opportunity, an adventure. The truth is, you don't know what may be around the next corner. It could be wonderful, not terrible. As the saying goes, *when the pupil is ready, the teacher will appear.*

Day 31
The three Self-Coaching facts of life

1. You can't change the past (many have tried and failed).
2. You can't control the future (many have tried and failed).
3. You CAN change the present (those who have tried have profited). Try! Profit!

Day 32
Feeling what it's like to be empowered

Regardless of your current belief or struggle, periodically during the day today, practice allowing yourself to believe that you already possess everything you need to have a happy, liberated life. Just permit yourself to relax and accept this fundamental notion—even if it's only for a few seconds.

Don't allow yourself to fight it. You can expect a struggle from your habit-loop of insecurity, but for now, accept it *as if* it's true. The important thing in this drill is to begin feeling what it's like to be empowered and not victimized by life. As you progress with this Self-Coaching exercise, you might be surprised at the lasting changes in your mood and your life.

Day 33
Getting your priorities straight

The Dalai Lama, when asked what surprises him most, responded, "Man! Because he sacrifices his health in order to make money. Then he sacrifices money to recuperate his health." Today, make the time to exercise, prepare good healthy meals, connect with friends and family, do something fun, and relax. Get your priorities straight today and avoid playing catch-up tomorrow.

Day 34
Perspective of the day

Time, and what we do with our time, is always a choice. If you feel you have no choice—think again! Starting today, choose to live each day as if it were the first day you ever knew and the last day you will ever have, as if there were no tomorrow.

Day 35
Yes, you can!

Talk about tenacity—Thomas Edison tried sixty thousand different filaments before he succeeded with the light bulb. Sixty thousand! What do you think would have happened if on trial fifty-nine thousand nine hundred ninety-nine he said, "The hell with this. Get me a candle"? In the end, psychological resiliency and tenacity will always prevail. When it comes to your emotional liberation, being tenacious with your Mind-Talk efforts will bring light into your life.

Day 36
Thoughts do matter—big time

You need to know that thoughts matter, and there's an emotional and physical price to pay for needless, shabby thinking. Recognize that "shabby" negative thinking is a choice of passivity—you sit back and allow your habits of insecurity to go on and on unimpeded. Instead, start to become a more active thinker, especially when you're feeling stressed and challenged. Starting today, take responsibility—one thought at a time. STOP dancing with negativity and choose to reject insecurity-driven thinking.

Day 37
Self-Coaching strategy of the day

When confronted with any challenge today, use this simple Self-Coaching strategy to help:
1. Do the best you can.
2. Never, ever, criticize your efforts.
3. Learn to celebrate your efforts rather than your successes.
Do this and you'll be guaranteeing ongoing, sustained motivation that will see you through whatever life throws at you. Remember, motivation is the fuel of liberation from struggle.

Day 38
You don't need permission to feel better

"The question," according to Ayn Rand, "isn't who is going to let me; it's who is going to stop me." No one—and nothing—can stop you from having the life you want. You don't need permission!

Day 39
Insecurity is NOT a fact of life

Most people confuse vulnerability with insecurity. The difference is simple but crucial. For starters, vulnerability is a fact of life. Insecurity isn't. Protecting yourself from vulnerability makes sense; that's why you buckle your seat belt, take vitamins, and learn to say *no*. The problem with insecurity isn't the seat belt, the vitamins, or the assertiveness; it's the worrisome anticipation of things going awry—a car accident, illness, or being victimized by others. It's anticipating what can go wrong in life and then worrying about it. It's like wearing a belt because you're worried your suspenders might break. Here's the key: insecurity was learned—it's a habit. Habits—all habits—can be broken! Here's today's answer: risk trusting your suspenders!

Day 40
Don't let overthinking become your excuse

The longer you ponder, scrutinize, and overthink your goals, the more likely you are to find excuses and begin to feel hesitant. Hesitation itself is just an excuse. When it comes to a happy life, you're NOT excused! Do it!

Day 41
What kind of thoughts are you accumulating today?

Sure, one thought isn't going to make a difference in your mental well-being. But ruminative, negative thinking has a cumulative, mind-body effect, depleting you both emotionally as well as chemically, and eventually contributing to anxiety or depression. The opposite is equally true: optimistic, positive thinking is cumulative and will begin to erode your habit-loop of insecurity.

Day 42
Be in charge!

If you can't be optimistic about the future, at least be neutral, but never concede to a worrisome, pessimistic anticipation of doom and gloom. Neither the optimist nor the pessimist knows the future, but let's be honest, the optimist lives a much happier life in the present than the pessimist, and this makes all the difference in the world! You're in charge of your life. BE in charge!

Day 43
Why you need motivation

Want a working, Self-Coaching definition of motivation? It's the moment you believe, with all your heart, that you *can*. This becomes the moment you unleash your energy. It's the moment that your hesitations vanish.

Day 44
Becoming courageous

It's never life that defeats us; it's always our reaction to life circumstances that does. When overwhelmed by life challenges and struggles, a courageous person is willing to fight the good fight. Nothing more, nothing less. Do this and you will never feel powerless or victimized.

INDEX